Marcia Muller and the Female Private Eye

35) Sharon Mc Cal S.J. fem detective
+ 1 st petit non white —
40) 1/8 Shoshone

Marcia Muller and the Female Private Eye

Essays on the Novels That Defined a Subgenre

edited by ALEXANDER N. HOWE
and CHRISTINE A. JACKSON

McFarland & Company, Inc., Publishers
Jefferson, North Carolina, and London

ALSO OF INTEREST

Alexander N. Howe. *It Didn't Mean Anything: A Psychoanalytic Reading of American Detective Fiction* (McFarland, 2008)
Christine A. Jackson. *Myth and Ritual in Women's Detective Fiction* (McFarland, 2002)

LIBRARY OF CONGRESS CATALOGUING-IN-PUBLICATION DATA

Marcia Muller and the female private eye : essays on the novels that defined a subgenre / edited by Alexander N. Howe and Christine A. Jackson.
    p.   cm.
    Includes index.

    ISBN 978-0-7864-3825-9
    softcover : 50# alkaline paper ∞

    1. Muller, Marcia — Characters — Sharon McCone.   2. McCone, Sharon (Fictitious character)   3. Private investigators in literature. 4. Women detectives in literature.   5. Detective and mystery stories, American — History and criticism.   I. Howe, Alexander N., 1973–   II. Jackson, Christine A., 1951–
PS3563.U397Z77   2008
813'.54 — dc22   2008024339

British Library cataloguing data are available

Front cover: TG Design

Manufactured in the United States of America

McFarland & Company, Inc., Publishers
    Box 611, Jefferson, North Carolina 28640
    www.mcfarlandpub.com

Contents

Genesis

Part III: Trauma

Introduction: Re-Reading Marcia Muller — Gender, Genre, and the Trauma of Interpretation

ALEXANDER N. HOWE

It is nearly impossible to mention Marcia Muller's name without recalling Sue Grafton's famous proclamation that "Marcia Muller is the founding mother of the female private eye," an epithet that Muller herself admits "gets a little old" (Ross). While the entry "Marcia Muller" appears in many a detective fiction encyclopedia, and numerous academic histories of the detective genre, there has been very little extended investigation of Muller's fiction. Indeed, reference to her parentage of the female private eye genre is often the extent of scholarship. By and large, Muller is merely a footnote to the genre that she herself helped create.

This collection has the distinction of being the first book-length work on Marcia Muller. As such, the goal of this volume is to open the field of Muller scholarship. This is fertile ground given the vast opus that Muller has produced over the past thirty years. To date, the author's catalog includes four series (Sharon McCone, Joanna Stark, Elena Oliverez, and Soledad County), collections of short stories, a number of standalones, and a few non-fiction works on the detective genre. The Sharon McCone series alone totals twenty-five titles, and counting.

It all began in 1977 when Marcia Muller published the first Sharon McCone mystery, *Edwin of the Iron Shoes*. Naturally, the climate of the publishing marketplace at the time made this a great accomplishment, a feat possible only with a great deal of effort from the author, and dozens of rejected manuscripts. In fact, Muller had difficulty finding a home for her second McCone novel, *Ask the Cards a Question*, which wasn't published until 1982. This was the same year that Sue Grafton and Sara Paretsky published their first novels featuring female private eyes —*A Is for Alibi* and *Indemnity Only*, respectively. Of course, the publication of these three novels proved to be a watershed for the mystery genre. The female hard-boiled detectives of Muller, Grafton, and Paretsky reinvigorate and revolutionize the mystery genre, resulting in what many have called a new "Golden Age" of mystery fiction (Walton and Jones 24).

When speaking of her entrance into the writing profession, Muller frequently recalls her early love for reading. She favored novels featuring private investigators, like those written by canonical hard-boiled writers such as Raymond Chandler, Ross Macdonald, and Dashiell Hammett, but she also found inspiration in the work of Dorothy B. Hughes, Lillian O'Donnell, and Patricia Highsmith (Bibel 1596; Muller, "Partners in Crime" 7). And yet in her early reading there was always something missing, namely, novels that told the story of a female private investigator. Muller realized that if she wished to read about such a character, she would need to create one herself ("Creating a Female Sleuth" 20).

In interviews, Muller has spoken at length of her self-conscious "adaptation" of the hard-boiled detective. Though she acknowledges a fond debt to her male predecessors, Muller insists that she had no interest in creating a female version of the stereotypical "hard-bitten loner with the whiskey bottle in the desk drawer" (Muller, "Partners in Crime" 8). Neither did she wish to create a "passive observer" who remained distanced from the world around her — a second hard-boiled formula that, if adapted outright for a female character, would significantly undercut the basic feminist gesture of Muller's project. What Muller chose to do instead was something much more interesting: a choice that no doubt has resulted in her longevity within the genre. As Muller relates, "Sharon McCone, I decided, was to be as close to a real person as possible" ("Partners in Crime" 8).

Muller refers to this decision elsewhere in the brief essay "What Sharon McCone Learned from Judy Bolton." Here, she recalls that a favorite author from childhood, Margaret Sutton, revealed the possibilities of a tough, self-sufficient female detective. Sutton's girl detective, Judy Bolton, is very much like McCone. Both characters are extremely intelligent and quick-witted, as well as "fiercely independent and often unresponsive to authority" (68). Without question, fans of the Bolton and McCone series favor these attributes. However, as a reader, Muller was drawn all the more to Judy's faults, such as stubbornness, insecurity, and having a temper. These character traits, which are shared by McCone, frequently get Judy into trouble; however, this is the saving grace of the heroine (67–68). She is "no paragon on a pedestal," but her failings make her all the more human (67).

A second decisive strategy that Marcia Muller drew from Margaret Sutton was opening her heroine to the effects of time — that most human of dilemmas. Through Sutton's series, Judy ages and changes, and Muller has demanded the same of Sharon McCone (68). As Muller recounts, "Like real people she [McCone] would age, grow, change; experience joy and sorrow, love and hatred — in short the full range of human emotion" ("Partners in Crime" 8). McCone is not frozen in the amber of art's "slow time," although she has aged more slowly than the rest of us over the past thirty years. (For example, in *The Ever-Running Man* [2007], McCone remains comfortably in her forties.) Nevertheless, McCone's passage through time has allowed Muller to explore the difficulties of, for lack of a better term, "growing up," or growing older. When we first meet Sharon McCone in *Edwin of the Iron Shoes*, she is in her late twenties and still very much an idealistic child of her time. As the series progresses, the reader watches McCone abandon her idealism and accept the compromises of success within her own field. Though she never loses sight of her moral obligations to others, she certainly revises the means of approaching these ideals — and, admittedly, she becomes skeptical of the possibility of *fully* achieving such goals. However, throughout her travels, she remains a professional, "and she won't let you forget it," as Muller has fondly noted (Isaac 30).

Interestingly, though Muller's name remains synonymous with the genre of the female hard-boiled detective, she professes to have little interest in remaining "true" to its structural requirements. As she has reiterated, "All good fiction comes out of character; plot doesn't work if you have to force the characters," and "plot comes strictly from the characters" (Ross; Bibel 1596). If we take Chandler at his word in his well-known work *The Simple Art of Murder*, there is a precedent for this emphasis upon character in the hard-boiled genre. Indeed, "the gradual elucidation of character is all the detective story has any right to be about anyway," according to Chandler (19). Muller evidently agrees. And this focus on character has allowed her to develop the genre like few other authors. At times, this innovation is found in re-reading traditional hard-boiled tropes; at others, this innovation comes through in pure invention within the genre. In 1984, obviously still early in Muller's career, Isaac called attention to the fact that Muller's concentration on character allowed her plots to "cross most of the genre's sub forms" (21). This is all the more true of Muller's work since that time. Beginning in the 1990s, Muller tinkers with the limits of the detective genre to incorporate adventure and thriller trappings more properly found in spy novels. Priscilla Walton and Patricia Maida's chapters in the current study provide excellent accounts of the logic of these border crossings.

Along with character, the guiding preoccupation of Muller's writing is the question of place. In many ways, this focus serves as a continuation of her character studies. As she affirms, "The characters depend on their surroundings, and the reverse is also true" (Isaac 27). Obviously, San Francisco, McCone's base of operations, is hardly an innocent detective locale. There is a long and distinguished list of detectives working in this city, beginning with

Hammett's Sam Spade. Muller makes ample use of this coding of San Francisco, its atmosphere, and also its political history — particularly the legacy of the Beat Generation and the student revolutions (Bairner 123).

Most importantly, Muller presents the city as the site of potential community, rather than scripting it as a simple adversary or figure of moral decay — a representation common to the original hard-boiled authors. For Horsley, in feminist crime fiction, "communal solidarity" is "not just a sustaining presence for the protagonist but the linchpin both for the plot and the protagonist's own self-definition" (264, 250). Throughout Muller's writing, this bond to others remains a guiding principle, even for the lone wolf McCone. Yet, Muller is careful to ensure that this "community" remains an open question. Like the space of the city, the place of community is always a contested site. The stakes of this dispute are found in the frequent references to San Francisco's past, and the recurrent description of the ways in which the topography of the city has changed during its history.

As was true with character, change is the only constant for the city. Throughout her years of writing about San Francisco, Muller has dealt with the numerous challenges facing the city, particularly those surrounding its immigrant and minority populations, as well as issues as varied as urban renewal, ecology, and terrorism. Here, too, the history of these trials is always reconnoitered as lived experience. Speaking of Muller, Grafton, and Paretsky, Dilley observes, "Cities and crimes have pasts, presents, and futures" (38). Muller unfolds this temporal expanse by confronting the reader with the often-traumatic effects these events have on individuals.

In the McCone series especially, this trauma is inevitable. To these ends, Muller affirms that history is important to her work (Bibel 1597), especially insofar as history "returns" to disrupt the present. Speaking of this unifying gesture in her work, Muller has said, "If the books have an underlying theme, it would be about how a past event can trigger a present explosion" (qtd. Martin 226). Naturally, such disruptions are the stock in trade of the detective genre. However, Muller's emphasis upon the experience of her characters and the lingering effects of crime and betrayal ensure that there are never any simple solutions. History is not a puzzle to be solved by the detective. Rather, it is an enigma that demands that we always retell and re-imagine the stories of our survival. Thus, the reader is forced to confront the arbitrary nature of convention and the ethical — and the potentially redemptive — component of interpretation.

Perhaps Muller's most important contribution to the hard-boiled genre is McCone's sense of empathy. McCone often shares her compassion equally with criminals and victims, which complicates the notion of the detective as a strict moral compass. Crime remains linked with larger social problems that cannot be resolved through the solution to a mystery and the apprehension of the malefactor. In nearly all her adventures, McCone is faced with the issues of racism, sexism, and bigotry. As a female investigator of Shoshone ancestry, she is doubly open to such violence, and all the more sympathetic to other victims of such treatment. Always acknowledging the enormity of these societal ills, McCone does not lose sight of the effects these struggles have on individuals.

Given the nature of this project, before concluding this introduction, it behooves me to say just a word about Muller's relative invisibility within detective fiction criticism. One of the more insightful comments on the scholarship of the female private eye genre was made by Linda Mizejewski in her *Hardboiled and High Heeled: The Woman Detective in Popular Culture* (2004). Here is Mizejewski's view of Sue Grafton and Patricia Cornwell's success and longevity:

> The Grafton and Cornwell series in some ways exemplify the 1970s tough-chic school of feminism, in which women succeed on male turf without changing the rules of the game. But they might also exemplify the residue of mainstream feminism *and* its backlash at the end of the twentieth century. After all, both sides can claim this strong female character as their own. She can be proof that women can succeed without the help of a cause or politics; and she can be proof that 1970s feminism *did* succeed, with the result that this character is now possible. That's why critics who debate the politics of the woman detective character often use the same evidence to come to different conclusions, a clue about why this character has such a wide appeal [23–24].

From the beginning in the 1980s, when academic interest latched onto the female private eye, critical response has fallen into these two camps. Either the female private eye is celebrated as a powerful representation of feminist demands (and perhaps successes), or she is scorned as a compromise formation of the worst kind.

Klein's *The Woman Detective: Gender and Genre* (1988) remains an influential point of reference in this debate. Klein famously claimed that gender and genre are necessarily at odds in the female detective text. Klein's often-cited summary of this situation is that "the detective script and the woman script clash because the necessary condition for each are the inverse and contradiction of the other" (57). This assumes that the detective text remains a conservative narrative that defends the status quo against corruption. Thus, the solution to a mystery always justifies current relations of power and the objectification of women. Should a woman refuse to be the object of a masculine narrative, the result can only be the rupture of the normative discourse. Unfortunately, this refusal would also take her outside the boundary of detective fiction. This subtle co-option is so powerful that Klein claims "women readers have to adopt an antifemale as well as an antifeminist stance unless they become self-consciously resisting readers" (132). The latter possibility seems remote at best. For Klein, the game of female detection is inevitably scripted according to the ominous proposition of all forced choices: "Heads I win; tails you lose."

In the opposite camp, in their equally influential *Detective Agency: Rewriting the Hard-Boiled Tradition* (1990), Walton and Jones have argued that the female hard-boiled detective actually "normalizes" a certain brand of feminism for readers who would not ordinarily read in this way (60). As the title of their valuable work suggests, the authors have much more faith in the reader's ability to read *otherwise*, that is, beyond the normative conventions that keep a woman "in her place." Rereading a masculine genre like hard-boiled detective fiction from a female perspective requires that readers critically negotiate several texts simultaneously. In so doing, readers (and authors) become "generic outlaws who, in appropriating powerful linguistic conventions, resituate and redirect power" (195). Walton and Jones conclude that this redirection reveals the rhetoric of both gender and genre, as well as the possibility of altering the "generic — and gendered — conventions of both literary and social behavior" (46). Focusing on the complexity of these issues, female hard-boiled texts necessarily disclose "less easily resolved endemic injustices and oppressions, making possible a level of social or psychological inconclusiveness and thus critique" (211). For Walton and Jones, this brand of feminist reading is actually authorized by the female hard-boiled detective.

The issue of Muller's politics is especially interesting in light of Mizejewski's claim that identical evidence is so often used to support the two opposite perspectives just discussed. Indeed, Muller is alternately accused of being either "too political" or not political enough. Sharon McCone's leftwing views are immediately established in the series by her position as lead investigator at the All Souls Legal Cooperative, an organization that provides low-cost legal help to those in need. The Cooperative is born of communal aspirations of the 1960s and 70s, a program that McCone will continue to defend even after leaving All Souls. Reading this aspect of McCone, Jean Swanson and Dean James write, "Fans of Sharon McCone generally enjoy Sue Grafton's Kinsey Millhone novels, though McCone is a little older and more consciously political than Kinsey" (156–157). Similarly, Mizejewski herself finds Sharon McCone to have an "edgy, liberal conscience" that leaves her, along with Paretsky's V.I. Warshawski, "at one end of the political spectrum in this genre, just left of center" (25).

Not surprisingly, Klein has found McCone's politics not radical enough. Klein admits that Sharon McCone (like most other female hard-boiled detectives) has "feminist inclinations," but these remain compromised, particularly insofar as McCone is tied to the legal system, at work and at times in her personal life (203). Klein goes so far as to say that "Sharon has no sense that both [the police and legal systems] are part of a larger, flawed system needing to be changed" (209). Similarly dismissive, Bertens and D'haen find McCone to possess "very little of the admittedly rather unfocused social concern and compassion with the downtrodden that we find in Marlowe, Archer, and their countless successors and that also characterizes the great majority of female PI's" (23). Like so many female detectives, Sharon McCone has been read alternately as an example of the solution *and* problem of the larger issues raised by female detection.

The contributors to this anthology — many of whom are well-known participants in the ongoing debates on the female detective — take up these issues in detail throughout the following chapters. The anthology is divided into three parts: Gender, Genre, and Trauma. As the discussion above indicates, the combination of gender and genre has served as a productive framework for reading the female detective. The essays of these sections reexamine Muller's own critical reading of the rhetoric of gender and genre, and explore the multitude of ways in which she has attempted to write something "new" in response to these strictures. The essays grouped in the third section of the anthology focus upon an aspect of Muller's writing that is more idiosyncratic, that is, Muller's insistence that the trauma of history cannot be assuaged. Muller elaborates this experience in a number of ways in her fiction, but her strategy might be summarized as confronting the reader with the trauma of interpretation. When the categories of gender and genre fail — and fail they must — the result is in effect an interpretative trauma for the reader. However, it is precisely through this fragmentation that Muller endeavors to rewrite convention, inviting us to take up this agency in turn.

Part I: Gender

Chapter 1, "Changing the World, One Detective at a Time: The Feminist Ethos of Marcia Muller and Sharon McCone," by Winter S. Elliott, reads Muller's *The Dangerous Hour* (2004) and discusses how the McCone series represents modern feminism and serves as a barometer for measuring the changing status and concerns of the modern American woman.

Chapter 2, "Crime, Punishment, and Some Change in the McCone Series," by Chin-jau Chyan, explores Muller's strategic appropriation of hard-boiled sympathy for the underprivileged to include issues of gender and ethnicity. This interest brings Muller's work into dialogue with other women writers working with issues of diversity and difference within the tradition of American literature.

Chapter 3, "Imagining the Margins: Muller's Explorations of Race," by Maureen T. Reddy, discusses the issue of race in Muller's Sharon McCone and

Elena Oliverez series. In *The Dangerous Hour*, Muller brings these two detectives together, highlighting the odd fusion of essentialist perceptions of race as a biological given and more progressive conceptions of race as a social construction—two perspectives that are evident in each series.

Chapter 4, "Gender and Genre Stretching in the Non-McCone Novels," written by Pamela E. Bedore, reads Muller's *oeuvre* as a key to understanding the development of gendered and ethnic representations in detective fiction over the past several decades. Reading Muller's well-versed use of the history of detective fiction, Bedore focuses on three of Muller's lesser-known series: the Joanna Stark books (1986–1989), the Elena Oliverez books (1983–1986), and the Soledad County books (2001–2005).

Part II: Genre

Chapter 5, "Taking *Edwin* to Lunch: Developing the Female Hard-Boiled Detective in the Early McCone Novels," by Patricia P. Buckler, examines the development of Sharon McCone's character in the first four novels of the series, and at the same time reads the parallel development of Muller as an author. Concomitantly, Buckler examines the rapidly changing gender politics of the 1980s.

Chapter 6, "Sharon McCone: From PI to Anti-Terrorist," written by Priscilla L. Walton, claims that Muller maintained her popularity throughout the 1990s—a time when public interest in the female private eye waned—by producing a generic hybrid: part PI novel, part thriller. The essay explores the context of these "new" McCone novels of the mid–90s, a time that brings both a shift in audience, as well as a shift in the political climate surrounding the feminist investigator.

Chapter 7, "Searching for the Past: Nostalgia in the McCone Novels," by Kelly C. Connelly, argues that Muller inventively redirects the nostalgia at the heart of all detective narrative to explore questions of identity and the social relation in a postmodern world. Providing an insightful reading of *Listen to the Silence* (2000), in which McCone uncovers the truth about her Native American heritage, Connelly then uses the category of identity to focus on Muller's own nostalgic references to the history of detective fiction.

Chapter 8, "The Journey of Sharon McCone, Private Investigator," by Patricia L. Maida, analyzes McCone's postmodern femininity as it develops over the course of the series. Citing the violent action of Muller's *Wolf in the Shadows* (1993), the author discusses Muller's foray into the "high tech thriller genre," and assesses how this adaptability figures the present challenges of the postmodern woman.

Part III: Trauma

Chapter 9, "Anxious Authorship: The Detective Fiction of Marcia Muller and Gertrude Stein," by Jessica V. Datema, provides a comparative study of the way in which Marcia Muller and Gertrude Stein negotiate their authorial identifications with their creations. This inquiry examines doppelganger figures in Muller's *While Other People Sleep* (1998), *Point Deception* (2001), and Stein's *Blood on the Dining Room Floor.*

Chapter 10, "The Lost Child: Haunting Motif in the McCone Novels," by Harriette C. Buchanan, focuses on the motif of the "lost child" in the series. The author of this chapter argues that the figure of the lost child parallels questions crucial to the McCone series, namely, origin and family — McCone's own family, of course, but also the "human family," as well.

Chapter 11, "Muller Earth: Mythic Topography in the Soledad County Trilogy," by Christine A. Jackson, analyzes the production of space and its symbolic encodings within Muller's fiction. Early McCone novels set in San Francisco create topographical metaphors of frontier, which clearly work to figure McCone's own "exploration" in the predominantly male space of detection. While such figurative devices in the McCone series obviously serve to develop character, propel narrative, and foreshadow solutions in other works, Muller's topography shifts focus to a space beyond the individual, the realm of myth.

Chapter 12, "The Deafening Silence of the McCone Series," by Alexander N. Howe, explores the series' dominant tropes, "silence" and "echo," in terms of the "object voice" of psychoanalysis. Muller's development of these figures is read as the key to the critical epistemological gesture at the heart of her revisions of the hard-boiled narrative.

The conclusion, "Marcia Muller in the American Tradition: Still Breaching Our Insecurities," by Christine A. Jackson, synthesizes the various critical approaches of the anthology, placing these in a broader context of American literary tradition. Jackson uses these insights to examine Muller's latest McCone mystery, *The Ever-Running Man* (2007), and comments on the future of Muller criticism.

Works Cited

Bairner, Alan. "Sharon McCone's San Francisco: The Role of the City in the Work of Marcia Muller." *Irish Journal of American Studies* 6 (1997): 117–138.
Bertens, Hans, and Theo D'haen. *Contemporary American Crime Fiction.* New York: Palgrave, 2001.
Bibel, Barbara. "The Booklist Interview: Marcia Muller." *Booklist* (May 1, 2000): 1596–1597.
Chandler, Raymond. *The Simple Art of Murder.* New York: Ballantine, 1950.
Dilley, Kimberly. *Busybodies, Meddlers, and Snoops: The Female Hero in Contemporary Women's Mysteries.* Westport, CT: Greenwood Press, 1998.

Horsley, Lee. *Twentieth-Century Crime Fiction*. Oxford: Oxford University Press, 2005.

Isaac, Frederick. "Situation, Motivation, Resolution: An Afternoon with Marcia Muller." *Clues: A Journal of Detection* 5, no. 2 (1984): 20–34.

Klein, Kathleen. *The Woman Detective: Gender and Genre*. Urbana: University of Illinois Press, 1988.

Martin, Rebecca. "Marcia Muller." In *American Hard-Boiled Crime Writers*, ed. George Anderson and Julie Anderson, 267–282. Detroit, MI: Gale Group, 2000.

Mizejewski, Linda. *Hardboiled and High Heeled: The Woman Detective in Popular Culture*. New York: Routledge, 2004.

Muller, Marcia. "Partners in Crime." *The Writer* (May 1997): 7–10, 46.

_____. "What Sharon McCone Learned from Judy Bolton." In *Deadly Women: The Woman Mystery Reader's Indispensable Companion*, ed. Jan Grape, Dean James, and Ellen Nehr, 67–70. New York: Carroll and Graf, 1998.

Ross, Michele. "How Mystery Masters Plot Their Craft." *Christian Science Monitor* (July 31, 1997): 89, 172. http://www.epnet.com/ (accessed October 3, 2007).

Swanson, Jean, and Dean James. *By a Woman's Hand: A Guide to Mystery Fiction by Women*. New York: Berkley, 1994.

Walton, Priscilla, and Manina Jones. *Detective Agency: Women Rewriting the Hard-Boiled Tradition*. Berkeley: University of California Press, 1990.

Part I

GENDER

1

Changing the World, One Detective at a Time: The Feminist Ethos of Marcia Muller and Sharon McCone

WINTER S. ELLIOTT

In her most recent Sharon McCone novel, Marcia Muller placed her character in what is possibly her most surprising and challenging role yet: marriage. After twenty-four books and myriad revelations and changes in Sharon McCone's character, the detective has evolved into a complex, resilient, and socially responsive woman. In the thirty years spanning from the publication of the first McCone novel in 1977 to her most recent outing in 2007, McCone has grown and changed, experiencing many of the subtle cultural shifts pivotal to the rapidly evolving American society. Consequently, McCone's reactions and participation in the various facets of modern life in America have rendered her a "touchstone" for current events. As Muller recognized in a 1990 interview: "[E]ach book is "about something" ... I have made more of a conscious effort to define to myself what I'm trying to say in a given book. Muller's "statements" on contemporary American life are always accompanied by expeditions into the past, particularly the pivotal decades of the 1960s and 70s" ("The Real McCone" 263).

McCone has thus dealt with everything from environmental activism, to gay rights, to the pros and cons of the death penalty. One issue, however, has remained almost a constant throughout the entire series. Although various writers created different female detectives before the publication of Muller's first novel, *Edwin of the Iron Shoes*,[1] in 1977, Muller is widely credited with launching the concept of the *hard-boiled* female detective. Sharon McCone adapts herself to what had been a primarily masculine genre and job — and she also adapts both that literary category and occupation to her own femininity. With Muller as with other modern authors of the genre, her main character represents a careful negotiation between the strictures of the original genre and the needs and differences of a specifically female detective (Walton and Jones 99). Therefore, the series consistently, if often implicitly, questions the relationship between the female McCone and an apparently patriarchal society. Accordingly, the character of Sharon McCone not only measures the changing status and concerns of the modern American woman over a period of several decades, but she also reflects the changing meanings and objectives of the feminist movements of those same years.

The nineteen sixties and seventies — the two decades immediately before and during which Muller began writing the McCone series — coincided with the rise and pinnacle of second wave feminism. In keeping with the times, second wave feminism was a highly politicized construct, contesting economic disparity and embracing issues as diverse as reproductive rights and sex discrimination. Often remembered for "bra burning, protest marches, and the sexual revolution" (Jacob and Licona 201), "'second wave' feminism is characterized at least in part by the practice of activism: getting real things changed in the name of feminism" (Meredith 126). Sharing historical similarities with first wave feminism, which flourished at the end of the nineteenth century and coincided with the abolitionists, second wave feminism followed another social upheaval, the civil rights movement. Third wave feminism, in turn, responded to perceived failures of those attempts to advance women's rights. Whereas post–civil rights movement feminism can be characterized as an incensed and reactionary movement, intent upon identifying and rectifying social evils perpetrated upon women, third wave feminism employs a very different — and harder to define — tone. Second wave feminism adopted a proprietary attitude towards women, attempting to coalesce all women and all feminist issues under a single umbrella. In contrast, third wave feminism welcomes different genders and different understandings of gender (Jacob and Licona 200). Additionally, this mind-set has adopted a more celebratory attitude toward femininity, distinguishing itself from prior mind-sets often criticized for portraying women as victims of patriarchal society.[2] Third wave feminism, in essence, celebrates female independence and power and aspires for more — power, that is. Significantly, neither of these concerted efforts to enact social change occurred in an academic vacuum, as each movement was interested in improving the everyday lives of women. Although second wave feminists are perhaps caricatured due to some extremist positions, both movements in feminist thinking enacted profound and long-lasting attitude shifts in our culture.

Marcia Muller freely admits that Sharon McCone enjoys decelerated aging. In other words, although the series has existed for twenty-nine "real-time" years, Sharon McCone has not aged at that same rate.[3] Nevertheless, her character and its evolution do reflect actual changes in feminism from her first appearance to the most recent chapter in her life. McCone, in effect, portrays the shift from the highly political, reactive second wave feminism to the more congratulatory, triumphant third wave feminism.[4] As contemporary society revised its view of women and feminist issues, McCone also changed, in her attitudes, dreams, and even her job. Throughout the series, the reader finds evidence of changes in McCone's development to parallel the shift in feminism itself, thus demonstrating Muller's consistent awareness of women's issues.

In the first few books of the series, it is questionable whether McCone may even be called a feminist. Plummer, for example, argues that Sharon McCone is not at all a "feminist," in the social or political sense: "Although aware from the first novel that discrimination against women exists, initially she could not be called a feminist" (245). Plummer acknowledges, though, that McCone's "feminist awareness, as well as her social consciousness, generally grow as the series progresses" (245).

Klein is more critical of Muller's inconsistencies:

> Midway through the first McCone novel, Muller suggests her character's feminist inclinations.... However, this motif fades away in subsequent novels. Sharon is specific about her relationships with men, wanting equality but not marriage. However, she has little to say about her consciousness of women's position in society except as men exasperate her with patronizing remarks [209].

But Klein also comments that "Sharon McCone might best be described as having feminist inclinations without explicitly defining [herself] that way" (202). This assessment comes closer to the reality of McCone's nature and the truth of her relationship with the feminist movement. Significantly, neither McCone nor her creator stand at the forefront of the feminist movement; Muller writes crime fiction, not feminist theory. As the novels indicate, McCone shows annoyance over people involved in social causes. For example, in *There's Something in a Sunday*, McCone disavows participation in organized group movements, from community activism to protest of the Vietnam War.[5]

Both Muller and McCone, however, have proven extremely receptive to cultural developments. Muller, in creating her female detective, responded to a perceived gap in popular fiction (Walton and Jones 19). As Walton and Jones perceptively observe:

> Trends in popular fiction, especially realist fiction, are driven by changes in society and in what readers are willing to "buy" in both the literal and metaphoric sense of that word. In one sense, realist fiction defines and conventionalizes the limits of its audience's shifting conceptions of reality at the same time that it allows its readers to explore, mediate, and manage their fantasies and fears about those limits [12–13].

Unsurprisingly, popular fiction followed this same course, creating characters responsive to the feminist movements of the 1960s and 1970s (Walton and Jones 12–13). Thus, it does not matter whether McCone is or is not a self-aware feminist character. Created in response to cultural stimuli of the "real world," McCone faces societal problems and responds to them, not as a feminist, but as an actual American woman. McCone's pulse, therefore, beats along with the heartbeat of the everyday woman — and her shifting attitudes and perceptions of feminism are also similar to those of everyday women. Ultimately, McCone's attitudes towards authority, physicality, and personal relationships demonstrate her connection to the ongoing shift from second to third wave feminism.[6]

In the third book in the series, *The Cheshire Cat's Eyes*, Sharon McCone quite correctly tells a listener, "I'm not very responsive to authority" (54). Indeed, throughout the course of the series, McCone frequently breaks rules, laws, and social strictures — although she grows less willing to risk her license as she matures. Despite her anti-authoritarian nature, in *Edwin of the Iron Shoes*, the first book in the series, we find McCone firmly within what could easily be regarded as a patriarchal structure: The All Souls Legal Cooperative. Muller explains this decision in an interview, stating that the organization provided Sharon with a sort of ready-made family. As an All Souls Investigator, "she wouldn't just be sitting in an office with a bottle in the desk drawer. All Souls gave her associates and friends. It gave her relationships" ("Marcia Muller: 'The Time Was Ripe'" 361). Despite the warm and fuzzy family feelings at All Souls, the association also appears to mimic, if benignly, the traditional protective, yet confining, and controlling function of any patriarchal organization. In *Edwin of the Iron Shoes*, for example, Greg Marcus, the initially challenging and insulting police lieutenant who confronts McCone, comes to conciliatory terms with the detective only as a result of the intervention of McCone's boss, Hank Zahn. In the same book, McCone is careful to seek Zahn's approval and permission — which he generously gives — before pursuing her investigation in the murder of Joan Albritton.

More telling, though, is McCone's relationship with the police in this same novel. McCone's interactions with Greg Marcus reflect a familiar version of authority that results in an equally as familiar patriarchal relationship. At first, Marcus is solidly dismissive of McCone's abilities; he is patronizing as well as sexist. Asking McCone about her job, he inquires, "Do you really have an investigator's license?" (*Edwin* 20). A little later, in response to her description of security work, he says, "Yeah, a nice business. So now you're out on your own, on the way to becoming a super-sleuth" (*Edwin* 21). However, undoubtedly the most telling evidence of Marcus's attitude towards the "super-sleuth" comes later in the book, when he remarks, "Yes, papoose, I can see you're learning a lot. It's a pity it hasn't improved your temper — or your appearance, for that matter. You look like you could use a bath" (*Edwin* 68). This snide remark about McCone's appearance criticizes her body — and implicitly, her sexuality. At the same time, Marcus manages to insult McCone's professional capabilities by at once mockingly praising her — "you're learning a lot" — and diminishing her through the comparison to a helpless infant. When McCone first challenges the term, demanding "What's this 'papoose' bit?" he smugly responds, "That's what they call little Indians, isn't it? Or would you rather I called you 'squaw'?" (*Edwin* 68). The use of "squaw" further emphasizes McCone's femininity and ethnicity, underscoring Marcus's challenge of her competence and suitability for her profession. Admittedly, near the end of the book Marcus laughingly acknowledges the derogatory term "papoose" manages to be racist, sexist, and ageist at once (*Edwin* 149). Thus, Marcus employs language as a descriptive tool, attempting to remake McCone into someone he can easily dominate. As Wilson observes, Marcus's "use of the name marks a structure of power within the relationship which positions Marcus, the figure of the law, as a dominating father rather than a sympathetic lover" (151). Significantly, both Hank Zahn and Greg Marcus enact very different paternal roles, and both, either mildly or caustically, attempt to control McCone's actions and temperament.

Notably, McCone responds neither to her professional situation nor to her relationship with Marcus with what could be called self-aware feminist reactions. Indeed, she is happy with her job at All Souls precisely because of the freedom she believes it grants her. Moreover, when Marcus repeatedly uses the term "papoose" over the course of the book, she frequently responds with controlled anger and attempts to reason with him. For example, "You have no business calling me either [papoose or squaw]. I don't have to listen to your comments on my ancestry or on the way I look. I can imagine you wouldn't look so great yourself if you'd spent the night on that couch" (*Edwin* 68). When she finally demands that he stop using the word "papoose," she interprets it as a "racial slur," and it is Marcus, not McCone, who acknowledges it as also "sexist and ageist" (*Edwin* 149). McCone, thus, doesn't react as a second wave feminist herself — but the situation she finds herself in is, nonetheless, one easily recognizable to a second wave feminist.

In fact, McCone in *Edwin of the Iron Shoes* finds herself in situations which represent the very problems second wave feminists contested. Confined within a benign patriarchy, McCone doesn't actively resist its limitations until its strictures cease to be comfortable. McCone constantly challenges Marcus, who as a police officer aptly figures the power fought through political activism in the 1960s and 1970s. She finds her physicality, her strength, and her professional abilities challenged throughout the book — always on the basis of her femininity. Thus, while McCone might not qualify as a feminist herself, the challenges she faces are undeniably informed by that same activist feminist movement.

McCone consistently demonstrates that, while she is willing to cooperate with authority, she considers it something to be disregarded and subverted the moment it infringes upon her own desires or sense of ethics. Significantly, McCone did not stumble onto her profession; she worked in department store security before earning a degree in sociology at Berkeley, and then joined "one of the big detective agencies here in the city" (*Ask the Cards* 55) after college. But McCone did not remain with that agency very long. She explains:

> I'm not on my own; I'm an employee of All Souls. I joined them after the detective agency fired me for refusing to jump at a special assignment that would have humiliated me and set up an innocent man for a very messy and expensive divorce. And I don't know about being what you call a "super-sleuth." I'm competent. I'd say my strong point is knowing how to ask the right questions. Without trying to cram my words into other people's mouths [*Edwin* 21].

As McCone tells Marcus, she lost her first real job because of an unethical "special assignment," one that, she infers, might have depended more upon her sexuality than her competence. In her response to Marcus, McCone demonstrates several attitudes at once — opinions coinciding with second wave feminism. McCone resists authority; she rejects identification of her profession with her sexuality; she is comfortable within a group setting. Similarly, second wave feminists also identified with a group, all women, and rejected both patriarchal authority and traditional interpretations of female sexuality. When challenged, McCone assumes an activist stance, willing to oppose and destabilize authority the moment its strictures become uncomfortable.

Ultimately, McCone finds the investigator's job at All Souls too confining, as her position there often forces her into a traditionally female role. *Wolf in the Shadows*, written in 1993 and the fourteenth in the series, begins with a subtle confrontation between McCone and her boss, Hank Zahn. As McCone scurries past on the stairs of All Souls, Hank grasps Sharon's shoulder, bringing her to an abrupt halt (*Wolf* 7). Setting her jaw, McCone demands to be let go, leaving Hank stammering a "befuddled" apology in her wake (*Wolf* 7).

Over the length of the series, McCone and Zahn seldom experience severe confrontations; they remain friends after her departure from All Souls. But the language of this first chapter of *Wolf in the Shadows* proves prophetic in suggesting the state of McCone's current relationship with her boss and the All Souls organization. Escape is implied twice in this short passage. Zahn wants to know where McCone is going, and she herself hopes to make a "getaway." Zahn also, literally, tries to hold McCone back, grabbing her shoulder, jerking her to a halt. Control and restriction, along with a need for escape, reverberate from this encounter to the later meeting between McCone and the firm's partners.

McCone feels suspicious about the meeting from the first, and it becomes increasingly clear that the firm intends to control what it regards as McCone's lack of discipline. Humorously, Ted, the firm's openly gay office manager, whispers "*Noli nothis permittere te terere,*" which he translates as "Don't let the bastards get you down" (*Wolf* 26). McCone is thus placed in a very loose alliance with another socially transgressive individual. Ted feels sympathy for her, not just because he is her friend, but because, as her friend, Ted understands that McCone will not be able to tolerate the limitations of the job her other supposed "friends" want to inflict upon her. As Hank reluctantly explains, the firm has decided to make McCone administrator of a department including both the investigators and the paralegals. McCone responds, "You want to confine me to a desk job?" (*Wolf* 31). Later, she imagines that the proposed job "would also mean stultifying boredom and a hell of a lot of clock-watching. It would mean surrendering the freedom I loved" (*Wolf* 35). Of course, the firm interprets McCone's prized freedom as a liability, a lack of discipline that can be remedied by giving McCone a raise and chaining her to a desk. The administrator's job, McCone observes, is what she *should* want. She reflects, "I wondered what was wrong with me. Substantial salary increase, profit sharing — the American dream. So why did I feel so confused and resistant?" (*Wolf* 32). McCone resists the job because it conflicts with who she is and the profession she has chosen. McCone values independence, freedom, and the ability to determine her own schedule. The proposed "promotion" would instead place her within a safe and controlled position, one much more traditionally acceptable for a female.

By the end of the book, the firm has bent to McCone's desires, but, no longer needing the safety net of All Souls, she opts for a permanent change — a change that in later books will become total independence and a firm of her own. McCone avoids compromise, refusing her "superiors'" concessions.

By the time of *The Dangerous Hour*, written in 2004 but set only a few years after *Wolf in the Shadows*, McCone has evolved into a full-fledged third wave feminist. McCone appears to have accomplished total success. She seems to have realized a feminist ideal and a myth of the twentieth (and now twenty-first) century: a woman's ability to succeed in both personal and professional spheres. McCone manages her own stable of detectives who double as good friends and sometimes protégés, but she also possesses a stable, healthy relationship with a man who both understands and complements her nature. McCone observes, "During the past two years our business had tripled. Last year we'd taken over all the offices fronting on the north-side second-story catwalk at Pier 24½" (*Dangerous Hour* 3). She has come a long way from her small office in that converted closet at All Souls where her career began (*Dan-*

gerous Hour 4). Initially, it appears that McCone's decision to buck authority and establish her own business has been uniformly successful. But McCone quickly learns that her complacency is dangerous.

A forgotten enemy from her past hatches a complex and clever plan to destroy her business and her life. Reynaldo Dominguez, the man McCone eventually tracks down and apprehends, constructs a plot around his own specifically misogynistic aims and beliefs. Effectively, McCone learns that while it may appear that authority no longer presents a problem, other misogynistic forces still necessitate conscious feminism. Indeed, the encounter with Reynaldo Dominguez suggests another recurring consideration McCone has dealt with over the course of her career: being female.

As a woman detective, McCone faces different challenges from her various male counterparts. Although Muller seldom stresses the limitations of McCone's size and build, both men and women consistently challenge that same body. These challenges range from relatively benign incredulity at the seeming incongruity between McCone's body and her profession to outright attacks on her sexuality. As the series progresses, both the nature of these challenges and McCone's reactions to them change, again paralleling the culture's progression from second to third wave feminism.

In the third book in the series, *The Cheshire Cat's Eye*, a prominent woman, Eleanor van Dyne, reacts to the hazards of McCone's profession with horror:

> "Good gracious!" she put a bejeweled hand to her throat. "What a grisly business! Why would a young woman of your looks and apparent intelligence want to involve herself in such sordid goings-on?"
> "It beats sitting behind a desk shuffling paper."
> She studied me for a moment. "Yes, I expect it does" [*Cheshire* 59].

Eleanor van Dyne's initial incomprehension of McCone's career choice fades to understanding and something very close to shared empathy and agreement. Initially, she correlates McCone's looks with her ability to find an appropriate job; by the end of the short exchange, she acknowledges that a desk job might not be all that a woman might want. Eleanor van Dyne and McCone do not, of course, accomplish anything remotely like the sisterhood so ardently desired by second wave feminists. McCone is talking to van Dyne, after all, under false pretenses. However, the shift from van Dyne's initial surprise at the discordance between McCone's appearance and occupation to a very limited understanding of McCone's desire for excitement does suggest the difficulties second wave feminism faced in forcing all members of society — including other women — to accept and acknowledge new roles for women.

Notably, although McCone continues to face similar challenges in later books, these confrontations often come from very different sources. For example, in *The Dangerous Hour*, McCone encounters Boydston, an old conservative Texan, who tells her that she drives "right good, for a girl" (244). Rather than become angry, she decides that it is "useless to go on resenting his genial sexism" (244).

Boydston embodies several interesting characteristics: he is male, older, and harmless. McCone, like many young third wave feminists, regards his version of misogyny as relatively innocuous. Boydston, in turn, considers McCone and others like her — including Rae Kelleher, McCone's former assistant — amazing but not particularly troubling. Upon hearing that Rae, whose husband is famous for his music, has just published a novel and is "an artist in her own right," Boydston shakes his head, saying, "Women these days — ain't it amazin'" (*Dangerous* 246). Although Eleanor van Dyne and Boydston share similar preconceptions, they also suggest very different societal realities. Eleanor van Dyne initially responds to McCone's appearance; Boydston responds to Rae's accomplishments. Additionally, Eleanor comes to terms with McCone's nontraditional profession, while Boydston remains in perpetual, if harmless, wonder. At the same time, Boydston represents an "antiquated" minority, whereas Eleanor's opinions were then a majority preconception. Effectively, McCone has moved from regarding such challenges as a typical fact of life to an unfortunate aberration.

More complicated still are physical challenges faced by McCone. In *Ask the Cards a Question*, McCone meets with the ironically named Mr. Hood — one of the few men in the book who is not, in fact, a criminal — who expresses (conventional) surprise at her appearance: "You look like you could be someone's very efficient secretary" (*Ask the Cards* 167). More interestingly, he also bluntly asks, "Know Judo? Know how to slap thugs around?" (*Ask the Cards* 167). McCone confirms that she has used judo, one of the very few references in the series to her martial abilities. Indeed, McCone typically relies upon mental toughness that denies or refuses to recognize any physical inferiority and, of course, upon her gun. Regardless, her ability to both recognize and deal with sexual aggression progresses as she matures and as her character develops. In *Ask the Cards a Question*, McCone relies upon a "calm response" to defuse Neverman's sexual belligerence. Neverman tells her, "You're really a pretty lady," words which "chill" McCone (*Ask the Cards* 76). Neverman proceeds to push "up the sleeve of my sweater and began stroking me with his fingers" (*Ask the Cards* 76). McCone responds by removing his hand and adjusting her sweater. Similarly, in *The Cheshire Cat's Eye*, McCone falls victim to a stronger male attacker — judo apparently failing her:

> I was so busy reaching for my find that I didn't take note of my surroundings. By the time I became aware of the footsteps behind me, a dark figure loomed up. It slammed me into the side of the archway. I cried out as my cheek scraped against the bricks, and a hand clamped over my mouth. An arm circled me, and

my attacker began to drag me into the alley. I tried to wrench free. I tried to get into one of the holds I'd learned in self-defense class. Nothing worked [*Ask the Cards* 118].

Despite her training, McCone is unable to defend herself against her attacker — much less defeat him.

In *The Dangerous Hour*, McCone faces an even more dangerous opponent, but she has also changed her strategy. Fighting with Dominguez, McCone first hides, then realizes, "This could go on all night, unless I took the offensive" (286). When she later interrogates — and provokes — Dominguez, McCone says:

Well, I can guess your plans for me. At first it was enough to ruin me professionally, but when you realized I'd identified you, it turned into something different. You wanted me to die, but first you wanted me to suffer [*Dangerous* 297].

McCone's limited ability to defend herself in *Ask the Cards a Question* corresponds with an issue second wave feminists stressed — female vulnerability. Third wave feminists, while recognizing continued violence against women, also celebrate female potential. By *The Dangerous Hour*, McCone has learned to employ her strengths effectively — her intellect, determination, physical fitness, language — and she has also moved beyond self-defense to active offense. Whereas in *Ask the Cards a Question* McCone can barely articulate why Neverman so alarms her, in *The Dangerous Hour* she has mastered those words and concepts — humiliation, torture, rape, murder — and in two languages. By expressing those possibilities, she negates some of their power.

Humiliation, torture, rape, and murder represent McCone's awareness of what can happen to ill-prepared or unlucky women, but they also haunt her ideas of personal relationships and marriage. While McCone herself does not verbalize a strictly feminist stance, she consistently recognizes and encounters the downsides of female participation in the institution of marriage. McCone herself goes through a number of rocky relationships before she encounters Hy Ripinsky, whose need for independence equals her own.

As early as *Ask the Cards a Question*, Muller begins to develop the dangers of marriage and sexual relationships for women into a recurring motif. The book contains not one, but two, women suffering as a result of their disastrous marriages: Linnea Carraway, who has landed at McCone's doorstep and litters McCone's apartment with evidence of her emotional disarray, and Madame Anya, the fortune teller at the heart of the book's plot. While Madame Anya uses blackmail to lure her husband home, Linnea has been abandoned by her spouse. Linnea "had a broken marriage, two preschool kids parked with Grandma, and a full-blown nervous breakdown over the prospect of her support running out in three years when, by the court's reckoning, she should have become self-supporting" (*Ask the Cards* 46–7). Undoubtedly Linnea's marriage and kids contribute to her lapse into drunken depression, but McCone sees money as the root issue. Linnea has lost not only a husband but also an income, and she is ill-prepared to earn her own living. Obviously, Linnea's situation underscores the difficulties facing women who depend on men for their sole economic support.

In *There's Something in a Sunday*, Muller fully expands her discussion of marriage and its drawbacks. McCone sees almost nothing but dysfunctional relationships over the course of the book; the debris of broken marriage after marriage surrounds her. Irene Lasser is raped by her husband's son and gives birth to his child; Jane Wilkonson's husband expects her to raise Irene's child (along with her own five) because he falsely believes the child is his; Vicky Cushman's husband wants an "open marriage" and treats her with scorn; Rae Kelleher's parasitic husband manipulates her with a fake suicide attempt and drains her of time, money, and energy; and even Hank Zahn and his wife, Anne-Marie, can't seem to exist in matrimonial harmony. McCone can hardly turn around without stumbling over some unhappy couple, and she is no exception to the rule, as she still suffers from her breakup with her former boyfriend, Don Del Boccio, the disc jockey. At the end of the book, McCone finds that she feels a distinct sympathy for the murderer. Jane Wilkonson brokenly explains:

> "Never even wanted all the kids I've got. Love them, but every time I'd wish.... But Frank had this need ... something to do with proving himself, I guess. Never cared that I had needs too. Something for myself. Sick of giving. Getting nothing in return. After Frank had her, he didn't want me anymore. Never came near me. So I didn't even have that. And then he wanted me to give some more ... to his bastard [*There's Something* 207].

Although Jane does not directly reject the traditional roles she has played for most of her life — wife and mother — her words testify to how ill-fitting she has found those responsibilities. Her final words in the book suggest an eerie, if unintentional, reflection of the title of Virginia Woolf's *A Room of One's Own*: "All I wanted was something of my own. Everybody's got to have something. Is it wrong to want that?" (*There's Something* 208). McCone considers the women and men she's seen throughout the book — Irene, Vicky, Gerry, Anne-Marie, Hank, Rae, and herself — and responds "'No,' I said firmly, 'it's not wrong at all'" (*There's Something* 208). Unfortunately, the prevailing lesson of *There's Something in a Sunday* does not seem to be the damages marriage may inflict on women — and on men, in the case of Hank. Instead, the book underscores the individual need for privacy and private ownership. Rae leaves her husband and moves into All Souls, and McCone plans to present her with a baboon flower as a "good housewarming — well, closetwarming — present" (*There's Something* 213). Despite the matrimonial carnage throughout the book, it ends optimistically, with the suggestion that freedom of some sort — even if it's found in a closet instead of an apartment or a house — is integral to individual development and health. McCone, therefore, is progressing from merely witnessing the dangers marriage presents to women to recognizing a sort of solution.

Significantly, the few successful sexual relationships sustained over the course of the series are unconventional in nature, often highly so. Hank Zahn and his wife, Anne-Marie, do survive their inability to live together, and in *The Shape of Dread* the two reconcile, with Hank moving into the apartment directly above Anne-Marie's. The two may not exactly live in the same space, but their marriage survives.

Similarly, despite the age difference, McCone's nephew Mick shows all signs of successfully continuing his relationship with his older lover, Charlotte Keim. Most significant, however, is McCone's marriage to Hy Ripinsky in *Vanishing Point*, published in 2006. McCone agreed to marry Ripinsky on impulse, and at the beginning of *Vanishing Point,* she is comfortable and pleased with her decision. Yet the book opens with various warnings about the dangers of marriage and the changes it will inflict upon both McCone and her new husband.

Gage Renshaw, who works with Ripinsky, dourly warns that "in my experience … a man gets married, he gets cautious, loses his edge. In our business, that makes for mistakes. And mistakes can be fatal" (*Vanishing Point* 6). McCone's friend Rae gives her a similar warning, telling her to "wait and see" the changes marriage will effect upon her life. At least at first, it seems that Rae's warning is justified. Ripinsky makes ominous noises about selling their various properties, including McCone's beloved little house, and buying a joint residence.

Vanishing Point, however, makes it apparent that the alternative to marriage can be far worse. Hired to find a vanished mother, McCone finds her — and makes a grim discovery. Not only did the woman willfully and consciously abandon her husband and daughters, but she also committed several murders. The woman has chosen a poisonous solitude, rejecting all familial relationships as well as possible friends. In contrast, McCone decides at the end of the book that marriage *can* embrace compromise: "*I won't have to give up this house that I love. He won't have to give up his ranch that he loves. And this house will become* ours" (*Vanishing Point* 323; italics in orig.). Neither McCone nor Ripinsky yield their individual passions; both maintain their individuality. Unlike the problematic relationships littering *There's Something in a Sunday*, both McCone and Ripinsky maintain a considerable measure of freedom, which seems to be the key ingredient in Muller's recipe for a viable marriage. McCone has thus evolved from merely observing the ills of marriage to a conscious realization of how little she really knows. She ends *Vanishing Point* with the excited and wondering words, "*Damn, I'm so new at this!*" (323; italics in orig.). She has moved from recognizing a problem to suggesting a solution and actively participating in that answer — a move reminiscent of the transition from second to third wave feminism and the corresponding cultural shift in attitudes towards male and female relationships.

Over the course of her career, McCone's role as a detective has required her to observe, to investigate, and, to some extent, to judge. In many ways, she has acted as an outsider, an onlooker, and an involved participant. As such, she has been in a unique position to weigh others' actions and choices and to formulate her own opinions. In regards to the feminist movement, McCone has taken on that same role of spectator. She has responded to events with passive vulnerability, suggestive of the attitudes second wave feminists fought against. McCone's attitude of hopeful strength in more recent books also reflects the tone of more recent feminism. Consequently, McCone has both experienced the problems second wave feminists so harshly and justifiably identified and, more recently, embodied the progressive, positive outlook embraced by third wave feminism. McCone ultimately insists upon individuality and freedom as necessities. It remains doubtful, however, whether McCone will ever specifically designate herself a feminist. After all, she considers herself first and foremost a detective.

Notes

1. For an expansive discussion of the history of the female detective, see Munt 1–29.
2. See especially Katie Roiphe, *The Morning After: Sex, Fear, and Feminism on Campus*; Naomi Wolf, *Fire with Fire: The New Female Power and How It Will Change the Twenty-First Century*; and Camille Paglia, *Sex, Art, and American Culture*. As Jennifer Gilley notes, "These three books claimed that contemporary feminism had devolved into what they called *victim feminism*, in which women derived all of their rhetorical power from claiming to be victims, particularly of sexual violence ... although they are not considered part of the third wave, they are part of the historical and cultural milieu third wavers have to negotiate in constructing contemporary feminism" (188).
3. See "The Real McCone" (263).
4. Discussing Patricia Highsmith, Ruth Rendell, and P.D. James, Sally Munt observes that these authors "all write within the historical context of the Women's Liberation Movement, developing particularly during the 1960s and 1970s and explicitly political ideology: modern feminism. This Second Wave of 'Queens of Crime' signifies another era of female achievement" (19). Although Munt does not discuss Muller during this time, Muller also began to write during the 1970s, and Sharon McCone, her main character, certainly came of age during this time.
5. McCone states, "I was uncomfortable enough with NIMBYism to have wriggled my way out of attending a block organizing meeting the week before. But that was true to form: in the sixties I'd done a lot of talking against the Vietnam War but very little protesting. Now I was merely hoping that somebody else would protect my property values for me. I wasn't proud of myself in either instance, but I was self-aware enough to have little real hope for change" (56).
6. Notably, in a discussion of female detectives in crime fiction, Munt comments that "as fantasy figures, these heroines facilitate a politicized vision of Woman. Female agency is assumed as these super-sleuths sally forth, suitably sanctioned by the literary institution, to strike down

crimes committed against humanist definitions of society. Functioning within a fantasy environ of post-feminist opportunity, these powerful detectives resolve three unstable forms close to the liberal feminist heart — the individual, the family, and the state" (31). McCone could be said to respond to and adapt these categories as well; but the two areas chosen above closely respond to her particular history and character.

Works Cited

Gilley, Jennifer. "Writings of the Third Wave: Young Feminists in Conversation." *Reference & User Services Quarterly* 44, no. 3 (2005): 187–198.

Jacob, Krista, and Adela C. Licona. "Writing the Waves: A Dialogue on the Tools, Tactics, and Tensions of Feminisms and Feminist Practices over Time and Place." *NWSA Journal* 17, no. 1 (2005): 197–205.

Klein, Kathleen Gregory. *The Woman Detective: Gender and Genre.* Urbana: University of Illinois Press, 1988.

Meredith, Fionola. "Where Do We Go From Here?" *International Feminist Journal of Politics* 5, no. 1 (2003): 126–129.

Muller, Marcia. *Ask the Cards a Question.* New York: Mysterious Press, 1990.

_____. *The Cheshire Cat's Eye.* New York: Mysterious Press, 1990.

_____. *The Dangerous Hour.* New York: Warner Books, 2004.

_____. *Edwin of the Iron Shoes.* New York: David McKay Company, 1977.

_____. "Marcia Muller: 'The Time Was Ripe.'" *Publishers Weekly* 241, no. 32 (August 8, 1994): 361–362.

_____. "The Real McCone." *Armchair Detective* 23, no. 3 (1990): 260–269.

_____. *The Shape of Dread.* New York: Mysterious Press, 1990.

_____. *There's Something in a Sunday.* New York: Mysterious Press, 1989.

_____. *Vanishing Point.* New York: Mysterious Press, 2006.

_____. *Wolf in the Shadows.* New York: Mysterious Press, 1993.

Munt, Sally R. *Murder by the Book? Feminism and the Crime Novel.* London: Routledge, 1994.

Plummer, Bonnie C. "Marcia Muller." In *Great Women Mystery Writers: Classic to Contemporary,* ed. Kathleen Gregory Klein, 244–248. Westport, CT: Greenwood Press, 1994.

Walton, Priscilla L., and Manina Jones. *Detective Agency: Women Rewriting the Hard-Boiled Tradition.* Berkeley: University of California Press, 1999.

Wilson, Ann. "The Female Dick and the Crisis of Heterosexuality." In *Feminism in Women's Detective Fiction,* ed. Glenwood Irons, 148–156. Toronto: University of Toronto Press, 1995.

2

Crime, Punishment, and Some Change in the McCone Series

CHIN-JAU CHYAN

> She was not the kind of private detective who has a bottle stashed in the desk drawer. She was not emotionally immune to the depressing and often tragic events she encountered on San Francisco's mean streets. She did not operate out of a shabby, one-woman down-town office. She was not a loner.
>
> Marcia Muller, *McCone and Friends*

Since the late 1970s, Marcia Muller has been praised as the "founding mother"[1] of female private eye fiction. This creation of an "authoritative new model of the detective" (Knight 167) has been placed alongside the accomplishments of Arthur Conan Doyle and Dashiell Hammett; however, the above passage reveals that Marcia Muller clearly differentiates her heroine, Sharon McCone, from both her iconic male predecessors and also her contemporary women counterparts. This chapter argues that Muller has distinguished herself in the genre by constantly and sophisticatedly attending to the issues of gender and race throughout the McCone series. These categories are uniquely examined as the detective goes through the aftermath of death and violence, being forced to shoot or kill under extreme circumstances. I suggest that the portrayal of McCone, someone who is aware of the destructive power of bloodshed and capable of scrutinizing her conscience, further challenges the generic tradition of many hard-boiled heroes. While this line of inquiry forcefully raises questions of diversity and difference, by frequently interrogating the experience of various minority populations in America, McCone's transformation into a "super detective" later in the series significantly diminishes this critique.

The central theme in most detective novels has always been the disclosure of crime. In Golden Age mystery fiction, as Stephen Knight observes, the crime is in some way socially contained: it often takes place in a secluded area, and the perpetrator is likely to belong to the same social class as the vic-

tim. Professional criminals or working-class characters never really play important roles, and "social conflict outside the murder scene" is rarely explored
(86–87). The process of investigation usually comes to an end after the identification of the murderer, and the result "brings a satisfying sense of com-
pletion and closure" (Horsley 12). To some extent, the traditional analytic
detective is interested only in "who done it" instead of "why," and thus overlooks the wider social-political context. Edward Margolies points out that such
genteel detectives defend the status quo because they believe in it (5). Similarly, Anne Cranny-Francis also notes that the detective "conceals the nature
of crime in bourgeois society even as s/he detects its perpetrator"; when an
"aberrant individual" is caught and then purged, social order will be restored
and, thus, shown to be innocent (152).

While the Golden Age mystery is frequently set in a bucolic landscape
with a seemingly harmonious society, the hard-boiled detective story is located
in the seedy urban streets dominated by lawless gangsters and permeated with
institutional corruption. As Lee Horsley puts it, the hard-boiled world is a
"contrast between the containment possible in the classic form and the dark
open-endedness of the alleyway, a location never conducive to the confident
act of bringing forth order from confusion" (71). Without the possibility of
"containment," the private eye's search for an individual criminal simultaneously shows that the wrongdoer is the product of a larger social construction
and a symptom of the illness of America. There is a sense of ubiquitous evil
and moral degeneration residing in society, and no one is immune to its malig-
nant influence. Although the alienated detective serves as the upholder of values and the righter of wrongs, he is unable to correct the social system as a
whole. There is never a guarantee of a perfect solution and, more often than
not, readers are left with more questions than answers.

In Muller's fiction, the identification of the lawbreaker often leads to the
exposure of social injustice and the predicament of the minorities in society,
particularly in the early part of the series. If this consideration for the underprivileged is similar to the male hard-boiled detective tradition, Muller places
greater emphasis on the issues of gender and ethnicity. In *The Cheshire Cat's
Eye*, for example, discrimination against homosexuality is the cause of three
homicides. Paul Collins who "fled the Midwest to find freedom and acceptance in San Francisco" does find love (66–67), but his partner's father humil-
iates him by offering him money to leave the city, saying that "no ... faggot
could possibly be good" for his family (197). Desperately trying to keep hold
of the relationship, Collins kills the father and commits two other murders
to cover up the evidence.

After McCone confronts him at the crime scene, Collins tries to run
away but unfortunately breaks his neck. When the heroine explains what has
happened to the police, McCone realizes that she actually sympathizes with

the killer: "I discovered I'd liked Paul Collins in spite of his murders. He was a gentle man, ill at ease with his nature, and ultimately the rough world had driven him too far. While knowing that did not excuse his crimes, it made them more understandable" (203).

McCone completes the investigation, but she knows there are still people like Collins suffering from prejudices because of their sexual identity. The novel also describes the antagonism between the affluent middle class families, including gay couples, and the relatively poor black community in the historical Western Addition area in San Francisco, where gentrification had "displac[ed] the blacks who have lived here for generations" (77). In this way, the story offers an alternative perspective on the situation of the sexual minorities in the city: while they may be the victims of discrimination, they can also play the role of the oppressors — whether knowingly or not — of another marginal group.

The plight of women in marriage is the central theme in *There's Something in a Sunday*. Irene Johnstone suffers domestic abuse from her wealthy, alcoholic husband and an incestuous rape by her stepson, which results in a child. She also has a short affair with Frank Wilkonson, an employee on her husband's ranch. But Frank's wife, Jenny, is trapped at home with six young children and endless housework. When McCone first visits Jenny, she is shocked that the wife knows almost nothing about her husband's life outside the house: "Plain Jane — that's what they think of me. The brood mare who only cares about her kids. I'm Frank's wife, and Randy's mother, and so on and so on. But take Frank and Randy and the rest of them away, and I'm nobody at all. So nobody ever tells me anything" (81).

Meanwhile, McCone's new assistant, Rae Kelleher, is struggling between her career and her possessive husband, who goes so far as to fake a suicide attempt to force her to quit the job. McCone sees the potential in Rae and is quite annoyed that she would let her husband's failings stand in the way of her professional goals. "Didn't she know that husbands might stay or go," McCone laments, "but a profession that would make use of the talents she seemed to possess would stand her in good stead for a lifetime?" (33).

Toward the end of the story, Jenny learns about the affair and shoots her husband out of despair. McCone helps Irene and her child leave for the women's protection center and manages to put the stepson on the stand during the trial. Motivated and encouraged by McCone, Rae decides to leave her husband and give herself a chance: "I've got a right to a dream, too!" Rae says, "Doug's got to learn he can't manipulate me like that.... Right now I'm not counting on anything — or anyone but myself" (212). This statement aptly summarizes a general critique of the novel, at the same time as it speaks to McCone's own program for empowerment.

The rich cultural and ethnic diversity of San Francisco provides the background for *There's Nothing to Be Afraid Of.* The story depicts in detail the difficulties of Vietnamese immigrant families living in the derelict Globe Apartment Hotel, as they strive to cope with their life in a new country. The tenants in the building are troubled by suspicious harassment, and later a teenager is even found dead in the basement. When the city Refugee Assistance Center asks McCone to work on the case, she finds the Vietnamese adults work hard to better their lives, but that the younger generation has a serious identity crisis. While a girl changes her name to Dolly and wants to bleach her hair blonde because she "admires Dolly Parton" (73), her brother Duc stoutly refuses to be assimilated into the materialism of the American dream: "My people settle in America. They look around them, and suddenly they must *have.*" "Have what?" asks McCone. "Everything," the angry young man exclaims:

> My sisters — you've seen them. The designer blue jeans, the T-shirts with stupid things written on them. Makeup. Hairdos. High heels. My parents are no better. They say we must save to move to the Sunset District. We must have a big house, and a car. They will fill the house with furniture and ... and ... things! [...] Comfortable, yes! But they choose the worst things about America to make their own. They are so anxious to fit in here. And in order to fit in, they must erase all the differences. They must erase who we really are. [...] We have a culture, an identity. And that is what they would throw away [54].

The central problem the Vietnamese family faces is, coincidentally, quite similar to that of the Changs in Gish Jen's *Typical American.*

Jen's novel examines and challenges the notion of an American dream through the Chang family, which has emigrated from China. Like the Vietnamese adults and little Dolly, Ralph Chang yearns to melt into American society by living, talking, even walking like a "typical" American. It is not until he almost loses his sister that he realizes the importance of family over material success. But no such understanding is achieved among the Vietnamese community in Muller's story. McCone discovers that the teenager has been killed by a mentally unstable vagrant who considers the immigrants as intruders. The collision between the two marginal characters in the city is tragic, and the only thing McCone can do is bring some limited support to the disoriented community.

Muller foregrounds the issues of assimilation and identity experienced by immigrants again in *Eye of the Storm.* In the story McCone goes to her sister's rescue and finds out about the grotesque history of Locke, a closed and forgotten Chinatown in rural California:

> Tourists are always poking around their town and treating the Chinese as if they're curiosities. Developers keep trying to take it over and turn it into some sort of Asian Disneyland. They seem to look at the people as stage props; one of them said in a newspaper interview that she hoped the Chinese would stay after redevelopment because they "need these people for local color" [37].

Angela Wong, an ambitious and hardworking woman from Locke, works for McCone's sister Patsy in her bed-and-breakfast business. Although she has been seen as the hope of the third generation from the Chinese community, she has trouble coming to terms with her racial identity. According to one of her colleagues, Angela feels "her ethnicity has kept her out of the mainstream of American business life," and her being a woman further "keeps her from having any real power or influence" (71). Angela's yearning for success and anxiety about exclusion lead her to embezzle money from the business, which in turn makes her a prime suspect for the murder in the inn. McCone proves that she is innocent of the killing, but the future of the Chinese people in Locke remains grim. Throughout the Muller series, the inequities of race and gender offer no simple solution.

In contrast to the confused and tormented Angela Wong who gets stuck in small-town America, Muller offers a very different version of the Chinese immigrants in *Where Echoes Live*. Investigating a suspicious plan to reopen a long-forsaken goldmine in California, McCone learns that Lionel Ong, a "moneymaking machine that's fueled by greed and instant gratification" (135), is actually trying to twist the project and make a fortune by property development. Lionel has good connections with City Hall and the state legislature and belongs to one of the "real movers and shakers in San Francisco finance" (133). However, McCone also knows that by naming the development project "Gum San," Land of the Golden Hills, Lionel "wanted to raise public awareness of the hardships and discrimination" which his people had suffered in the goldfields in the eighteen fifties (224). It is this strong sense of identity that "makes him go to any length to ensure it succeeds" (203–204). The story of Lionel makes McCone and a Chinese American friend ponder their own identities:

> "Our people have taken a lot of shit in this country. Remember the Exclusion Act of eighteen eighty-two? The 'heathen Chinee' are the only ethnic group in history to be specifically denied entry to the U.S." [As McCone responds:] "I remember. But in a way don't you think that all the discrimination helped sustain your ethnic identity? Look at me, for instance: I'm seven-eighths Scotch-Irish plus one-eighth Shoshone, and I don't identify with any group" [203].

Readers of the series know that McCone's racial identity will be significantly complicated in *Listen to the Silence* later in the series,[2] but race as it is represented in *Echoes* is not quite the non-issue that McCone's remarks suggest. Here again, there are no simple answers to the issues of racism, ethnic identity, and integration.

Muller's interest in the experiences of Asian immigrants, Chinese and Vietnamese in particular, and the complex problem of their cultural and ethnic identity, in fact mirrors the emerging voices of Asian American literature in recent decades. Maxine Hong Kingston published *The Woman Warrior* in

1978 — one year after Muller's first novel *Edwin of the Iron Shoes* — and received wide attention. In 1989, Amy Tan came to the fore with *The Joy Luck Club*, the same year in which Kingston published her *Tripmaster Monkey*. Two years later, Tan produced *The Kitchen God's Wife* and Gish Jen published her debut work *Typical American*. American writers of Vietnamese descent have been few until recently, but Lan Cao's semi-autobiographical book *Monkey Bridge* in 1997 delineates the clash and confusion between two generations in two different cultures, endeavoring to construct new American identities. These women writers, along with others of Indian, Japanese, Korean, or Filipino heritage, have been trying to negotiate the conflict between their cultural roots and American values, and the desires for individual happiness and the expectations from their parents. In this context, Muller joins her contemporary fellow women writers in exploring and recording the stories of those "who have historically been confined to the margins of white Western male experience" (Kinsman 156). While working within the hard-boiled detective tradition and challenging her mainstream male predecessors, Muller also enters into a dialogue with other female writers across a range of different genres in an attempt to provide more possibilities of diversity and difference within the tradition of American literature.

　　Continuing her departure from the male hard-boiled tradition, in the middle part of the series McCone turns her thoughts inward and scrutinizes her conscience on the issues of violence and taking life — an unavoidable experience in her line of work. Throughout the series, the heroine is conscious of the destructive influence of bloodshed and tries hard to deal with the consequences. In contrast, death and violence are all too common for "tough guy" detectives. The prototypical American hard-boiled hero of course does not play the subtle game of ratiocination, as did the classical detective. Walking down the mean streets, the private eye — like the frontier hero — needs quick wit and physical strength rather than intellectual superiority. For example, when the Continental Op tries to save a woman from a cult fanatic, he shows no sign of hesitation. "I fired," the Op narrates unfeelingly. "The bullet hit his cheek. I saw the hole it made." The wounded person then attacks the Op with a carving knife, but is killed by his own knife instead: "I drove the heavy blade into his throat, in till the hilt's cross stopped it. Then I was through." After the brutal combat, the detective simply concludes: "Thank God he wasn't really God" (Hammett 271). Nor does the private eye trust the system of law and order represented by the police. "Until you guys own your own souls you don't own mine," Marlowe tells the two cops in *The High Window*. "I have a right to listen to my conscience, and protect my client the best way I can" (Chandler 122–123). The private eye tends to work outside the conventional rules of society, "preferring his own instinctive justice to the often tarnished justice of civilization" (Grella 106). In effect, as Porter notes, the hard-boiled detective "often acts as his own judge and jury," particularly in the case of Mike Hammer (167–169).

To perform her investigation, McCone does not rely on physical strength as much as her male counterparts. Although she may not completely believe in the effectiveness and efficiency of the justice system, she is willing to cooperate with the law enforcement agencies in a practical and realistic way. In doing so, she avoids rivalry with the police and reduces the risk of personal injury. Compared to Kinsey Millhone and V. I. Warshawski, two of her most famous fellow private eyes, McCone more frequently cooperates with the police, content to leave the criminal to the deliberations of the judicial system. While more than capable of handling herself, McCone prefers not to carry a firearm unless a situation demands it.

Throughout the series, the detective's experiences with death and violence change her character in significant ways. When she first sees a dead body at a crime scene, the heroine trembles and fears that she might "start to hyperventilate" (*Edwin* 175). Yet over the years, her close encounters with bloodshed have gradually changed her: "I'd often been in extreme danger, had coped as best I could with violence and death, had even been forced to kill a man. I was more cynical, more judgmental, more prone to anger" (*Trophies* 139).

Perhaps the most significant example of this change occurs in *Trophies and Dead Things*, when Hank Zahn, McCone's boss and mentor at All Souls Legal Cooperative, is shot and nearly dies in front of her because of her investigative work. Feeling guilty and enraged, McCone chases after the shooter and pins down the man with her gun. The whole process is witnessed by her colleagues, and she quickly realizes that her fierce outrage has somehow distanced herself from them. In *Where Echoes Live*, McCone reflects on this incident, acknowledging that, though this rage is a part of herself that she would like to keep hidden, it is hers nevertheless.

The lesson seems learned, when on the desolate Mexican coast in *Wolf in the Shadows*, McCone becomes the only person to protect her partner Hy, who is seriously wounded and unable to move. McCone has the opportunity to eliminate the killer first, and she knows she cannot waste her chance:

> Everything I believed in told me this was wrong. Everything I cared about told me this was right. One shot, two at most. Shoot to kill. A gun has only one purpose: if you use it, be prepared to take a life. [...] I sighted on him. Waited until he was completely still. And pulled the trigger [358].

Although deep down McCone still has doubts about killing, she knows what she is doing and is willing to accept the consequences. In *A Wild and Lonely Place* the detective considers the difficulties she experienced when she first took a life to save a friend. This act had weighed on her conscience, but as McCone explains, "last spring I'd cold-bloodedly shot another man and called it justice. I wasn't sure that I liked the woman I was becoming, but she was formed of life experiences I couldn't eradicate" (16).

While the detective may become increasingly familiar with death and violence, she never forgets about their devastating consequences. In the recent book *The Dangerous Hour*, a drug dealer-turned businessman tries to impress McCone with his "bravery," telling the detective, "It takes a brave man to kill. I am a brave man. And proud of it." For McCone, however, this "lack of humanity" is exactly what separates her from people like him. Though she too had taken human life, this was done only in self-defense, or in defense of loved ones. McCone takes no pride in these actions, and remains hounded by her choice to use lethal force (130–131).

Muller's McCone is equally distinguished from her female colleagues, a fact that sheds light on the development of the sub-genre itself. Since Grafton and Paretsky respectively launched their private eye series in 1982 — five years after Muller's *Edwin of the Iron Shoes*— McCone has inevitably been examined alongside Paretsky's and Grafton's eye characters, V.I. Warshawski and Kinsey Millhone, respectively. In terms of academic interest, Warshawski has always been in the spotlight of literary, cultural, and sociological research.[3] In terms of commercial success, although Muller is a prolific writer with devoted fans, her sales figures never match up to those of Grafton and her best-selling "Alphabet Series."

One wonders if these differing levels of success and recognition are a function of the unique aspects of Muller's series. While Millhone and Warshawski start out as independent private eyes, McCone begins as the staff investigator at All Souls. No matter how idealistic and loose the organization, McCone can pursue investigations only with the approval of Hank Zahn (her boss and mentor). The ambivalence of the position may, as Hans Bertens and Theo D'haen suggest, cost the heroine the "independence and autonomy traditionally associated with private investigating" (19). "Through her affair with a cop and her employment by a legal cooperative," Kathleen Gregory Klein also notes, speaking of McCone's first romantic relation with Lieutenant Greg Marcus, McCone is "tied to the police and legal systems," failing to recognize that these two institutions are "part of a larger, flawed system needing to be changed" (209).

As far as characterization is concerned, McCone may appear to be less hard-boiled than her fellow private eyes. She does not talk tough and crack wise like Millhone, nor does she act as streetwise and physically strong as Warshawski. It may be true that "Sharon McCone's busy amiability [...] eased the transition from male to female private eyes" (Knight 167), but this leaves McCone looking "soft-boiled" compared to the strong characteristics of her sister investigators. To make up for the "soft-boiledness" of her heroine, Muller may have decided to let her detective renounce, in her own words, the "rather confining position at All Souls Legal Cooperative" and set up McCone Investigations in *Till the Butchers Cut Him Down*, the fifteenth installment in the series. This may also be the reason McCone gains more power and authority throughout the remainder of the series. "While not a superwoman," Muller comments on the recent development of her detective, "when forced to confront extraordinary situations, she reaches beyond her normal capabilities and grows and changes accordingly" (A. Muller 775). But, on the contrary, the strengthened and empowered McCone sometimes looks like a superwoman, a drastic change in her characterization that requires that previous successes of the series be reassessed.

This transformation into a super-heroic detective is most obvious in *A Wild and Lonely Place*, the second novel after McCone leaves All Souls. To rescue the child of a foreign diplomat kidnapped by organized criminals from a remote Caribbean island, McCone bests the heavily armed gangsters, and then swims for a long distance to safety with the girl on her back. After this feat, she single-handedly pilots a plane, overcoming gusty winds and a broken engine to make a perfect emergency landing. In her final confrontation with the "diplo-bomber," the detective miraculously dodges bullets and fires distress flares — as she is without her own weapon — in return. In pursuit of sensational action and thrilling adventure, McCone has somehow "uncritically fallen in love with a superwoman of her own creation" (Bertens and D'haen 23). Money matters also cause problems in this novel. McCone is involved with RKI, an international agency specializing in corporate security. To find the bomber, she accepts the deal offered by the agency. Gage Renshaw, a founding partner of RKI, promises to pay her expenses and ten times her ordinary fee if she is successful. However, if she fails, she gets nothing and must work nine additional jobs for RKI with no remuneration (170). This is a far cry from the previous modest means of the detective, and it is hard to believe that she can quickly afford to take this gamble without jeopardizing her own business. What is even more implausible is that after solving the case, McCone is rewarded with a quarter of a million dollars from the FBI. It is big money for a small agency, but the detective does not appear much bothered by it. Indeed, in the next installment of the series, McCone nonchalantly indicates that she has the reward "tucked away in various conservative and easily liquidated investments" (*Broken* 20). Both her newfound talents and financial means seem out of character for the detective.

Appropriately, McCone's growing renown is acknowledged. For example, when McCone goes to see an owner of a check-cashing store in connection with the bomber case, the man knows her as soon as he sees her business card. "You're not unknown in this city, Ms. McCone," he says, an answer that McCone readily accepts: "No, I guess not" (*Wild* 167).

In *While Other People Sleep*, this "celebrity status" is such that there is even an impostor trying to imitate her way of investigation going so far as to take cases under McCone's name. When McCone goes to her old friend Hank for help, the experienced lawyer tells her that it is not easy to prove the damage because she is already a "public figure": "Shar, your name and picture have been in the paper how many times? To say nothing of that *People* article. And then there were those TV and radio talk-show appearances" (68–69). While McCone maintains that she did these things to benefit her business, she cannot deny the impact it has had on her reputation. This success (and perhaps self-importance) are again at the forefront of the recent book *The Dangerous Hour*. As the novel begins, the reader finds that Sharon's business has "tripled" in two years, and her agency has moved from a shabby downtown Victorian building to a posh workplace on the pier with her office window overlooking San Francisco Bay (3). McCone appears satisfied with her current status.

McCone's departure from All Souls has indeed marked a significant step in her professional career, and it has also fulfilled Muller's desire to differentiate her detective from her other sister investigators. But one point worth noting here is that after establishing McCone Investigations, what matters to Muller is how her heroine keeps her independence and effectiveness by expanding the business and, if necessary, defending it. In doing so, however, McCone's earlier concern for minorities and the issues of gender, race, and class are somehow lost. Unfortunately, these causes seem to be replaced only by her increasing self-interest and defense against external threats.

As the "founding mother" of female private eye fiction, Muller uses the McCone series to bring to the fore the issues of gender, race, and class, infusing the genre with diverse voices in a manner in keeping with other contemporary female writers. Emphasizing the effects of crime and the trauma of bloodshed, Muller's series questions and revises the male generic tradition, by producing a more compassionate and self-reflective private eye. However, as Muller modifies McCone's character later in the series, turning her into a veritable "super-sleuth," many of these achievements seem left by the wayside. Since the publication of *Edwin of the Iron Shoes* in 1977, McCone has so far appeared in more than twenty novels and several short story collections. The sheer volume of the stories may serve as a testament to Muller's passion and devotion to the unique genre that she has helped develop and flourish for the past three decades. McCone has turned from a young, inexperienced staff investigator into a competent leader of her own agency. Along the way, she manages to retain her courage and integrity, her love and support of family, and her generosity in friendship and love. However, most importantly, she never loses her hard-won independence. In this way, Sharon McCone has secured a special position in the history of the genre, and she has every reason to continue to be loved and remembered by her readers.

Notes

1. In the blurb printed on many of the covers of Muller's novels, Sue Grafton is quoted as saying that "Marcia Muller is the founding 'mother' of the contemporary female hard-boiled private eye." The title follows Muller and has been widely used.

2. McCone's Native American heritage is in many ways equivocal: although she talks about her Shoshone blood throughout the series, Muller foregrounds the issue of her racial identity only in *Listen to the Silence*. Priscilla L. Walton and Manina Jones acknowledge that McCone's "gender and racial marginality are, in effect, conflated" (200), and Maureen T. Reddy argues that *Listen to the Silence* "deals with race over-simply, treating it as a biological rather than a cultural fact" (205).

3. Apart from being referred to as the "founding mother" of the female private eye, Muller attracts less academic attention than either Paretsky or Grafton. For example, two critical anthologies published in 1995, *Feminism in Women's Detective Fiction* edited by Irons and *Women Times Three: Writers, Detectives, Readers* edited by Klein, respectively feature two articles on Paretsky and Grafton, but none specifically on Muller. The same situation applies to Panek's *New Hard-Boiled Writers, 1970s-1990s* (2000).

Works Cited

Bertens, Hans, and Theo D'haen. *Contemporary American Crime Fiction*. Basingstoke, UK: Palgrave, 2001.

Chandler, Raymond. *The High Window*. London: Penguin, 2005.

Cranny-Francis, Anne. *Feminist Fiction: Feminist Uses of Generic Fiction*. Cambridge: Polity, 1990.

Grella, George. "The Hard-Boiled Detective Novel." In *Detective Fiction: A Collection of Critical Essays*, ed. Robin W. Winks, 103–120. Englewood Cliffs, NJ: Prentice-Hall, 1980.

Hammett, Dashiell. *The Four Great Novels*. London: Picador, 1982.

Horsley, Lee. *Twentieth-Century Crime Fiction*. Oxford: Oxford University Press, 2005.

Irons, Glenwood, ed. *Feminism in Women's Detective Fiction*. Toronto: University of Toronto Press, 1995.

Jen, Gish. *Typical American*. London: Granta, 1998.

Kinsman, Margaret. "A Band of Sisters." In *The Art of Detective Fiction*, ed. Warren Chernaik, Martin Swales, and Robert Vilain, 153–169. Basingstoke: Macmillan, 2000.

Klein, Kathleen Gregory. *The Women Detective: Gender and Genre*. 2nd ed. Urbana: University of Illinois Press, 1995.

_____, ed. *Women Times Three: Writers, Detectives, Readers*. Bowling Green, OH: Bowling Green State University Popular Press.

Knight, Stephen. *Crime Fiction, 1800–2000: Detection, Death, Diversity*. Basingstoke, UK: Palgrave Macmillan, 2004.

Margolies, Edward. *Which Way Did He Go?* New York: Holmes & Meier, 1982.

Muller, Adrian. "Marcia Muller." In *St. James Guide to Crime and Mystery Writers*, 4th ed., ed. Jay P. Pederson, 774–776. Detroit, MI: St. James Press, 1996.

Muller, Marcia. *Ask the Cards a Question*. London: Women's Press, 2000.

_____. *The Broken Promise Land*. London: Women's Press, 1996.

_____. *The Cheshire Cat's Eye*. New York: Mysterious Press, 1995.

_____. *The Dangerous Hour*. New York: Mysterious Press, 2004.

_____. *Edwin of the Iron Shoes*. London: Women's Press, 1999.

_____. *Eye of the Storm*. New York: Mysterious Press, 1988.

_____. *Listen to the Silence*. New York: Mysterious Press, 2001.

_____. Introduction. *McCone and Friends*. Norfolk, VA: Crippen & Landru, 2000. 11–13.

_____. *Pennies on a Dead Woman's Eyes*. London: Women's Press, 1995.

_____. *There's Nothing to Be Afraid Of*. New York: St. Martin's Press, 1985.

_____. *There's Something in a Sunday*. London: Women's Press, 1995.

_____. *Till the Butchers Cut Him Down*. London: Women's Press, 1995.

_____. *Trophies and Dead Things*. London: Women's Press, 1995.

_____. *Where Echoes Live*. London: Women's Press, 1995.

_____. *While Other People Sleep*. London: Women's Press, 1998.

_____. *A Wild and Lonely Place*. London: Women's Press, 2000.

_____. *Wolf in the Shadows*. New York: Mysterious Press, 1994.

Panek, LeRoy Lad. *New Hard-Boiled Writers, 1970s-1990s*. Bowling Green, OH: Bowling Green State University Popular Press, 2000.

Porter, Dennis. *The Pursuit of Crime: Art and Ideology in Detective Fiction*. New Haven: Yale University Press, 1981.

Reddy, Maureen T. "Women Detectives." In *The Cambridge Companion to Crime Fiction*, ed. Martin Priestman, 191–207. Cambridge: Cambridge University Press, 2003.

Walton, Priscilla L., and Manina Jones. *Detective Agency: Women Rewriting the Hard-Boiled Tradition*. Berkeley: University of California Press, 1999.

Wilson, Ann. "The Female Dick and the Crisis of Heterosexuality." In *Feminism in Women's Detective Fiction*, ed. Glenwood Irons, 148–156. Toronto: University of Toronto Press, 1995.

3

Imagining the Margins: Muller's Explorations of Race

Maureen T. Reddy

With *Edwin of the Iron Shoes* (1977), Marcia Muller opened what many critics consider to be the most significant and extensive revision of the hard-boiled genre since its beginnings in the post–World War I pulps, challenging the genre's insistence on masculinity as one of the detective's most important attributes. By the late 1980s, Muller's Sharon McCone was at the center of a feminist counter-tradition in American crime fiction. A curious critical over-sight, barely noticed at the time the McCone series began in earnest in the early 1980s or even later as Muller achieved wide recognition as the creator of the first feminist private detective,[1] was Sharon's doubled outsider status as a woman of color. Until the mid–1990s, when several women of color detectives created by authors of color finally appeared in print, Muller remained a lonely pioneer, with Sharon McCone the sole female private eye who was not white. The lack of critical attention to Sharon's race may be related to Muller's own downplaying of race in the novels. Throughout the series, which now includes twenty-five novels plus the co-authored (with Bill Pronzini) *Double*, Sharon's racial identity seems generally far less significant in her work as a detective than does her gender, a pattern that is common for *white* women (fictional) detectives but not for detectives of color created by authors of color. Further, until *Listen to the Silence* (2000), Sharon is only occasionally raced; that is, her Indian appearance makes no difference in her life except when others comment upon it or it is otherwise drawn to her attention, usually by racist whites. Before that novel, her Indianness is *wholly* a matter of appearance, as she has no tribal affiliation or social/cultural connection to Indians. For nearly a quarter century, Muller seems not to have known what to do with her detective's race beyond using it as one among many characteristics and experiences that individualize Sharon, such as her love of her cats or her pursuit of a pilot's license, or as a quick way to place other characters beyond the pale of progressive social attitudes.

Nevertheless, Muller clearly is interested in exploring race, especially non-whiteness, as she has built another series around a woman of color, amateur detective Elena Oliverez. In this essay, I examine the racialization of Sharon McCone in relation to the more central racial identity Muller constructs for Elena Oliverez, who is featured in just two books plus the co-authored (also with Bill Pronzini) *Beyond the Grave* (1986). Oliverez also briefly appears in a recent McCone novel, *The Dangerous Hour* (2004). In both the Oliverez and the McCone series, Muller alternates between two mutually incompatible understandings of race, treating it sometimes as a biological given and at others as a social construction. In contrast, both series clearly present gender as entirely social; nowhere does Muller fall into the essentialist trap when it comes to gender. Consequently, her revision of the masculinist discourse of the hard-boiled with the McCone series is more coherent and powerful than is her revision of the racial codes of either the hard-boiled or of the broader crime genre. Indeed, "revision" is an overstatement when it comes to Muller's contribution to rethinking race's role in crime fiction; instead, her work offers sporadic critiques of the centrality of whiteness in crime fiction. Those critiques tend to appear as set pieces in the McCone series, where overt white racism briefly disrupts a novel's action and provides an occasion for Sharon to express outrage at racism, which is typically portrayed as personal prejudice. In contrast, the Oliverez series more fully integrates such critiques into the novels' plots, which are built around elements of Mexican American history and culture.

Unlike the McCone series, the two main Elena Oliverez novels, *The Tree of Death* (1983) and *The Legend of the Slain Soldiers* (1985), are amateur detective novels in which the narrator/protagonist is a museum curator who accidentally stumbles into the profession of investigating murders. These novels do not draw on the tradition of the hard-boiled but instead on the less ideologically coherent and consequently far more capacious tradition of the amateur sleuth. Although certainly amateur detective fiction has also frequently worked to valorize whiteness and to dramatize supposed threats to whiteness, that has not been its central concern, as it has been with the hard-boiled. Repeatedly proving the detective's masculinity/heterosexuality/whiteness through violence against sexual/racial others is not traditionally the major action of amateur detective fiction, whereas it is of the hard-boiled, which helps to explain why the majority of fictional detectives of color and white female detectives have been amateurs.[2]

Beginning with *Edwin of the Iron Shoes*, Sharon McCone presents herself as not quite white but also as not quite not white: she describes herself as just one-eighth Shoshone, yet often asserts that she appears Indian to others. At least once in every book, Sharon reflects on her Indian appearance, whether prompted by a mirror or by a stranger's comment — for example, a

Latino in *The Dangerous Hour* telling Sharon about native people adds, "You look Indian" (99). An early romantic interest, police officer Greg Marcus, calls her his "little papoose," a supposed endearment that foregrounds Sharon's Indian appearance while also infantilizing her in a deeply significant double-othering. Both women of all races and non-white men, perhaps especially American Indians, historically have been positioned as children vis-à-vis the white/male/adult world. Marcus's nickname for Sharon is part of a pattern of his failing to treat her as an equal, which dooms their relationship. That Sharon's supposed Indianness, even if only phenotypical, makes little differ-ence in either her professional or her private life is perhaps the least believ-able element of the series; only white people can afford the luxury of forgetting their own race and of believing that race does not matter. Race shapes every aspect of life for all of us, a truth driven home to people of color daily but easily denied by whites, because white experience is represented in media and other social institutions as *unraced* experience. At one point in *Listen to the Silence*, the novel in which Sharon discovers that she was in fact adopted and that her birth parents are both Indian, an Indian man calls her a "white-thinking woman" (81). Although he is criticizing her impatience, the man's comment aptly describes Sharon's general worldview and perception of her-self throughout the series.

In contrast to Sharon, Elena Oliverez is acutely aware of her otherness in white America, thinking often about Mexican American differences from Anglo culture. Rather than being merely one among many characteristics that serve to individualize the detective, race/ethnicity — and the two are collapsed in Muller's novels as in U.S. society — is the central fact about Elena. The two Oliverez novels offer extensive introductions to Mexican American his-tory and culture and are clearly aimed at Anglo audiences that presumably do not know even about Cinco de Mayo, which Muller has Elena explain in a paragraph that would be at home in a guidebook:

> El Cinco de Mayo — May fifth — marks the day in 1862 when the Mexican army defeated the invading French forces at the town of Puebla, near Vera Cruz. The victory was accomplished against incredibly high odds, and the would-be con-querors were driven back to Vera Cruz and the sea. The holiday has taken on special significance for Mexican-Americans, becoming a symbol of their growing cultural awareness and pride, and for that reason we had scheduled our opening gala for the night of May fifth, only three days from now [*Tree* 15].

Similarly, in *The Legend of the Slain Soldiers*, Elena tells readers about the ori-gins of Fiesta in Southern California, including a brief history of Spanish rule and the use of Indians and Mexicans as low-paid labor on ranchos. This method of conveying cultural information corresponds closely to "scenes of instruc-tion" in black women writers' crime novels, where direct discussion of race mat-ters clearly aimed at a white audience frequently disrupts narrative flow.[3]

Not only these scenes of instruction but also Elena's entire narration of both novels seem aimed at an Anglo audience, which creates an interesting gap between the world of the novels' action and the world of their narration. Almost all the important characters in both texts are Mexican American — the sole exception being a white police detective — and the action takes place in and around the fictional Museum of Mexican Arts in Santa Barbara and the mostly (Elena says three-quarters) Mexican American mobile home park where Elena's mother lives. Given her immersion in Mexican American communities, Elena's narrative voice might be expected to assume a Mexican American audience, but that is not the case. Instead, as narrator, Elena serves as a cultural translator, explaining Mexican American life to Anglos. Whites, then, remain central to the series, despite their being on the margins of the action within the novels. This assumption of a white/Anglo audience makes sense for Muller, given the majority readership of crime fiction, but it does not make sense for Elena, who supposedly is telling "true" stories, not consciously constructing fictions. These logical contradictions in how Elena is presented and how she is socially positioned in the texts are rooted in a mainstream ideology that regards whiteness as normative and that consequently undermines or at least limits Muller's critique of whiteness's centrality in crime fiction.

Sharon, in contrast to Elena, is tokenized as the sole person of color in an otherwise white world in most of the novels in the McCone series. Whiteness remains normative and unanalyzed in the McCone books, and therefore addressing a white audience in Sharon's first-person narration seems consistent. *The Dangerous Hour* brings in several characters of color in addition to a brief appearance by Elena Oliverez; in every case those characters' racial "difference" is foregrounded. This novel's plot revolves around a scheme to destroy Sharon's agency by setting up one of her employees to be accused of credit card fraud by a former client, charges that could result in Sharon's losing her investigator's license. The employee is Julia Rafael, whom Sharon describes as "my only Hispanic operative" (6). Sharon hired her after Julia submitted "the most off-putting [job application] I'd ever seen," including listing two stints with the California Youth Authority on drug-related offenses (15). The client, who claims Julia stole his credit card after he "rejected her sexual advances," is an up-and-coming politico, hoping to be San Francisco's "first Hispanic mayor" (6). When Sharon calls her own lawyer to act on behalf of Julia, she insists that Julia could never have done what she is accused of but goes on to claim that "sometimes she does display a curious pattern of behavior." (9) McCones observes that Julia's shyness at times comes across as haughty, though, she is for the most part, able to maintain a professional, even assertive, demeanor in business situations. However, "if someone says or does something — no matter how innocent — that she interprets as an ethnic, class, or gender slur, she'll lash out." (9) McCone had warned Julia about this behavior on a number of occasions.

The lawyer, a white Jewish man who expresses sympathy for Julia based on his own experiences of discrimination and isolation, responds by identifying this "curious pattern" as "passive-aggressive," and Sharon seems to agree, adding only, "With a wide swath of middle ground" (9). As in the rest of the series, here Sharon is presented unironically, and I think readers are meant to accept her analysis of Julia's behavior uncritically. However, if one steps outside the demands of normative whiteness, which include the demand that whites be accepted as unbiased authorities on race matters, problems with Sharon's analysis are glaringly obvious. First, the pattern she describes is not at all "passive-aggressive," although it perhaps might be passive and aggressive by turns, and so her accepting the lawyer's summary is perplexing. Second, and far more important, Julia's pattern of behavior is not at all "curious," but a completely understandable response to minority status, where "shyness" may result from anxiety about being out of place/othered and where the target of slurs is the sole person likely to speak out against such slurs. Why Muller would assign to Julia a behavioral style likely to make whites nervous (at least) and then have Sharon interpret the behavior in a "white-thinking" way (to quote her Indian critic from *Listen to the Silence*) is for me the true curiosity.

The function of race within *The Dangerous Hour* diverges from its function in earlier McCone novels. In this text, Muller makes a serious, sustained attempt to portray a multiracial environment in which people of color play more than minor roles; however, that attempt is sharply limited by an understanding of race that is unthreatening to white ideology. Sharon's commentary on the Mission District comes close to directly stating the book's ideological foundation. A full paragraph describes the sights, sounds, and smells that greet her as she drives along Mission Street, with an emphasis on ethnic diversity. Sharon then gives a brief history of the area from its late-nineteenth-century role as the first stop for European and then Hispanic immigrants. She notes that the Mission is changing again:

> Now yet another ethnic transition is taking place as Asians, blacks, and Caucasians move in. The result is a melting pot in the truest sense of the word. The area has its problems — gentrification that threatens to displace longtime residents, drugs, crime, homelessness, and lack of funding for critical services — but it's also a place where ground for community gardens is broken, where colorful street fairs celebrate diversity, where clubs and restaurants and boutiques take hold and siphon off money from more advantaged parts of the Bay Area. Many years ago I lived near the heart of the Mission, and I'm not all that far from it now; it was an interesting place back then, but today it is positively vibrant [52].

The perspective here — Sharon's, of course, but one that the text itself follows and seems to endorse — is a liberal, celebrate-difference, apolitical variety of multiculturalism. Ideologically, this perspective assumes that ignorance, as opposed to deliberate racism and white supremacism, is at the root of the racial divide; the way to heal that divide, then, is for individuals and groups to interact across color lines. That interaction here is figured as a neighborhood version of the familiar schoolroom "holidays and heroes" approach to racial/ethnic diversity, not as concerted political or social activism: there are grassroots parades but no mention of grassroots organizing.

The notion that Americans have now entered a multicultural/multiracial age is one long promoted nationally by conservative politicians and insufficiently challenged by the media. Beginning with the Reagan era, we have seen a sustained assault on gains made by the Civil Rights Movement, with affirmative action particularly vilified. The Equal Employment Opportunity Commission (EEOC) and the U.S. Commission on Civil Rights (USCCR) were stripped down to the bone in the 1980s under Reagan and Bush, with ever fewer discrimination cases pursued. At the same time, conservative Republicans promulgated the idea that affirmative action constituted "reverse discrimination" and unfairly benefited people of color to the detriment of whites. A quarter century on, that view is now the mainstream one, as the right wing-led backlash against affirmative action has thoroughly succeeded. *The Dangerous Hour* includes an anxious-seeming defense against implicit anti-affirmative action attitudes in Sharon's description of her friend, Adah, a black female member of the San Francisco Police Department:

Adah liked to refer to herself as the department's "poster child for affirmative action," but that alone didn't account for her rapid rise through the ranks. She was a damn good investigator, and in the past year she'd also proved herself a good diplomat, having tactfully distanced herself from a rash of scandals that threatened to cripple the already troubled department [163].

Nowhere does Muller have Sharon make any parallel remarks about white police officers; we do not hear, for example, that Greg Marcus may be a white man, but that alone does not account for his success in the SFPD. A moment's reflection makes it obvious that whiteness and maleness are always assets in seeking promotion in police departments, yet only in relation to Adah does it seem necessary to claim that success is both deserved and earned, not conferred on the basis of her race and gender "alone." Muller is an astute social observer when it comes to gender, judging from the rest of the McCone series, and so her lack of clarity on race matters and her incorporation of logically flawed, deeply conservative assumptions about race can be disturbing. Perhaps Muller's acceptance of that fantasy of a multiracial/multicultural triumph is limited to cities like San Francisco, which is indeed more racially diverse than most areas of the U.S., but that geographical limitation does not explain the odd comments about Julia's behavior or Adah's job qualifications.

Certainly celebration of racial/ethnic difference is preferable to persecution of differences, just as Muller's inclusion of people of color in her work is preferable to the exclusively white casts of characters in much white-authored crime fiction. However, it is quite possible to celebrate difference while unconsciously reproducing the racial status quo, particularly when racism is reduced to mere personal prejudice rather than seen as pervasive and systemic, foundational to U.S. social hierarchy. Julia's "curious pattern of behavior" is indeed problematic if one's analysis of racism assumes that racism is largely an anachronism that lingers only among the consciously evil on the one hand and those innocents or social throwbacks who have not yet learned to appreciate difference on the other.

There is a suggestion in one of the Elena Oliverez books that Muller has long taken this view of racism. In *The Legend of the Slain Soldiers*, an old white woman comments that she enjoys taking care of a small boy and asserts, "I don't even mind that Tommy is part Mex." Suddenly realizing that Elena is Mexican, the woman apologizes (149). Elena is not offended, noting that "she was the product of a different time, when people thought it all right to refer to us as Mexes. The ones of her generation who used that term actually liked my people; if they didn't, they called us Spics" (149). Reflecting on her response to this woman, Elena thinks, "It was strange.... She had said something offensive to me and I was trying to make up for her discomfort. But maybe what I was really trying to make up for was the fact that times had changed and left her behind — and all alone" (149). Like Sharon, Elena is never treated ironically in the texts in which she appears; no gap ever opens between author and character or reader and character to suggest problems with Elena's analyses; indeed, readers are encouraged to share her perspective and to acknowledge her reliability as a guide not only to the particular crimes she investigates but also to Chicano culture and to other matters. Although Elena is not in the mold of the masculine/white voice of authority that dominates conventional crime fiction, she nonetheless is the primary figure of authority in the text. Her view that this old white woman has been left behind by changing times and is to be pitied rather than criticized is of a piece with the perspective on multiculturalism offered by Sharon in *The Dangerous Hour* nearly twenty years later and therefore possibly represents Muller's own view, or at least a view that she finds congenial.

That attitude about race/ethnicity helps to explain the portrayal of inter-racial relationships in both series as no big deal to those involved in them. For instance, Adah Joslyn, the black female police investigator who appears not only in *The Dangerous Hour* but also in other McCone novels, lives with a white former FBI agent who now works for Sharon, and their racial difference goes unremarked. All of Sharon's romantic relationships in the series are with white men, but none of those relationships — including the one with

Greg Marcus, "papoose" comments notwithstanding — are figured as interracial. In fact, interracial romantic relationships remain sufficiently unusual in the U.S. that those involved in them are unlikely to be able to ignore racial difference, even if they would prefer to do so. According to the 1980 U.S. census (the census closest to the dates of the Elena Oliverez novels), 2 percent of all households had a householder of one race with a spouse/partner of another race. In 1990,the latest decennial census fully analyzed by race as of this writing, that figure had climbed to just 2.9 percent.[4] Since the census figures count only live-in partner households, not other relationships, they therefore likely understate the frequency of interracial romance. But even if we assume that interracial romance figures are double those of interracial live-in relationships, the incidence of interracial couples would be below 6 percent of all couples. By any standard, that is a small minority. Logically, then, interracial couples are likely to attract some attention and, more importantly, to experience themselves as violating social norms, an assumption that is borne out by the few studies of interracial couples available, including my own interviews with members of interracial couples in the early 1990s.[5] For Sharon never to experience her various romances with white men as significantly shaped by race beggars belief and strikes me as a rent in the realistic fabric of Muller's fiction. The absence of attention to — or even acknowledgment of— the interracial character of Sharon's romantic involvements makes sense only if considered as part of the apolitical multiculturalism that serves as the ideological center of the McCone series.

Interracial romance is directly addressed in the Elena Oliverez novels. Early in *The Legend of the Slain Soldiers*, we learn that Elena's mother strongly disapproves of exogamy and therefore even of dating outside her own racial group. Explaining to Dave Kirk, the white homicide detective introduced in *The Tree of Death*, how she knows that her mother's trailer park is predominantly Chicano, Elena says, "When my mother moved here, she was looking for widowers, and since she doesn't believe in interracial dating, she chose the place with the highest proportion of our own kind" (20). At one point, Elena briefly considers that the murder in her mother's trailer park that she's helping Kirk to investigate — his idea in enlisting her assistance is that Chicanos are more likely to speak to a Chicana than to a white cop — may have been motivated by anger at the victim's opposition to interracial/interethnic marriage. The victim, an historian who specialized in local history, told a group of neighbors that interracial marriages do not work out due to cultural differences. One of those neighbors — the Anglo/white partner in an interracial marriage — remains furious at the comment years afterward, and Elena regards him with some suspicion. Another suspect criticizes Elena for her supposed lack of authentic Chicano-ness, saying that her "Anglo boyfriends" show that she must be "not too proud of being Chicano" (94). Interestingly, none of the opposition to interracial relationships we hear about in this book comes from whites. Elena herself has mixed feelings about interracial relationships, wondering if she wants to get involved with an Anglo (130) and describing the Anglo in question, Dave Kirk, as looking around her house "as if he'd just walked out of the airport in some exotic foreign land" (164). Elena immediately forgives Kirk his fascination, thinking that she sees his world as exotic also: "I supposed that had always been part of the attraction Anglos held for me; they thought and lived differently than I did. Becoming involved with one was, in a sense, a ticket out of the life I'd known and into an exciting new realm" (164). Elena initially resists her attraction to Kirk because she wants to "come to terms with my heritage," which means "sticking with the people and customs I knew best" (164–56). Ultimately, however, Elena does date Dave Kirk, after ending a relationship with an older man, Carlos Bautista.

Nomenclature presents difficulties in the two Oliverez books and is worth some attention because of the political implications of the various terms used. In *The Tree of Death*, Elena uses "Mexican American" or just "Mexican" but in *The Legend of the Slain Soldiers* she refers to herself as "Chicana." Muller has Sharon use "Hispanic" in *The Dangerous Hour* to describe Julia. These terms are all politically loaded and not interchangeable; further, although Elena describes dating non–Mexican Americans as "interracial" dating, Mexican American people or Hispanics may be of many different racial groups but have a shared ethnicity. "Chicano/a," as its synonym "La Raza" implies, stakes out a *racial* unity regardless of phenotype by claiming that Chicano is a racial identity, not solely an ethnicity. The U.S. government uses "Hispanic" and "Latino" as interchangeable generic terms meant to include any people with origins in the South and Central Americas. The U.S. Office of Management and Budget (OMB), which has responsibility for the census, recognizes two ethnicities: Latino/Hispanic or non–Latino/Hispanic. Official government forms ask one to specify both a race *and* one of these two ethnic categories. However, as the 2000 census results demonstrate, many of those who identify themselves as Latino/Hispanic see that category as a racial one, and they do not choose white or black as their race but instead choose "other." The category Hispanic was essentially created by the OMB in the 1970s; Latino is an older term that began in colonial politics but that now tends to indicate a type of unity among all peoples from South and Central America. Mexican American is of course more specific than either Hispanic or Latino and has moderate or conservative implications, especially when juxtaposed with the more politically freighted "Chicano. " The modern use of Chicano has its roots in 1960s leftist organizing, which led to a major movement (the Chicano Movement) and is a reclaimed term, one that originally had negative social implications (similar to "black" in the same time period). For Elena to describe herself as Chicana, then, as she does several times in

Legend, is to identify herself with leftist political struggles and to place herself in a class/race/ethnic category.

Interestingly, Elena mentions being Chicana — as opposed to Mexican American — specifically when she thinks of herself in contrast to wealthy Anglos. The first time is when she recalls her college days, when "there had been little distinctions I'd been aware of, such as the sororities that didn't take Chicanas; and the wealth of my Anglo classmates who didn't have to work, while I often came to lectures with my hair still smelling of grease from the drive-in where I served hamburgers part-time" (26). These distinctions hardly seem "little," but Elena is contrasting them with earlier, more widespread discrimination and exclusion. At a party with Carlos Bautista, Elena notices that the other guests are older than she is, affluent, and mostly Anglo. She reflects, "These Anglos accepted Carlos and Alicia and Ramon [the hosts] because of their wealth and — in a manner they probably considered extremely tolerant — overlooked their Hispanic origins.... It made me uncomfortable to be in a situation where I wasn't simply taken at face value — indeed, where my being a Chicana was something to be ignored or even forgiven" (41). Chicano/a identity politics are rooted in class politics, so Muller's depiction of Elena as feeling most Chicana when in a *wealthy* Anglo environment is astute. Later at that same party, Elena is put off by Alicia's complimenting her on her sense of solidarity with farm workers by saying "I think it's good she's concerned about her people." Elena thinks, "*My* people. Not hers, in spite of having one hundred percent Mexican blood" (44). But "blood" does not a Chicano/a make — politics do. Alicia does not consider herself a Chicana because her politics place her outside "La Raza," comfortably chatting about decorating styles with the owners of the farms, not planning a strike for higher wages with the farm workers.

The political awareness that Elena evinces in *The Legend of the Slain Soldiers* is a long way from her thoughts about Mexican Americans in *The Tree of Death*. In the latter novel, Elena worries about Anglos' views and is distressed by anything that might seem to reinforce Anglo stereotypes of Mexican Americans. For instance, she is appalled by the massive Tree of Life a wealthy supporter gives the museum and says, "It's all the stereotypes about junky Mexican art rolled into one. It'll make the museum look like a cheap souvenir shop. We might as well hang up a piñata or two.... Do you want to make us a laughing-stock?" (*Tree* 25). Similarly, when Elena discovers a smuggling ring that has been using the museum as a cover to deal in artifacts, she expresses concern that the scandal will ruin the museum because "the papers will put racial overtones on it" (*Tree* 131).

The history of racial categories and divisions in the U.S. follows social practice in being all about the white/not-white binary, with many groups moving from not-white to white across the past two centuries and thereby acquiring the privileges of whiteness.[6] Those privileges have varied considerably — from voting rights to property ownership to employment and educational opportunities and so on — but they have been constant in their relation to the lack of privileges of non-whiteness. In making her two detectives not white and members of racial categories unlikely to become white any time soon, Muller disrupts the discourse of normative whiteness within which crime fiction has traditionally operated. However, that disruption is not accompanied in either case by an alternative discourse that would refuse to reproduce conventional racial hierarchies. As a consequence of that limitation, neither the Sharon McCone nor the Elena Oliverez series achieves the promise of innovation in the genre that their conception seems to hold out.

Notes

1. See, for instance, *Women of Mystery*, dir. Pamela Beere Briggs. In fact, P.D. James is the inventor of the modern female private eye, with her Cordelia Gray first appearing in *An Unsuitable Job for a Woman* in 1972, but since James wrote just one other novel featuring Cordelia, her impact, especially on U.S. writers, is far less significant than Muller's.

2. For the ideological underpinnings of the hard-boiled, see my *Traces, Codes, and Clues: Reading Race in Crime Fiction*, especially chapter one, and Bethany Ogdon, "Hard-Boiled Ideology."

3. See *Traces, Codes, and Clues*, 66–68.

4. Interrace Tables at www.census.gov/population/www/socdemo/interrace.html (accessed on July 12, 2006).

5. See my *Crossing the Color Line: Race, Parenting, and Culture*, especially chapter two.

6. See, for example, Noel Ignatiev, *How the Irish Became White*, or Karen Brodkin, *How Jews Became White Folks and What That Says about Race in America*.

Works Cited

Brodkin, Karen. *How Jews Became White Folks and What That Says about Race in America*. New Brunswick, NJ: Rutgers University Press, 1999.

Ignatiev, Noel. *How the Irish Became White*. New York: Routledge, 1996.

Muller, Marcia. *The Dangerous Hour*. New York: Warner, 2005.

_____. *The Legend of the Slain Soldiers*. New York: Signet, 1987.

_____. *The Tree of Death*.New York: Signet, 1987.

Ogdon, Bethany. "Hard-Boiled Ideology." *Critical Quarterly* 34, no. 1 (1999): 71–87.

Reddy, Maureen T. *Crossing the Color Line: Race, Parenting, and Culture*. New Brunswick, NJ: Rutgers University Press, 1994.

_____. *Traces, Codes, and Clues: Reading Race in Crime Fiction*. New Brunswick, NJ: Rutgers University Press, 2003.

4

Gender and Genre Stretching in the Non–McCone Novels

Pamela E. Bedore

Marcia Muller, described as "the founding mother of the contemporary female hardboiled private eye" by Sue Grafton, is best known for her creation of female private eye Sharon McCone. McCone is a highly attractive detective figure who becomes increasingly self-reliant throughout the span of the series — 30 years and counting — as she makes new choices about relationships, gains professional independence, and develops a stronger network of friends and family. Her growing self-awareness has made her exemplary of — because influential to — shifts in representations of female detectives within the American detective genre. Adrian Muller, in fact, characterizes Marcia Muller as "haunted" by the legacy of Grafton's famous comment (26).

Muller is both less and more than the "founding mother." The contemporary female private eye comes from a long history of female detectives. Muller herself points to P.D. James's Cordelia Gray as a precursor (Taylor 262) and mentions Dorothy Uhrak and Lillian O'Donnell as creators of early policewomen (James 58). In addition, American dime novels — late nineteenth- and early twentieth-century cheap books that marked the beginning of mass-market bookselling — are peopled by female detectives of various kinds. Certainly, Muller did not invent the notion that fictional representations of women as strong and resourceful detective figures could be effective in both aesthetic and economic terms.

But Muller is also considerably more than the creator of Sharon McCone. She has co-edited several anthologies and written excellent introductions on popular fiction in general and detective fiction in particular. Her grounding in the history and breadth of the genre of detective fiction is evidenced by her familiarity with the key detective writers that precede her, her exploration of the influence of women writers in dime novels — especially western dime

50

novels in *She Won the West*— and her lucid explanations of the relationships of detective fiction to the genres of westerns, ghost stories, and horror fiction (Taylor 264).

Muller's power as a writer comes from her innovation in stretching the limits of the detective genre, especially with regard to questions of gender. With Sharon McCone, she reworks key conventions of the hard-boiled genre with an attention to gender politics, a move central to the establishment of the feminist hard-boiled detective subgenre. The McCone novels clearly reveal the rich intersections of detective and feminist concerns around structures of power, questions of identity, and the nature of knowledge.

Explorations of such intersections shape all of Muller's work, albeit with varying levels of success. Muller has also written a number of novels featuring detectives other than Sharon McCone. While her recent Soledad County novels (2001–present) are highly successful, her two early non–McCone series are, rightly, less well regarded by the author herself as well as by publishers (and presumably other readers and critics). The Elena Oliverez (1983–1986) and Joanna Stark (1986–1989) novels, in fact, are among the only of Muller's works to be long out of print. Why were the two early non–McCone series ultimately unsuccessful? Muller herself addresses this question with reference to the conditions under which they were produced, explaining that both series emerged out of financial need on her part before she moved to the Mysterious Press (A. Muller 28). Certainly the market realities cannot be ignored, and Muller's explanation goes a long way towards elucidating why Elena Oliverez and Joanna Stark elicit little name recognition among even hard-core detective readers. But these six books (three in each series) — despite and perhaps because of their failings — actually demonstrate Muller's deep engagement with the historical as well as philosophical development of the detective genre.

Although the Elena Oliverez and Joanna Stark novels can be seen as aesthetic and even narrative failures, and it may be perfectly appropriate for publishers and the reading public to allow them to lapse from attention, critics of detective fiction should not ignore these books. Late twentieth- and early twenty-first-century American detective fiction is marked by an increasingly articulated and deliberate exploration of the potentials of genre fiction to engage political issues. Muller's responses in interviews to the issue of politics in detective fiction are not as definitive as arguments made by Carolyn Heilbrun (Amanda Cross), who claims that the genre allows authors "to dabble in a little profound revolutionary thought" (7), or by critics like Anne Cranny-Francis who argue that the popularity of genre fiction offers politically motivated writers the opportunity to communicate a message to a widespread group of readers who would be otherwise unlikely to receive it. Muller says that a detective writer must balance politics and character development to be successful: "I think you can explore issues and perhaps, while you are entertaining your reader, you can get the person to think about this, but if you are only using the novel to further some political point it's not entertainment, you're not telling a story" (A. Muller 28). She is aware, then, of the need to balance between the impetus of the detective narrative and the interest of political concerns. Her success in creating Sharon McCone as a complex and dynamic character whose detective investigations often raise her own awareness — and thus the awareness of readers — regarding political issues provides an example of just such a balance, especially at the site of gender politics.

Muller's non–McCone novels participate in a similar move: they demonstrate not only the rich potential of detective fiction to explore issues of personal identity and socio-cultural power dynamics, but also serve to demonstrate the logical limits of the detective genre. Like the exploration of the hard-boiled in the McCone novels, each of Muller's other series explores key moments in the development of the detective genre by overlaying questions of gender on the detective narrative. Although the success of the execution of these tropes varies across the three series, Muller's explorations illuminate several of the challenges intrinsic to the politics of the detective genre.

Joanna Stark

The late nineteenth century saw a great deal of anxiety around both the real-life figure of the detective and the multiplication of fictional representations of that figure. This social anxiety arose from a number of concerns, not the least of which was the notion of contamination: a fear — articulated repeatedly in *New York Times* editorials and other periodicals — that the detective, by the very nature of his continuous contact with institutions of crime, might become a criminal. Hard-boiled writers of the 1930s and 1940s continued the work of early dime novels as they explored the fine line between the detective and criminal in complex ways.

In her Joanna Stark series, Muller takes the trope of dangerous proximity between detective and criminal even further than most detective narratives that were criticized for this move during the early evolution of the genre. Although the series is far from being a success, it encapsulates the point at which detective-criminal doubling can topple a narrative into something that might be more accurately categorized as *noir*, for here the detective's doubling of the criminal leads her not only to be contaminated by the criminal, but to become a contaminant to others.

Muller suggests that because the Stark books were based on a "personal story," she could not, despite her original intention, extend the series beyond a trilogy (Taylor 262). The genesis of the series, intriguing as it is, does not change its impact. I would argue that in many ways, perhaps largely because of the clearly articulated nature of her personality flaws, Joanna Stark is in fact a fascinating female figure who embodies the ideological foundation for early panic around the celebration of the detective.

The trilogy places Joanna in a situation often seen in dime novels and in the comic books that carried the cultural resonances of cheap fiction into the second half of the twentieth century. Joanna is constructed as a problematic hero facing a single villain throughout the series. Anthony Parducci is Joanna's archnemesis, and in the development of her story, Joanna faces the sort of character slippage often explored in detective texts that specifically narrate a pairing. The very notion of detective-criminal doubling means that, in order to function as opposites of one another, the detective and criminal share many of the same features.

Joanna Stark is perhaps Muller's least attractive character, constructed as she is in almost diametrical opposition to Sharon McCone. Whereas McCone works hard to manage her private investigator business and is therefore available to readers as a role model of ethical female entrepreneurship, Joanna is left free to pursue her obsessive vengeance by an inheritance from her deceased husband. Joanna, moreover, is a poor judge of character; she repeatedly overestimates her own abilities and she indulges in vengeful behavior against Parducci that puts not only her but also her long-time friends at personal and professional risk. Joanna's financial freedom, at odds with the typical world of the fictional private detective and repeatedly constructed as unearned, has two effects on the narrative: on one hand, it acts in concert with her lack of self-awareness to render her an unsympathetic character; on the other hand, it accounts for her ability to indulge in her personal obsession with Parducci and is intrinsically linked to her crossing of the line between criminal and detective that threatens to move her story out of the detective genre entirely.

The Cavalier in White, a third-person account given from Joanna's perspective, begins by constructing Joanna in opposition to Parducci. Throughout the first novel, the competition between Parducci and Joanna is one of well-matched opponents as they battle over *The Cavalier in White*, a painting that Parducci has stolen from a museum and that Joanna, a security-systems specialist, is trying to recover. Even from the beginning, Parducci seems to have the ability to make Joanna act irrationally. One of their first meetings involves a chase around a darkened museum whose security system Joanna has designed: "She knew she had mishandled the situation — mishandled it very badly. Parducci had been trapped there in the basement, and instead of summoning security to deal with him, she had tried to be a hero. And, as with many would-be heroes, she had gotten her comeuppance" (151). Despite the narrative condemnation — constructed as part of Joanna's own reflection — Joanna continues in her failed attempts at heroism and in receiving comeuppance as a result. In fact, Parducci — twenty years after abandoning a lost and pregnant young Joanna in Europe — becomes an obsession that simultaneously provides her with the meaning she's been lacking in her life as well as the opportunity for her narrative to explore the limits of revenge as a motive for detective activity.

By the end of *The Cavalier in White*, Joanna and Parducci are constructed as opposites slipping towards similarity as the legacy of their past sexual relationship overlays their present competition with a strong current of contamination as the professional, the personal, and the erotic meld at the site of their relationship. The conflict over the painting slides into a conflict over E.J., the young man who believes himself to be Joanna's adopted son but who is in fact the product of the union between Joanna and Parducci. By the final novel of the series, E.J. faces his mother with the consequences of her inability to focus on her son in the face of her obsession with Parducci:

> You protected me from Parducci when I was a baby. Okay, I know you had to do that, and I'm grateful. But then when you married David you "protected" me by letting me go on thinking I was his natural son and Eleanor my natural mother. And for the longest time after I suspected you and David had been having an affair before Eleanor died, long after I was old enough to understand, you denied that, too. Was that "protecting" me, Jo? Or was it really protecting you? [*Dark* 58].

Parducci disrupts Joanna's life, already constructed as lacking in meaning and direction, by approaching her son. And yet, this disruption is a problem only because Joanna has allowed it to be due to her ongoing secrecy, constructed as self-protection by her son.

Joanna's slide across the detective-criminal line is fully developed in *There Hangs the Knife*, a novel that pushes the very boundaries of the detective genre. Detective fiction, according to Tzvetan Todorov's seminal analysis, is by definition the story of a detective unraveling the anterior story of the criminal. In *There Hangs the Knife*, the detective figure is proactive rather than reactive, thus embodying a contamination of the detective position. Joanna commissions a painting, *There Hangs the Knife*, to be used as bait for Parducci. In making the opening move of the detective-criminal conflict, Joanna sets into motion a series of events that put into jeopardy not only her own career and professional standing, but also the reputations of several of her friends in Europe: a gallery owner who commissions and displays the forgery, a journalist who reviews it as genuine, and an ex-lover who uses his underworld art connections to ensure Parducci's interest. Joanna's dangerous trap ends badly, with Parducci killing an innocent man and escaping, and Joanna's old friends become angry and upset at her reckless obsession for revenge.

The Joanna Stark series puts forward two potent symbols of the threats inherent in the archnemesis trope: the painting Joanna commissions as bait and her apartment in San Francisco. Each symbol becomes imbued with a series of meanings — and thus emphasizes the epistemological uncertainty that accompanies the trope of detective-criminal doubling. *There Hangs the Knife*, whose very name suggests impending doom, initially symbolizes Joanna's anti-detective stance of provoking her nemesis along with her blindness in risking long-time friendships in her obsessive quest for revenge. After the disastrous conclusion of *There Hangs the Knife*, Joanna brings the painting back to California and hangs it in her home, renaming it *Stark's Dark Star*. She characterizes it as "the worthless painting that symbolized her own fool-hardiness — and whose creation had set in motion the events that had resulted in her present fear-crippled state" (22–23). The third novel in the series, *Dark Star*, involves further exploration of the detective-criminal doubling/competition as the novel opens with the theft of Joanna's *Dark Star*. The theft, of course, is the work of Parducci, and this time he is stealing Joanna's symbol of her self-knowledge rather than a valuable painting. Like the renamed painting, Joanna herself moves from the role of contaminated to that of contaminator as her actions lead to Parducci's eventual demise.

Joanna's ongoing struggle to gain a sense of self in the face of her continued obsession with her nemesis is also symbolized by the tiny apartment she rents in San Francisco. This is a space she has rented for about twenty years, since before her marriage to David, and which she has always kept for reasons she can't quite articulate. She seldom invites others into this space, and she characterizes it as "a sort of grounding wire that kept her connected to who Joanna Scherer Stark really was" (*Dark* 125). The apartment becomes a touchstone to Joanna's internal struggles as the series progresses. At the end of the first novel, her decision to share her secret space with fellow art security expert Steve Rafferty could be construed as Joanna making progress in advancing with her life; this decision is recast in the second novel, though, when Rafferty turns against Joanna during a confrontation with Parducci.

The secret apartment becomes, in the final novel, the site of Parducci's murder. Joanna is taking her new love interest to the apartment for a tryst when they find a bloody corpse wearing E.J.'s coat that turns out to be Anthony Parducci. Joanna processes the scene: "Relief came swiftly, followed by incredulity. Parducci — briefly her lover, long her enemy — dead? Here? *Dead in her apartment?*" (160, italics in orig.). Joanna's apartment, her grounding wire, has recently led her to understand her own identity: "she found she could no longer empathize with the lonely woman with the disreputable past who had inhabited these four walls — wasn't all that sure she would like her could they meet" (125). Parducci's death within Joanna's space is aesthetically elegant in that it captures the slippage between the detective and criminal figures in the series. Parducci's murderer is E.J.'s best friend, Joe, who killed Parducci in self-defense after going to the apartment to protect E.J. and Joanna. Joe becomes contaminated by Joanna's obsession and is forced into killing as a result of his strong ethical commitment to friendship. Joanna tries in vain to comfort Joe:

> "You killed him in self-defense," Joanna said.
> "I took a *life*. One minute he was moving and breathing and the next —"
> "Self-defense, Joe."
> He put his hands to his face and sobbed [*Dark* 242–243].

Joanna cannot comfort this young man who bears the masculine version of her name because he has a self-awareness she lacks: self-defense or not, he has become a killer and he must face that fact. This contaminated space — which turns Joe into a killer and Parducci into a corpse, and which may have begun Rafferty's betrayal — is clearly acting as a touchstone to the contaminant Joanna has become.

The Joanna Stark series weaves two potent images together with the arch-nemesis trope in demonstrating the limits of this detective motif. The two symbols, whose meanings are continually shifting, work together to provide the backdrop to a story that is difficult to maintain within the bounds of detective fiction. The Joanna Stark novels, though compelling stories, fail as *detective* novels because Joanna cannot negotiate criminal-detective doubling and becomes not only contaminated by her battle with a worthy opponent, but becomes a contaminant to others, most extremely to Joe. This embodies a threat — constituted as an ethical threat by nineteenth-century readers and perhaps as more an aesthetic threat today — that lies at the very roots of detective fiction.

Elena Oliverez

With Elena Oliverez, Muller explores two distinct but related detective tropes that were part of the initial development of the detective narrative and that have raised anxieties for critics of the genre: the overlay of a quest for personal identity on a detective narrative, and the notion of liminality in the detective figure. The Oliverez books fail not because there is a hard limit to either of these tropes — although the novels certainly push both motifs to extremes — but because Elena's character is not well enough balanced on the point of liminality in which she resides. As Maureen Reddy argues in her chapter of this volume, Muller sets up non-white racial identities with great narrative and politically nuanced potential for both Sharon McCone and Elena Oliverez, but she ends up offering only "sporadic critiques of the centrality of whiteness in crime fiction" (Reddy 40). Muller affirms that she had planned to write more Oliverez books than the three that were published (the last co-written with her husband, Bill Pronzini) and admits that she ended the series because she felt "burned out" on the young character and found that she had nothing more to say about her (A. Muller 28). It seems there might be much more to say about a figure as liminal as Elena Oliverez. And yet, frequent narrative slippages combine with unreliable first-person narration leaving Elena an unsatisfying character despite her rich potential as both a detective and a female role model.

The motif of paralleling the detective figure's professional and personal stories has its roots in early detective fiction. Even Poe's "The Purloined Letter" (1844) briefly explores this theme, and the dime novels are full of characters — usually men — who represent everyday people who briefly become detectives to solve a problem. In these early detective narratives, it is common for the detective plots to be literally about a search for the detective's identity; many of these novels share with mid-nineteenth-century sentimental fiction the plot of the mechanic character discovering his or her identity as an heir or heiress as a subsidiary element of the detective plot. As Catherine Ross Nickerson has found, domestic detective fiction (late nineteenth-century middle-brow women's fiction) often follows a similar pattern, with women finding themselves in positions that require detective work. When Kathleen Gregory Klein finds this trope in female detectives in dime novels, she argues that the overlay of the personal narrative on the professional serves to limit the power of the female detective by containing her in a single situation and usually in a single novel. In conceiving the Elena Oliverez novels as a series of distinct detective stories rather than as a single story spread over several volumes, Muller advances the notion that questions of personal identity can be explored without unduly limiting narrative potential in the way Klein discusses. Elena's quest for self-knowledge can be spread across several detective problems because her character pushes the liminality inherent to the detective figure to the extreme.

The detective is often constructed as a liminal character who regularly lives at the interstices of socio-cultural groups. Because a story of crime generally involves the crossing of one or more boundaries, so too must the story of the detective who unravels the criminal's narrative. The detective's identity, thus, is often constructed on a point of liminality. Raymond Chandler's definition of the hard-boiled detective may remain even today the most cogent account of the detective's liminality. The detective who goes down those "mean streets," remaining "neither tarnished nor afraid," is forever out-of-step with his surroundings. Yet, as Chandler suggested, this very fact makes the honorable detective "the best man in his world and a good enough man for any world" (237).

The female detective, as we see with Sharon McCone, is often placed in a liminal role by her participation as a woman in a world that is peopled almost entirely by men. In Elena Oliverez, Muller creates a character poised on the brink of several thresholds: not only is Elena a woman entering the male world of detection, but she is also negotiating her complex ethnic role as a Mexican-American living in southern California, her role as an arts administrator caught between downtrodden artists and powerful business-men, and her lifestyle choices between marriage and children on one hand and a fulfilling career on the other. The overlay of these heavily gendered concerns on detective work seems to have great potential in developing the trope of the detective seeking to resolve issues of personal identity toward a long-running series.

Elena's complex personal negotiations are encapsulated in *The Legend of the Slain Soldiers* as she processes an area of socio-cultural diversity when she accompanies one of the museum's board members to a party:

> I'd long ago realized that when one becomes as rich as Carlos or the Rodriguezes, one forms alliances with other rich people, rather than along ethnic lines. These Anglos accepted Carlos and Alicia and Ramon because of their wealth and — in a manner they probably considered extremely tolerant — overlooked their Hispanic origins. They accepted me primarily because Carlos had brought me, but also because I was in the arts field and therefore practically a conversation piece [28].

Here Elena acts as a naïve observer in explicating the rich identity grid in which she resides. She notes that the socioeconomic trumps gender and ethnicity in determining acceptance in some circles, and she also emphasizes her own liminality when she understands her exoticization as resulting from the intersection of her ethnicity and professional position as a curator.

Elena and the cases she encounters — as a museum curator/amateur detective — are very much wrapped up in her continuing negotiations of her ethnic identity. In *The Tree of Death*, Elena, a suspect in her boss's murder, is forced to investigate, showing intelligence and courage as she discovers a major Mexican-American art smuggling ring, and the killer, a Mexican-American woman who is a major patron of the arts. In *The Legend of the Slain Soldiers*, Elena solves the case because of her training as a curator, which encourages her to preserve art at all costs, and her understanding of the nature of art, specifically of the artist's ability to manipulate the viewer's perceptions. The final novel, *Beyond the Grave*, plays out Elena's difficulty in negotiating romantic relationships — a difficulty she repeatedly links to her bicultural identity — against the backdrop of a century-old mystery whose solution relies on Elena's ability to negotiate knowledge and intuitions about historical Mexican-American interactions. *Beyond the Grave* is easily the best book of the series, and where the other two are marred by too little reliability in the detective-narrator position, this novel reveals the potency of blending the quest for personal identity with extreme liminality in the detective figure.

Beyond opens with Elena reading the notes of John Quincannon, a nineteenth-century detective, partially as an avoidance mechanism to the twin traumas she faces: her mother requires surgery, and her white American boyfriend, Dave Kirk, has ended their relationship. Mama and Dave are crucial figures to Elena, for it is through her simultaneous relationships with them that she most often processes her own bicultural identity. The threat to Mama's health represents a threat to Elena's heritage, since her strong-willed, independent and intuitive Mexican mother has been a role model for Elena, especially as she has navigated her professional world. The end of her relationship with Dave reveals Elena's continuing struggle to transfer the qualities that make her a good detective to her personal life.

Elena's difficulties in negotiating her liminal identity are often explored at the sites of erotic relationships, a common trope to detective fiction, perhaps especially within the hard-boiled genre. Elena explains early in the series that her upbringing has conditioned her against seeking interethnic romantic involvement, as Mama "didn't approve of mixed marriages, and she was ominously silent whenever I dated an Anglo" (35). And yet, Elena has often dated white Americans, although always with ambivalence: "I supposed that had always been part of the attraction Anglos held for me; they thought and lived differently than I did. Becoming involved with one was, in a sense, a ticket out of a life I'd known and into an exciting new realm" (*Legend* 127).

Dave Kirk is a Santa Barbara homicide detective who meets Elena in *Tree* when she is a suspect in the murder of the museum director. The misunderstandings and tensions that arise naturally from the difficult circumstances under which they meet become emblematic of the difficulties of interethnic relationships. Elena and Dave are initially wary of each other, as befits a homicide detective and a murder suspect. The wariness, though, pursues them through the slippage of their professional relationship to their later personal one.

In narrating the continuing problems Elena faces in her relationship with Dave, Muller uses a potentially powerful technique seldom seen in detective fiction, a genre in which the reader normally relies on the detective to accurately and effectively mediate, process, and convey data. E.C. Bentley's *Trent's Last Case* (1930), which uses an unreliable and ineffective detective, is generally considered an anti-detective story in the way it demonstrates the limitations of deduction. In Elena Oliverez, we get a character who is effective in processing and articulating the detective narrative, but who struggles to accurately represent issues around her own liminality. I would argue that this disjunct in Elena's abilities is both a strength and a weakness. On one hand, Elena's lack of reliability violates reader expectations of the genre and may explain both why Muller tired of this character and why the books are out of print. On the other hand, the narrative provides space for the reader to seek a more nuanced view of interethnic relationships than Elena herself can initially provide, perhaps highlighting a reality about the complications of bicultural identity.

Muller cues the reader to Elena's unnuanced readings of interethnic relationships through a number of personal reflections in Elena's voice. At the beginning of *Legend*, for example, Elena reflects on Kirk, saying, "Kirk was brown and bland, the most nondescript, unreadable Anglo I'd ever met. Even when dealing with basics.... I was wrong where Kirk was concerned" (4–5). Even after they date for some time, Kirk remains difficult to read for Elena. When Elena solves the murder she has been dabbling in alongside Kirk in *Legend*, she explains her process of reasoning in a way that straddles her detective work and the ongoing personal issues. The exchange between Elena and Kirk about the solution of the mystery exemplifies the dynamics of their relationship.

> [Elena:] "That got me to thinking about how we sometimes see what we expect to see rather than what's actually there, and I guess I made some sort of mental leap from squash to squash blossoms." "The intuitive and creative side of detective work," Dave said. I glanced at him to see if he was being sarcastic, but his smile told me otherwise [171].

In a comment about overcoming the limits of observation, we nonetheless see Elena's difficulty in processing Dave, as she initially assumes that he is being sarcastic rather than supportive or admiring.

The break-up between Dave and Elena at the beginning of *Beyond* demonstrates Elena's continuing struggles with maturity and perception. As Dave enters her house, Elena tells the reader her understanding of Dave has changed: "But as our relationship had deepened and we'd become friends and then lovers, I'd learned to read him very well — every nuance of expression, every tone of voice. And what I was reading now was not encouraging" (24). Although Elena recognizes Dave's mood as negative, her ability to read him stops well shy of the truth. She is shocked when Dave says that their relationship has simply not been working out as if assuming Elena is aware of their problems:

> "It hasn't been working out," I [Elena] repeated flatly.
> The tension in his jaw relaxed somewhat. "I'm glad you agree with me."
> Was he deliberately misinterpreting my comment? I wondered. Couldn't he see how stunned I was? What did he mean, anyway — not working out? [25–26].

And yet, the weaknesses in Elena's identity are put aside in the quest for truth. Elena solves all three cases that she approaches, and she solves them using features that are both appealing to readers and typical to successful detectives. She draws upon specialized knowledge, works through intuitive flashes of perception, and approaches dangerous situations courageously towards her end of solving mysteries.

The immaturity that marks Elena Oliverez is a legitimate part of a liminal detective whose quest for personal identity resides alongside her detective work. In this series, perhaps because Elena's liminality extends over so many aspects of her identity — as a woman, as a Mexican American, and as an arts administrator — she is simply not attractive enough as a character to carry the series. Nevertheless, the exploration of the intersection of detective identity and liminality, and the challenges inherent in that intersection — especially when it involves questions of interethnic relationships — makes a valuable contribution to our understanding of the development of the detective genre.

Soledad County

Unlike the intriguing but imperfectly executed Joanna Stark and Elena Oliverez series, the Soledad County novels are valuable in their insights into the potential future of the detective genre. These books overlay issues of landscape and gender onto the detective formula. The framing of the series as exploring a geographical region that is part of the complex ethical network at the center of a detective story harkens back to highly respected hard-boiled writers like Dashiell Hammett, Raymond Chandler, and Ross Macdonald, who brought to life their California landscapes, and to police procedural grandmaster Ed McBain, whose "City" he articulates as a central character in his long-running *87th Precinct* series. In fact, this tradition goes back to some of the earliest roots of the modern detective genre. At the extreme, it draws upon the city-mysteries that grew from French *mystères* like Eugène Sue's *Les Mystères de Paris* (1842) and became popular in 1840s and 1850s America. More clearly within the detective genre, the motif of the geographical region as organizing principle for a series of books follows from various dime novel series that grouped disparate stories together under the rubric of a city or region, like the *New York Detective Library* in the 1890s.

The Soledad County characters are challenged by murders that are inextricably linked to the complex geographical and socioeconomic landscape in which they occur. In all three novels, we see dying communities whose residents are struggling to maintain harmony between the land and their lifestyles. In each, a cold case is juxtaposed with a current social crisis. In *Point Deception*, the trauma caused to the town by a thirteen-year-old mass murder is rekindled by the murder of a stranded motorist whom many residents ignored rather than helped as a result of the distrust that is a legacy of the old murders. *Cyanide Wells* explores the revisiting of the murder of a controversial mill owner whose decision to close the town mill has led to great economic anxiety. *Cape Perdido* casts a twenty-year-old murder against a predicament in which a small California town fights for control of its water rights in the midst of state-wide water crisis. In all three novels, it is the ability of the two central characters to successfully negotiate the complexity of their landscape and to move beyond traditional gender roles that leads to the resolutions of social problems as well as of murder cases.

In these novels, Muller moves away from her longstanding tradition of placing a strong female protagonist in the center of a text populated by complementary men and toward the formula Dan Brown has employed so successfully (perhaps especially in his *Deception Point*, released the same year as Muller's *Point Deception*, 2001): a man and a woman are paired together, both violating the expectations of heteronormative behavior, and together they form an impressive force that strategically diffuses gendered characteristics rather than delineating them in clearly gendered terms. In this series, Muller works from a liberal feminist perspective in which characters explore their gender potential by focusing on equality rather than on difference (as an essentialist feminist position might do). Each book splits the detective position into two, featuring one male and one female detective figure: one a local who knows the sociopolitical and geographical landscape, and one an outsider whose fresh observations are necessary in revealing the strengths and weaknesses of the community. These two characters, who can be seen as a landscape proxy and a reader proxy, each have qualities essential to both solving a mystery and resolving a problem.

Point Deception, the first Soledad County novel, demonstrates the manner in which a liberal feminist ideology can contribute to the successful handling of a case and a crisis. Guy Newberry is a New York City journalist whose specialty is writing about towns in trouble, and he has come to Point Deception to write a book about the town, whose social and political infrastructure was rocked by the mass murder thirteen years earlier. While Guy is clearly characterized as an outsider to the region bringing a fresh — but often limited — perspective to its problems, Rhoda Swift is practically part of the very landscape that has shaped both her personality and the complex sociopolitical system central to understanding the dynamics of the case they explore. In fact, in future Soledad County novels, Rho appears in her role as police detective as part of the landscape that other characters are negotiating. Rho, like the landscape she is part of and emblematizes, is a tangle of contradictions, at once delicate and powerful, competent and dangerous. Although he is an outsider to the details of the Soledad County geographical and sociopolitical landscape, Guy's experience as a journalist makes him a highly sensitive man whose arrogance and perceptiveness construct him as an excellent collaborator for Rho.

In *Point Deception*, the potency of place is explored partially through Guy's almost mystical ability to read emotion even in very cold crime scenes. Guy and Rho visit the long-abandoned crime scene of the mass murders and together intuit that two of the victims had realized that the murders were coming and had met them with resignation. Recalling Guy's argument that powerful emotions are indelibly written on the site where they are experienced, Rho argues that resignation does not seem to qualify as such a forceful experience. "Resignation — that's weak, passive," she concluded, yet Guy maintains his position: "Not always. I'd define it as powerful when it comes to allowing yourself to be killed" (178–179).

Guy's understanding that the landscape itself soaks up the emotional resonances of deep trauma becomes crucial in processing the crime scene long after the forensic evidence is gone, and his insight here — not only that the victims were resigned but that they took power in their resignation — becomes important in solving the case. The reading of the landscape itself, then, including the sociopolitical landscape that results from violent crime, is at the heart of not only solving the mystery of the old mass murder, but also of resolving the town's untenable level of distrust.

The potency of place combines with the ability of the two central characters to move beyond gendered roles in the climactic scene of *Point Deception*. Here, Guy and Rhoda together go after the killer, Ulrick, at Point Deception, an area that Rho knows extremely well. Rho tells Guy that he can accompany her, but only on the condition that he lay low and allow her to do her job as a police detective. She takes the lead role in their physical confrontation throughout, and Guy accepts her superior competence in this milieu. Even from the beginning, it is Guy who follows. When they reach a barbed-wire fence, "Rho held it apart so Guy could slip through, then followed" (329). As Rho prepares for confrontation with the male killer, she gives Guy the less dangerous job of checking if the killer has left his unarmed female accomplice as a lookout. Though Rho fears that Guy will try to stop her from taking on the more hazardous task, he obliges, saying only "Be safe" as he leaves (330). The narrative then takes the reader through Rho's competent tracking of Ulrick, marred briefly by worry for Guy and by the spookiness of the storm that masks the already difficult landscape. Rho calls upon her experience with that landscape to maintain her calm, reminding herself that it is "*her* territory, *her* advantage" (331).

The scene ends in a reversal of many climactic detective scenes in which a male detective saves his female love interest who is less prepared than he to deal with danger. Against the backdrop of the rugged landscape and the driving rain, the killer attacks Guy, who tries to yell and is unable to produce a sound. Guy fires wide at Ulrick and is saved when Rho appears and downs Ulrick with a single shot. The scene ends with Guy sobbing in Rhoda's arms. Though she begins to cry herself, Rhoda shrugs off Guy's assurances and offers her own final assessment: I know. The first thing *my* father taught me about guns: They've got only one purpose. If you have to shoot, shoot to kill." She drew a deep, fluttering breath. "And that's what I did. I blew the bastard's head off" [334].

This scene marks the end of the narrative, followed only by a brief denouement. The reader, then, is left with the image of a man and a woman holding each other and crying in the mud and the driving rain. The scene's violence, combined with the tears and the rain, suggests cleansing and rebirth for the characters and landscape simultaneously.

Cyanide Wells focuses closely on the motif of paired detective figures as it narrates the complex relationship between Matt Lindstrom, a photographer visiting the town, and Carly McGuire, the editor of the local newspaper. Although the murders of a mill owner and his gay lover a few years earlier serve as a narrative backdrop, the main characters work together in trying to locate a woman; she is both Matt's ex-wife (Gwen), who disappeared fourteen years earlier and left him under suspicion of her murder, and Carly's current lesbian lover (Ardis). Gwen/Ardis understands and can share with others the economic and sociopolitical landscape of Cyanide Wells; she comes to symbolize the changing landscape of Soledad County and the ways it must be negotiated through different perspectives to Carly and Matt. They in turn come to reconcile themselves with the multiple facets of her personality, with the fact that "she seemed like two persons encased in one skin" (26). Like *Point Deception*, *Cyanide Wells* ends with a moment of personal clarity for both detective figures as the mystery is resolved. Carly and Matt confront Gwen/Ardis, with Carly's thoughts presented in italics:

"Please!" she [Gwen/Ardis] said.
She's pleading for her life, and I don't feel anything.
She looked from Ard to Matt. He nodded, face grim.
He doesn't feel anything either.
We're both free [327].

Of the three Soledad County books, it is *Cape Perdido* that most forcibly examines landscape as a central theme. This novel opens, in fact, with a paean to the landscape that sets up the central conflict in the novel. The opening passage moves from a second-person journey along the beautiful Perdido River to the articulation of the threat it faces:

This is a place out of time — for now.
West, where the Perdido eases off to sea level, it moves lazily around sandbars and between white sand beaches, carrying with it kayakers, swimmers, and dogs splashing after Frisbees their owners have tossed.... You watch them and think it

is wonderful that all this has been preserved in its natural state for everyone's enjoyment.

Preserved — for now [2].

As the river is threatened by waterbaggers fighting for legal permission to harvest the area's natural resources, present-day sabotage and kidnapping are linked to a twenty-year-old murder. The two detective figures, a female New York City ecologist and a male local environmentalist, are vitally involved in the political movement to save the river even as they unravel the mysteries that plague the town. The novel ends as it began, with a contemplation of landscape, as Timothy McNear, who has given up his grandson as a murderer to save the river, comes to peace with his decision: "In the spring, when the egrets and great blue herons were nesting along the Perdido, work would begin. *And that, old man, will be your legacy*" (306).

In the Soledad County novels, Muller both splits the detective position into complexly gendered characters and combines that position with a focus on landscape. In this way, she develops the notion of landscape as potentially straddling the boundaries of setting and character explored by early hard-boiled writers. Perhaps especially with Rho, we see a woman who is continually linked to "Mother Nature," and who is simultaneously delicate and powerful, cruel and nurturing. By focusing on the danger, deception, beauty and potency of the landscape in combination with relationships in which strong men and women are comfortable in adopting a liberal feminist approach to gender roles, Muller achieves a highly successful formula built from a careful combination of diverse generic conventions overlaid by compelling gender representations.

Conclusion

Muller's work moves beyond that which garnered her the "mother of the female hard-boiled genre" appellation to an even fuller and equally important exploration of several ideologically fraught trends in American detective fiction. Muller has studied the period in which the detective genre was shaped and in her non–McCone narratives, she pursues some of the potential avenues of detective development to their logical extremes.

In the Joanna Stark novels, we see a feminist rewriting and undermining of the archnemesis trope that has its roots in the beginnings of detective fiction and that raised anxieties about detective-criminal doublings in the popularization of detective narratives through the dime novels. In the Elena Oliverez books, we find an example of the fruitful intersections of liminality and personal identity as Oliverez's negotiations within an ethnically and socio-economically heterogeneous climate are repeatedly clarified by her interactions with forces of law and order as she takes on an amateur detective role. The Soledad County series represents a new direction for Muller, one which we might anticipate becoming a highly successful exploration of multiple detective motifs played out against a landscape that becomes almost a character within the narrative. Here we see a liberal feminist ideology explored through multiple groupings of characters as detective work provides a forum for the development of complex relationships between simultaneously independent and interdependent men and women. The developments Muller explores in each of her non–McCone series offer readers insights into some of the key narrative tensions that have shaped and continue to shape the detective genre.

Works Cited

Chandler, Raymond. "The Simple Art of Murder." In *The Art of the Mystery Story: A Collection of Critical Essays*, ed. Howard Haycraft, 222–237. New York: Carroll & Graf, 1946.

Cranny-Francis, Anne. *Feminist Fiction: Feminist Uses of Generic Fiction*. New York: St. Martin's, 1990.

Heilbrun, Carolyn. "Gender and Detective Fiction." In *The Sleuth and the Scholar: Origins, Evolution, and Current Trends in Detective Fiction*, ed. Barbara A. Rader and Howard G. Zettler, 1–8. Westport, CT: Greenwood, 1988.

James, Dean. "Marcia Muller Interview." *Mystery Scene* 45 (1994): 24, 58–59.

Klein, Kathleen Gregory. *The Woman Detective: Gender and Genre*. Urbana: University of Illinois Press, 1988.

Muller, Adrian. "Marcia Muller." *Mystery Scene* 50 (1995): 26–29.

Muller, Marcia. *Cape Perdido*. New York: Warner, 2005.

_____. *The Cavalier in White*. New York: St. Martin's, 1986.

_____. *Cyanide Wells*. New York: Warner, 2003.

_____. *Dark Star*. New York: Worldwide, 1989.

_____. *The Legend of the Slain Soldiers*. New York: Walker and Company, 1985.

_____. *Point Deception*. New York: Warner, 2001.

_____. *The Tree of Death*. New York: Mysterious Press, 1983.

_____. *There Hangs the Knife*. New York: St. Martin's, 1988.

_____, and Bill Pronzini. *Beyond the Grave*. New York: Walker and Company, 1986.

Nickerson, Catherine Ross. *The Web of Iniquity: Early Detective Fiction by American Women*. Durham, NC: Duke University Press, 1998.

Reddy, Maureen T. "Imagining the Margins: Muller's Exploration of Race." In *Marcia Muller and the Female Private Eye: Essays on the Novels That Defined a Subgenre*, ed. Alexander N. Howe and Christine A. Jackson, 39–49. Jefferson, NC: McFarland, 2008.

Taylor, Bruce. "The Real McCone." *The Armchair Detective* 34, no. 3 (1990): 260–269.

Todorov, Tzvetan. *The Poetics of Prose*. Trans. Richard Howard. Ithaca, NY: Cornell University Press, 1984.

Part II
GENRE

5

Taking Edwin to Lunch: Developing the Female Hard-Boiled Detective in the Early Sharon McCone Novels

PATRICIA P. BUCKLER

Sharon and I have been together since 1972 when I penned my first, abortive attempts about her, and the connection grows stronger year by year. And she grows bossier.

Muller, *Interview*

Critics generally view Marcia Muller as the "mother" of female hard-boiled detective fiction based on the early appearance (1977) of her first Sharon McCone novel, *Edwin of the Iron Shoes*. Although, in retrospect, scholars recognize the McCone books as highly popular and influential, in the beginning the publishing world was not quite ready for a hard-boiled female private investigator. After the publication of *Edwin of the Iron Shoes*, it took Muller four years to find a publisher for her next McCone novel. (*Edwin*'s publisher went out of business, and novel two, *Ask the Cards a Question*, didn't appear until 1982.) While searching for an interested press, Muller reports that she was frequently told "No one's going to believe women in this profession" (Ross B1).

Nevertheless, with the publication of *Edwin of the Iron Shoes*, Muller celebrated what would eventually be acknowledged as an important turning point in the history of the detective series. She took *Edwin* out to lunch! In an interview posted on her website, she describes the "best moment" of her entire career: "Holding the first copy of my first novel in my hand. I was so excited I took it out to lunch and let it sit on the chair next to me." Women had arrived in the hard-boiled world. Lewis Moore cites Muller as one of several authors who transformed the hard-boiled detective genre in the late sev-

69

enties and early eighties, along with John D. McDonald, Brett Halliday, Richard S. Prather, Robert B. Parker, and Muller's husband, Bill Pronzini. By the early eighties, Sara Paretsky and Sue Grafton's female private eyes, V. I. Warshawski and Kinsey Millhone, respectively, had been launched as well. Shaking up the genre, the female private investigators re-shaped "the [hard-boiled] character of the detective in light of female experience and attitudes" (Moore 180). They exploited and subverted the male detective hero by encountering different problems and responding to them in a "self-consciously female way" (Van Dover 200, qtd. in Moore 180).

In *Detective Agency: Women Rewriting the Hard-Boiled Tradition*, Priscilla L. Walton and Manina Jones examine the feminist transformation of the genre in terms of the sociological, historical and political as well as literary environment. "Writing within the confines of both formula and series fiction, authors such as Sara Paretsky, Marcia Muller, Linda Barnes, Liza Cody, and Sue Grafton have strategically redirected the masculinist trajectory of the American hard-boiled detective novel of the 1930s and 1940s to what we would argue are feminist ends." They add that the authors apply an "established popular formula" as a means of exploring the offenses of the "patriarchal power structure" of modern life (Walton and Jones 3–4). In other words, these authors created and established the female hard-boiled detective genre.

Judgments made in retrospect are fair enough. And after twenty-five Sharon McCone novels, one can validate the claims that Muller's work re-shaped not only the hard-boiled genre but also the women's detective series in vast and deep ways. Moore, Van Dover, and Walton and Jones explore the changing nature of the genre as a whole. Within that sweep, Muller's works themselves change, sometimes leading and sometimes following the path of transformation.

Tracking the evolution of a series is itself a large undertaking, since the thrust of transition proceeds along many fronts. Moore's book explores a number of features whose changes benchmark the evolution of the hard-boiled genre: theme, violence, character, family, friendship, space, sexuality, love, work, and society. Tracing these indicators throughout the series would yield a comprehensive look at its transformations. A narrower list of points of reference is provided by Kathleen Gregory Klein who suggests that a series (specifically Dorothy L. Sayers's Peter Wimsey tales) transforms itself on three fronts: "character development of the protagonist, thematic development, and structural changes that hold political implications" (5).

Even more narrowly, I follow Muller's own lead, focusing on only one aspect of the novels — character. Within the turning kaleidoscope of the hard-boiled genre, Sharon McCone's character leads its evolution in remarkable and unique ways. Muller's series highlights a truth about the new shape of the detective novel — no longer does plot or puzzle drive mysteries: charac-

Bechard

ter does. As the author herself puts it, the genre's borders are fading, and mystery writers today experience "a real freedom to experiment [both] in types of characters and situations. We are no longer confined to a plot-driven novel. This is not what the mystery is about anymore" (Hoffert and Annichiarico 120). In fact, Muller says, "Flexibility is important to me…. I don't plan the ending of a book. I think all good fiction comes out of character; plot doesn't work if you have to force the characters" (Ross B1).

Right from the beginning, Muller lays out the types of challenges this new breed of PI will face — disapproval by her family, lack of trust by the police with whom she must work, skepticism by society as a whole, difficulty in her relationships with men, and her own self-doubts. Predictably, McCone's character responds to a range of personal conflicts concerning work, family, and romance and faces the other significant markers that Moore and Klein suggest. Each personal and professional quest changes her, although she never becomes finally and permanently complete.

Just how much *has* McCone changed over the course of the series? The mission of this chapter is to search for the original McCone, the "abortive" creation Muller mentions. Exploring McCone's early character yields some surprises. This groundbreaking, stereotype-busting, "hard-boiled" female detective is tentative, nervous, uncertain, fearful, and very sensitive about society's negative attitudes toward women sleuths. She sticks close to her employer, All Soul's Legal Cooperative, and works cases in her familiar turf, San Francisco. She seeks support from her extended family and friends and is subjected to patronizing remarks from her first lover, police detective Greg Marcus. But the core of McCone's character, the detective that we know today, shows itself even in this early period: When she is alone, facing the sharp realities of her profession, McCone confronts her own fears and finds the courage to complete her job.

The early McCone — young, nervous, and uncertain — frequently finds shelter under the wing of her boss, Hank Zahn, the head of All Souls Legal Cooperative, a poverty law firm that charges on a sliding scale and pays so little that some of the lawyers live in the big old Victorian house where their offices are located. They embody the ideals of the seventies in San Francisco, only a decade after the Peace and Love movement of Haight-Ashbury. McCone is the staff investigator for the firm, and the group at All Souls forms her surrogate family.

Her real family makes marginal appearances, although later they play larger roles in her tales. Muller does establish her detective as the oddball member of her large, Scotch-Irish family. She is smaller and darker in appearance, a peculiarity attributed to a Shoshone great-grandmother. Sharon's detective origins are humble. She had worked as a department store security guard to pay her way through college at Berkeley and then received training from a local private eye in San Francisco. She was fired for failing to conform, so the job as the staff investigator for All Souls gives her both an anchor and freedom from the demeaning divorce investigations that comprised most of her previous job.

The McCone of the first three books adheres to her familiar circle — she has a previous relationship with the victims and remains within familiar territory. The cases keep her in the Bay Area. Not until novel four does she finally take up the case of strangers on behalf of All Souls and pursue her investigation outside San Francisco.

In *Edwin of the Iron Shoes*, she probes the murder of an antiques dealer, Joan Albritton, one of All Souls' clients. The woman is found stabbed in her antique shop on Salem Street, an area of junk and antique dealers situated on property desired for more profitable real estate investment. The murder occurs after a campaign of arson and vandalism, followed by city condemnation, that persuaded most of the merchants to sell; Albritton, the victim, had been one of the holdouts. Earlier, McCone had looked into the vandalism on behalf of All Souls, although she failed to identify the culprits. Her work on that front, however, caused a bond to develop between herself and Albritton, along with other merchants in the area. This feeling of responsibility compels her to force her way into the murder case, in spite of her boss's reluctance and the local police department's unwillingness to have her involved. Additionally, Sharon feels guilty since she believes that by solving the problem of the vandals, she could have prevented the murder.

Her self-confidence is undercut repeatedly because she is a woman in a man's world. She expects police resistance to her involvement, as her first encounter with Lieutenant Gregory Marcus, Homicide, shows: "Marcus hesitated, the corner of his mouth twitching, and I braced myself for one of the variants of the usual remark, along the lines of 'what's-a-nice-girl-like-you-doing-mixed-up-with-an-ugly-business-like-this?'" (2). Later when they discuss the case, "His tone was needling and unkind. Back to my antiques, in my proper place. Damn it, why did Marcus go out of his way to annoy me? It was strange behavior for a high-ranking, professional cop, even given the traditional antagonism of his breed for private operatives" (53). After Marcus learns she is one-eighth Shoshone, he calls her "papoose," an appellation that McCone hardly finds endearing. Enraged, but with a steady voice, McCone tells Marcus that he has no business speaking of her gender or ancestry (84).

Marcus is not alone in doubting the suitability of this job for a woman. Even the "Spanish thug" who threatens her on behalf of one of her suspects calls her "little detective" and "Pobrecita" (116). Another potential suspect, a woman this time, accuses her of holding "girlish liberal sentiments" (130). When McCone tells her mother she kissed a homicide lieutenant, instead of expressing pleasure that her daughter is finding romance, she reacts by saying, "Oh, Sharon ... you're not mixed up in a murder, are you?" (194).

Muller also establishes that relationships with men will always be problematic for a female P.I. When Marcus asks McCone to see him "socially," he comments that she could teach him, "Things about a strong man and a strong woman ... how two such people can be together without diminishing each other or tearing each other apart"(180).

Although her competitive bouts with Greg Marcus continue throughout their relationship (three novels' worth), additional slams against her unconventional career choice are less frequent. In book two, *Ask the Cards a Question,* a neighborhood grocery owner comments on the fact that the police asked her to identify the body of her murdered neighbor:

> "And why would the police permit a pretty young woman like you to view such a horror?" His characteristic irony colored the words.
>
> "My job makes me tougher than I look. I'm a private detective, with All Souls Legal Cooperative, the legal services plan."
>
> "A detective?" Something flickered in the pools of the grocer's eyes and his lids, almost lashless, slid down, lending his face a faintly reptilian cast.
>
> "That's right." I watched him closely.
>
> "I did not know" [10–11].

McCone in the first books confesses her fear, self-doubts, and strong emotional responses to aspects of her work. She averts her eyes from the corpses and loses sleep over her cases. In the Albritton case, she investigates under the pretext of inventorying the shop's contents for the estate. She spends the night in the shop, trying to sleep curled up on a settee, recklessly overlooking the fact that she would be virtually alone in a dangerous and deserted commercial district. When an intruder does materialize, she impulsively jumps up and pursues him, "not stopping to think what to do..." when she caught him (71). In spite of her terror, however, she remains in the shop, frightened, trembling and panting. McCone is struck by the extremity of her situation (and profession), and Albritton's murder now feels both "intimate and horrible" to the detective (73). Nevertheless, she remains in the shop, facing her fears and waiting for the intruder to return.

In *Ask the Cards a Question*, McCone investigates the murder of another elderly woman, who lives in her apartment building. This woman is *not* a member of the legal cooperative, but Sharon again feels compelled to pursue the murderer of a friend. When she finds herself alone in the dark ruins of a church with an ex-convict she suspects of being the murderer, she has an attack of nerves and feels chilly and edgy when he comes near her (55). Before the end of the book, however, the murderer is holding her best friend Linnea hostage in this same ruined church, and McCone takes him out in one shot. Here is another example of how she overrides her fear in the execution of her duty.

McCone's oddest struggle with fright, however, occurs in this same novel, and it involves her desperate dread of birds, surprisingly. In this investigation she must interview the phony fortuneteller, Anya, whose husband is one of McCone's leading suspects. Anya has a large crow as a pet, and she uses the bird as a weapon against McCone. Anya tricks McCone into going into her bathroom and then shoves the large bird in after her. Even though the door is not locked, McCone is too terrified of the bird to deal with it directly. "I cringed against the wall, breathing hard.... The crow was between me and the door" (94). The window, she finds, is nailed shut. This is where her ability to think her way out of a dangerous situation, even when panicked, comes to the fore. She finds a corkscrew in her bag, uses it to pry the nails, and coaxes the bird to the open window, so it flies away. Tragically, while the detective has been trapped in the bathroom, someone has entered the apartment and murdered Anya. Here, again, McCone displays an intensely emotional reaction that we see through this argument with herself:

> Anya lay crumpled on the living room floor, like a rag doll a child has discarded after play.
>   I staggered and dropped the towel bar, then leaned in the archway, staring at her prone figure.
>   "This is too much," I said aloud. "Two people killed in two days."
>   No, maybe she's not dead. Go over and see if she's dead.
>   "I can't. I can't take any more."
>   Go on. You've got to.
>   "I can't!"
>   Go! [95].

Although McCone seems thoroughly shaken, she musters the strength to face the fortune teller's body, and in spite of the increasing sense of doom, to solve the case successfully.

In the third book, *The Cheshire Cat's Eye*, McCone once again pursues the murderer of a friend, Jake Kaufmann, her former boyfriend. Again she blames herself for the death. She and Jake had an appointment to meet in a Victorian house he was painting, but she arrives late and finds him murdered. If only she had come earlier, she thinks, she might have prevented his death. The trauma and sorrow of finding his corpse interfere with her ability to pursue her case. "I tried to focus on my observations and movements since I'd first arrived at the house, but the picture of Jake lying paint-smeared and dead kept flashing before me..." (5).

McCone keenly understands that her life is in danger throughout this novel. She is pursued by Ray-the-Hit Man, who attacks her in an alley: "'Now you listen, bitch,'" he says. "'You gonna get out of the Western Addition, you hear? You gonna stay away from that Wintringham and forget about everything. Or else you gonna get blown away'" (119). McCone is terrified.

But she nevertheless confronts the power behind the hit-man, former city supervisor and local "big deal" Nick Dettman. Although McCone is armed and uses her weapon to threaten Dettman, she talks with him, despite her fears that Ray-the-Hit-Man will show up at any moment and kill her. After she hears the information she wants from Dettman, she drives away, but her "accelerator foot began to tremble" and she has to "pull back to the curb. I leaned on the steering wheel, my head on my arms, trying to control the attack of nerves."

> The confrontation with Dettman had been a risk — a bigger risk than I'd wanted to admit when I went in there. And, although again I hadn't acknowledged it to myself at the time, during our entire conversation I'd been straining to hear Raymond's returning footsteps, steeling to defend myself against the two men.
>
> Well, I thought, raising my head and smiling faintly, I pulled it off. Sharon McCone, ex-cheerleader and homecoming princess, can get tough when she wants to [162].

In major ways, McCone's self-realization here in the third book refracts the issue of competence at the heart of the modern detective novel, and in particular, the female detective novel. The private eye, like the lone sheriff in the Western, must figure out what she is made of before she can hope to do good for society and live with herself. McCone questions and challenges herself at every turn. She allows herself to embrace fear and push through it to find the courage she needs to complete her task and solve the crime. As the series develops and her character expands, McCone also recognizes that she must grow a thicker skin, become hardened to protect herself psychologically from the horrors of murder and the malice of murderers. Yet she fears that such toughness will diminish her humanity. Here is the detective's ever-present dilemma.

The fourth novel, *Games to Keep the Dark Away*, marks a major transformation in Sharon McCone and in the series. The detective is ready to reject her restricted yet comfortable life. Her apartment depresses her, friends and family seem out of touch, and her romance with Greg Marcus has ended. She is lonely and restless. She searches for a bigger apartment, or possibly a house, while at the same time questioning her decision:

> It was time to move.
> Wasn't it?
> But I'd been here for years. I was settled.
> Wasn't I? [17].

Her boredom and lethargy interfere with her duties for All Souls. She keeps neglecting to file court documents (one of her responsibilities), provoking a rare, angry dispute with her boss and good friend, Hank Zahn.

This case involves a private hospice down the coast in Port San Marco, a place that incorporates a new concept in the care of the terminally ill. (The hospice model was new to the United States in the early eighties.) The approach is enlightened, although a local waitress calls it a place where people "play games to keep the dark away" (21). McCone wonders if her life so far hasn't been somewhat the same thing — playing games to keep her own dark away.

McCone is ready for a change, and so is the direction of the series. This quest takes her out of the safety of the Bay Area and away from the shelter of All Souls. She can't turn to Marcus for inside information. She must depend on her own research and investigative skills to carry her through.

Most of the snide comments about being a woman PI have evaporated, although one woman seems perplexed at the idea. "'A private detective.' She shook her head slowly. 'The kinds of jobs you girls will get into today'" (28).

Games to Keep the Dark Away signals a change in McCone's attitude about her career. Her new acquaintance, Don Del Boccio, recoils when he sees the gun in her glove compartment.

> "You're for real, aren't you?" he said.
> "What?"
> He motioned at the glove box. "It's one thing hearing you talk about an investigation, but seeing that..." [86].

Being a "real" hard-boiled detective means accepting the reality of giving and receiving violence. In creating the first female "hard-boiled" P.I. on the scene, Marcia Muller had to resolve this problem for the character and her readers. Sharon herself articulates this challenge of dispensing violence while remaining ethical and humane. After discovering the body of yet another victim, she struggles with the feeling that her investigation was the cause of the murder. Reflecting on the turn her career has taken, from snooping around department stores trying to catch shoplifters to her seventh murder investigation in three years, McCone muses that she could have handled just one murder if that were all:

> But there were other deaths, and the older I got and the more violence I saw, the more I wondered if I could go on like this indefinitely. And when I wondered that, I also wondered what I would do if I couldn't go on. What on earth *could* a former private eye with a useless sociology degree do for a living? [*Games* 49].

In spite of her increased experience, she remains sensitive to the horrible toll human beings extract from one another and reacts acutely to the discovery of a very bloody corpse. "Blood. So much blood. Not a clean killing, like Jane Anthony. A messy killing. Blood. A sickly-sweet smell. And the rising stench of feces.... My stomach lurched and I ran down the steps, fell to my knees, and retched" (103). This is the pivotal case, the novel that transforms McCone into the "real thing," and she manages to regain her composure and stubbornly carry the case to its conclusion.

Significantly, the murders take place near and in the sea, the classic site of death and rebirth. Patients at the Tidepools had chosen a hospice near the sea to die in comfort and peace. The crimes occur near an old marina in the area. McCone recognizes the power of water as she swims in the hotel pool. "I was firmly convinced there was some mysterious connection between water and the creative process.... I puzzled out cases in the swimming pool" (80). In the course of this investigation, she is twice forced into water, and both experiences result in a new sense of resolution for her.

In the first instance, she finds one of her prime suspects, the hospice director Allen Keller, taking refuge on his boat, where she tries to trick him into giving up some important evidence. He overpowers her and throws her overboard. " 'That'll teach you to be so goddam nosy!'" he shouts. She shouts back, " 'Fuck you!' (It was one of the few times in my life I'd ever said that.)" While she swims to the dock, she has resolved to get even. "By the time I'm through with this case Allen Keller won't be laughing at anything" (97–98).

The second incident is the climax of the novel. McCone has solved the case and is pursuing the murderer, a woman, through the cypress grove between the hospice and the bay. The murderer heads down the stairs to the beach, but the tide is coming in, and McCone rushes to save her. McCone swims through the icy, turbulent water, reaching the woman on one of two reefs that remain above the surface. The murderer grabs and strangles Sharon until "the gray blurriness gave way to red and gold flashes..." When Sharon regains consciousness, she discovers she had been left to die face down in a tide pool. She spots the woman on the other reef, thirty yards away, just as a large wave is about to engulf her. She shouts for her to get off the reef, but the other woman refuses, and a huge wave sweeps her away. McCone swims to safety.

The powerful images of water surrounding life and death in this work perform as more than background setting. Muller uses primal associations of water with woman as giver of life to signify the new life of Sharon McCone as she advances from tentative woman detective to full-fledged female private eye. The self-contained comfortable life she had been living had, like the tide pools themselves, been flooded with a new existence. By the end of the novel, McCone is ready to forge ahead with her personal life and her career.

This novel similarly marks the maturing of Marcia Muller as author. By moving Sharon McCone out on her own, Muller demonstrates her own deftness at creating a more fully realized character in the new genre she has designed. Like her character, she is confident that she can swim against the tide and overcome the public's (or at least the publishers' and critics') resistance to the birth of a new style of detective. She proves that "the ex-cheerleader and homecoming princess, can get tough when she wants to" (*Cheshire* 162).

Works Cited

Hoffert, Barbara, and Mark Annichiarico. "Backed by Popular Demand." *Library Journal* 119, no. 3 (15 February 15, 1994): 120.

Klein, Kathleen Gregory. "Dorothy L. Sayers: From First to Last." In *In the Beginning: First Novels in Mystery Series*, ed. Mary Jean DeMarr, 5–18. Bowling Green, OH: Bowling Green State University Popular Press, 1995.

Moore, Lewis D. *Cracking the Hard-Boiled Detective : A Critical History from the 1920s to the Present.* Jefferson, North Carolina: McFarland & Company, 2006.

Muller, Marcia. *Ask the Cards a Question.* New York: St. Martin's Press, 1982.

_____. *The Cheshire Cat's Eye.* New York: Mysterious Press, 1983.

_____. *Edwin of the Iron Shoes.* New York: Mysterious Press, 1977.

_____. *Games to Keep the Dark Away.* New York: St. Martin's Press, 1984.

_____. Interview. http://wwww.marciamuller.com/author/interview.asp (accessed August 25, 2007).

Ross, Michele. "How Mystery Masters Plot Their Craft." *Christian Science Monitor* (July 31, July 1997): B1.

Van Dover, J.K. *You Know My Methods: The Science of the Detective.* Bowling Green, OH: Bowling Green State University Popular Press, 1994.

Walton, Priscilla L, and Manina Jones. *Detective Agency: Women Rewriting the Hard-Boiled Tradition.* Berkeley: University of California Press, 1999.

6

Sharon McCone:
From PI to Anti-Terrorist

Priscilla L. Walton

In 1977, Marcia Muller's Sharon McCone burst onto the publishing scene, introducing readers to the first hard-boiled female private investigator (in a novel-length and serial form). The groundbreaking McCone was joined in 1982 by Sara Paretsky's V.I. Warshawski and Sue Grafton's Kinsey Millhone, and, by the mid–1980s, female PIs were sweeping the literary scene, effecting a cultural phenomenon that had never been witnessed in the history of genre fiction. Indeed, in "Murder Most Foul and Fair," Katrine Ames and Ray Sawhill suggest that the active female detective arose in part because female readers were clamoring for representations of strong women characters. They argue that this demand was made possible by the expansion of feminism itself: "as the women's movement grew, so did the demand for female protagonists. Carol Brener, former proprietor of the Manhattan bookstore Murder Ink, remembers customers so desperate 'they didn't even care if the killer was a woman, as long as it was a strong character'" (67).

Unfortunately, however, and in the way of most phenomena, female PIs (of all stripes, sexualities, colors, ethnicities, nationalities, and so on) saturated the market, and, by the mid–1990s most female dicks limped out of sight, with only a few left standing. McCone survived (as did her counterparts Warshawski and Millhone, along with a handful of others), but Muller, perhaps not content simply to be a survivor of the latest trend, began to bend the genre of her McCone series. It is this genre shift that interests me here, since it is a shift found in no other female hard-boiled texts, and perhaps in no other formula novels of any kind. Indeed, to switch genres is extremely unusual; most authors write in one format or another, and rarely crossover, or, if they do, the changed genre springs up in a different series. The changes in Muller's 1990s novels compose a modified genre shift, in that, where McCone had embodied the quintessential hardboiled dick (if in female form), the series transitioned into part-detective fiction/part-thriller, as the texts moved into an international and global milieu. In previous works, McCone had been an investigator for a legal co-operative, All Souls, based in San Francisco; however, in *Till the Butchers Cut Him Down* (1994), she leaves the co-operative to begin her own investigative firm, and, in so doing, becomes one of the first female thriller protagonists. Unlike other such protagonists, such as those created by Helen McInnis, Gayle Lynds, or Maureen Tan, McCone is not quite spy, not quite PI, but she ventures into new territory — territory rarely explored by a woman.

A hard-boiled detective novel consists of a tough-talking, gun-toting, private investigator, a character who works outside the law, since s/he is not a member of an institutional organization (such as the police); s/he generally solves a mystery — usually a murder — all the while uncovering systemic corruption of one sort or another (usually along local lines). The thriller protagonist shares some of these features but not others. Umberto Eco, in "The Narrative Structure in Fleming," begins his article by noting Ian Fleming's debt to Mickey Spillane (242), and John G. Cawelti, in *Adventure, Mystery, and Romance*, offers a definition of what he calls "the adventure genre" (and what I am labeling "the political thriller"):

> The central fantasy of the adventure story is that of the hero — individual or group — overcoming obstacles and dangers and accomplishing some important and moral mission. Often, though not always, the hero's trials are the result of the machinations of a villain and, in addition, the hero frequently receives, as a kind of side benefit, the favors of one or more attractive young ladies... [39–40].

Ernest Mandel attempts to define the differences between the detective novel, the spy story, and the political thriller. He suggests, in *Delightful Murder*:

> In the spy story, unlike the usual detective story, the villains are normally well known from the outset, although occasionally their identification is one of the elements of the plot. They are agents of the Main Enemy of the State. The problem is not to identify them, but to undo their machinations... .
>
> But state crime is by no means limited to espionage. Just as espionage spills over into more general political intrigue, so the spy story pure and simple spawns the political thriller. Plots to kidnap or rescue opposition politicians under dictatorships ... conspiracies to organize military coups, or control the American president have all been the subjects of political thrillers [62].

Muller's 1990s novels incorporate elements of the political thriller: they include kidnappings, bombings, international conspiracies, and so on. Consequently, her genre shift is partial, since McCone is still a P.I. and still solves crimes; however, the nature of the crimes changes, just as the scope of the novels broadens.

In the earlier novels, McCone's position at All Souls Legal Co-Operative reflected the series' basis in the 1960s and '70s, since it embodied many of the values that accrue to the counter-culture: communal living, collective endeavors, alternative lifestyles, or anti-materialism. Conversely, the novels of the 1990s are situated clearly in a different era. This is a period of international terrorism (yet still pre–9/11), market downsizing, globalization, multinationalism, and confrontational environmentalism. To a large degree, the transformed political and social climate leads Sharon to consider changing her life.

In *Wolf in the Shadows* (1993), the camaraderie of All Souls begins to break down, and the co-op's convivial ambiance starts to dissipate. As Sharon is called into a partners' meeting, she is certain that she herself will now be a victim of the restructuring of the new All Souls, a project that had already resulted in many changed job descriptions for her reassigned colleagues (8). Sharon laments to Rae Kelleher, her assistant, "I miss the good old days" (19), and goes on to note the changes that she sees in the "reorganized" co-op actually run counter to their original mission: "In the old days All Souls had possessed a certain laid-back ambience as well as an excitement about the challenge we were presenting to the legal establishment. Now we were establishment" (19). The co-op, purchased by its members, Sharon's friends, is now an incorporated, for-profit business. The mainstreaming of All Souls bothers Sharon, but, even more, she regrets the differences that affluence has engendered in the composition of the law firm. She fondly remembers the days when she knew all of her colleagues, many of whom lived free of charge in the vast All Souls Victorian. The days of employee community, with "frequent potlucks, parties, and poker games," are now gone, and newer, anonymous employees have taken the place of departed friends (*Wolf* 20).

Just as the lifestyle of All Souls is shifting, so is the structure of the co-op. Indeed, at the partners' meeting, Sharon is offered a "promotion" to a desk job: She will serve as the chief administrator of the investigative and paralegal research branches of the operation. Sharon is horrified at being tied down: "It would mean surrendering the freedom that I loved" (*Wolf* 28). She asks for time to consider and then leaves — without notice — to tackle an unauthorized case (a tendency that has already been criticized). And, when she solves the crime she uncovers (by killing one of the perpetrators, an act atypical of the old Sharon), she returns to All Souls to discover her "promotion" has changed in order to utilize her "unique abilities," although she would still have to supervise staff (*Wolf* 296). At the conclusion of *Wolf in the Shadows*, she has not accepted the offer, and announces that she is due for a "change" (294).

One of the major changes in Sharon's life is the addition of Hy Ripinsky, first introduced in *Where Echoes Live* (1991). Hy, as Sharon describes him, is something of a Renaissance man. He is a "gentleman sheep rancher" who also serves as the director of an environmental foundation. A polyglot pilot and political activist — with an accompanying arrest record — he is also a "book collector, naturalist, sometime diplomat." In appearance he is "Tall, lanky, hawk-nosed, with shaggy dark-blond hair and a droopy mustache. Given to rugged outdoorsman's clothing, but also at home in formal fund-raising attire" (*Wolf* 9). Through Hy, Sharon also encounters the security firm Renshaw and Kessell International, or "RKI," with which she deals increasingly from *Wolf in the Shadows* on.

RKI, Sharon discovers, in *Wolf in the Shadows*, is an international security consulting firm, which employs (and is run by) "people whose past you really don't want to know too much about" and hired by people who have no other alternatives (41). Hy is a former colleague of the owners, Gage Renshaw and Dan Kessell, both former government officials: Renshaw was DEA, Kessell was in "Special Forces in 'Nam'" (41). When she first hears of them, Sharon is warned "you're not in RKI's league. These people have been around — everyplace. They're tough and they're dangerous" (42). Yet, while she is distrustful of them and wary of their methods, Sharon works with the security firm.

By the end of the novel, this association nets her a job offer from Renshaw, who is duly impressed with Sharon's creative work in the field (294). Apparently, and regardless of the protests her friend voiced earlier, Sharon *is* in their league; however, she turns down Renshaw's proposal. At the same time, Hy, who has known Renshaw and Kessell since childhood, and worked for them years before (when they were engaged in shady operations in Southeast Asia [*Wild* 77]), is offered a partnership in RKI, which he ultimately accepts. *Wolf in the Shadows* ends with Sharon contemplating her future.

At the opening of *Till the Butchers Cut Him Down*, Sharon has decided to go out on her own. At this point, her departure from All Souls is partial, since she plans to rent office space at the All Souls Victorian, an arrangement that will keep her close to her coworkers whom she describes as her "extended family" (9). This move has the added benefits of keeping her from a desk job (as head of the Investigative Services Department proposed by the new All Souls leadership) and allowing her to reject the lucrative job offer from the ethically suspect Renshaw and Kessell International security firm.

Intriguingly, however, her view of RKI has changed. She remarks, "I'd always have a soft spot for RKI, however: the cash bonus they'd given me last July, prompted by my saving them from a disastrous situation, had put McCone Investigations in business" (9). On this uneasy note, McCone Investigations is born.

While, professionally, Sharon is no longer a part of All Souls, she still rents office space there; yet, the difficulties she now confronts revolve around the nature of her former relationships. Sharon fears that the camaraderie she had enjoyed at the co-op was an illusion, when, in *Till the Butchers Cut Him*

Down, she realizes she has not lately received invitations from her friends/colleagues for the usual All Souls social activities:

> Maybe all these years I'd mistaken what were essentially business relationships for friendships. Maybe now that I no longer worked for the co-op those relationships would cease. Sure, old friends like Hank, Ted, and Rae would still come around — but what about the others?… I didn't regret my decision to fly solo, but it saddened me that it might involve such a big trade-off [107].

By the opening of the next novel in the series, *A Wild and Lonely Place* (1995), she contemplates moving out of All Souls entirely. Her few close friends are the only tie that keeps her tethered to the co-op, and McCone recognizes that both she and All Souls have changed. As she reflects, "The days whose memory I cherished, when the co-op had been a laid-back, unconventional institution where the old me fit perfectly, were gone forever" (26).

One novel later (*The Broken Promise Land* [1996]), Sharon does leave All Souls, and opens new offices in Pier 24½, taking with her Ted, Rae, and a few other operatives. Conveniently, her new offices are alongside the legal firm just opened by Hank Zahn and his partner, Anne-Marie Altman.

Somewhat disturbingly, as Sharon moves away from the co-op, she drifts closer to RKI. She finds the differences she had perceived between her and the international security firm dissolving: "Lately … I'd had a sense that the distance was shrinking, as if I stood on the edge of a cliff whose ground was eroding beneath my feet, forcing me to repeatedly step forward…. And in the dark hours of the night, when my misdeeds preyed upon my wakeful mind, I became convinced that I'd already evolved into the kind of investigator I detested" (*Broken* 49). Her fears that she herself is becoming more like the unscrupulous operatives at RKI continue to haunt her, and, in *A Wild and Lonely Place*, she admits: "I thought about my fear of becoming too much like Renshaw and his cohorts. Realized that if I accepted the proposed contract I would have taken one more step toward the line that separated us" (25). But she takes the proffered assignment from RKI anyway, conceding: "I didn't wholly approve of their method — it involved too much risk for my taste — but I had to admit that more often than not it worked" (84). Moreover, she begins to see merit in the methods to which she had previously objected: "I knew that my fears of becoming like Gage Renshaw and his cohorts were one step closer to being realized" (*Wild* 109), a possibility that to her is no longer so objectionable.

In *A Wild and Lonely Place*, Sharon starts to realize how much she has changed, and, looking back on the person she had been, she thinks, "she was someone I hardly knew anymore, distanced by a number of eye-opening years" (51). McCone recognizes that her idealism and compassion are not what they once were. Like all hard-boiled detectives, she struggles to be honorable when honor has long since gone out of style. She admits, "I wasn't sure that I liked the woman I was becoming, but she was formed of life experiences I couldn't eradicate. You work with what you are, I often told myself on those dark lonely nights when my misdeeds caught up with me" (11).

In the next novel, *The Broken Promise Land*, she admits: "Now there were emotional doors that I no longer dared to open, and I sometimes wondered what kind of woman I'd become" (67). Earlier, in *A Wild and Lonely Place*, countering these upheavals, she tries to build a safe space for herself, "nest-feathering" in the cottage she shares with Hy. In part, the cottage is important because she wants to "[c]reate a new structure, a new shared home. That and the fact that I sensed a number of my old friendships at All Souls and elsewhere to be fading away" (125).

Increasingly, throughout the 1990s novels, Sharon voices both her dissatisfaction, as well as her discomfort, with the person she is afraid she is becoming. Her client in *Till the Butchers Cut Him Down* is an old friend, "Suits," from her UC Berkeley days. He, too, has changed and become a "turnaround specialist" ("One of those people who bring corporations back from the edge of bankruptcy" [23]). She is surprised that the former drug dealer has become a corporate savior, and wonders: "But had Suits changed that much? By extension, had I?" (215). As if in an answer to her own question, she later recalls: "Once I wouldn't have been party to such a sham [she helps cover up aspects of the crime involved], but as I'd told Mick, that was what life did to you. Old loyalties, as well as new ones, were at work there" (328).

In addition to everything else, in *A Wild and Lonely Place*, Sharon starts to feel old with her fortieth birthday on the horizon (177). One novel later, in *The Broken Promise Land*, she searches for some kind of emotional security: "Change. Recently there had been too much change in my life. The demise of All Souls, the new offices, a deepening commitment to Hy that still held little of the security of a full commitment" (52). Again, to emphasize her feelings: "Everything was changing. Everything" (*Broken* 179).

In *Both Ends of the Night* (1997), McCone observes an FBI colleague: "He was teetering on the same invisible line I'd crossed so many times. Some of those crossings I regretted" (162). In this novel, she and Hy help to cover up a murder (280), and she asks him: "'What does that say about us?' Hy answers, 'Maybe that we're human, but our experiences have made us colder and harder than most people'" (311). She also wonders: "Do you think we'd have acted any differently if we'd confronted [the murdered man]" (324). But, at least on some levels, she also holds onto her former ethical code. In *A Wild and Lonely Place*, she announces: "Once I'd given my word I wouldn't retract it," an effort at "moral purity" that she hopes distinguishes herself from RKI (251).

By 1999, in *A Walk Through the Fire*, Sharon seems to be more at peace with herself. As she remarks, "Sometimes ... I thought I must have tossed out my ethics along the way, but other times I thought I'd grown up enough to accept the fact that there are situations and people who won't be saved if the letter of the law is followed" (256). In this novel, her struggle is personal, not political or ethical, in that she is drawn to a Hawaiian pilot and must choose between him and Hy. Similarly, in the novels following, *Listen to the Silence* (2000) and *Dead Midnight* (2002), the plots revolve around personal identity — identity theft (*While Other People Sleep*), loss of her own identity (*Listen to the Silence*), and, later, searches inside herself — the suicide of a family member, the trustworthiness of an employee, among others. These novels shift again, then, losing their international scope, and perhaps reflecting, at least in the latter case, a post–9/11 effort to grasp some kind of (personal) security.

Given all of Sharon's self-doubts, her anxieties regarding change, and her professional upheavals, it should come as no surprise that the series begins to transform. Although it is unlikely that an espionage hero like James Bond would ever be as self-reflective as McCone, she does move into the international milieu that Bond might inhabit. While I am not trying to suggest that the novels transform into spy fictions, that is, Sharon does not suddenly begin to work for the state, I am arguing that they hybridize, becoming part detective fiction and part political thriller.

When McCone goes over her old work files in *The Dangerous Hour* (2004), she reflects, that, with few exceptions, her former cases consisted of relatively mundane matters:

> I'd sent con artists and embezzlers to jail, returned children to the custodial parent, unmasked insurance fraud, recovered stolen property, and, in a few cases, allowed people whose misdeeds had really harmed no one to retreat into obscurity. In the end, I had to conclude that none of the cases I'd worked during my tenure at All Souls could have provoked serious retaliation. The majority of them were simply not important enough and had happened too long ago [155–56].

As her readers know, if Sharon's assessment were accurate, hers would not be one of the most successful hard-boiled series in recent years. Nevertheless, from *Wolf in the Shadows* on, Sharon's cases change. Some revolve around political kidnapping plots, a staple of political thrillers, as Mandel suggested; others concern an "important and moral mission," as Cawelti suggested in his delineation of adventure stories. Perhaps most interestingly, on occasion, Sharon's cases involve the machinations of a villain, who, unlike Mandel's distinction of the villainous knowability of the espionage genre, is often unknown. As Sharon (erroneously) self-describes her earlier work as "pretty ordinary stuff" (*Dangerous* 155), the series takes on a more distinctly global edge, in moving to encompass issues of greater social and political significance. For example, in the earlier McCone novels, the case in question usually involved a murder (or two), but the setting was local, and while it concerned the individual parties involved, rarely did the case make a statement about the world at large. All of this changes in *Wolf in the Shadows*— in large part due to Sharon's relationship with Hy —when McCone moves into the world of international terrorism.

In *A Wolf in the Shadows*, Sharon becomes concerned about Hy's recent disappearance, and she sets out to find him. To do so, she tracks him back to RKI (it is in this novel that she first hears of the security firm), and contacts Gage Renshaw, whom she dupes into hiring her as an independent operator. The case revolves around the kidnapping of a CEO, who, Renshaw admits, had refused an anti-terrorism policy, choosing instead to hire RKI for security. Though the firm originally suspects the kidnapping to have been staged, they begin investigating the possible involvement of "lunatic-fringe animal-rights groups" that made threats against the corporations research labs (53). The authorities are not contacted because RKI believes that it can better handle the situation by itself.

Renshaw goes on to explain that the kidnappers did eventually communicate with RKI, and demanded a ransom of two million dollars in cash; RKI decided to pay them with an "irrevocable international letter of credit" or "LC" (54). Since the LC can only be cashed at a firm in Mexico City, Renshaw is afraid that the CEO had been taken into Mexico. It was at this point that he asked Ripinsky to deliver the letter of credit at a drop off point in San Diego. Since Hy disappears after the planned exchange (along with the LC), Renshaw believes that he was in collusion with the kidnappers, that the CEO is dead, and that Hy is hiding out until it is safe to cash the LC.

Of course, Hy has not behaved as Renshaw believes, and Sharon sets out to prove his innocence, as well as to find the CEO. Over the course of the investigation, she gets involved with illegal immigrants, the "coyotes" who help the desperate cross illegally into the United States, and becomes more familiar with the nature of international terrorism, as this pre–9/11 work labels the situation. The novel, like McCone's other mysteries, does turn back into a more local affair, as it were, for the kidnapping was arranged by the CEO's spouse. However, the spouse is then duped by a corrupt Mexican businessman (and drug lord), who uses her and her arrangement to try to steal the two million dollars, attempting to kill her in the process.

This novel is unlike McCone's earlier mysteries, in that it involves a cross-border crime, huge sums of money, and speaks to the increasing terrorist threat of kidnapping for ransom, which, at the time of publication, was becoming common practice in Latin America. In effect, while Sharon is not an ordinary citizen "overcoming obstacles and dangers," she does accomplish an important mission, and confronts larger social issues: kidnapping for ransom and the plight of illegal immigrants in California.

In *Till the Butchers Cut Him Down*, the next novel in the series, Sharon again confronts corporate terrorism. She is contacted by on old acquaintance, who believes someone is trying to kill him. But "Suits," as Sharon's client was called in their shared Berkeley days, is no ordinary businessman. He is a "turnaround man." As he explains it (and note the broadened scale of his operation compared to those of Sharon's earlier clients), when a corporation is facing bankruptcy: "the turnaround man ... comes on board. There aren't all that many of us — maybe nine, ten, tops, in the country — who're first-rate. The Board pays maximum dollar, maximum options and non-cash perks to get me. They agree to let me call all the shots. I'm a dictator with a license to kill — and that's exactly what I do. The first step is the bloodbath" (24). Sharon is appalled by his actions, but Suits tries to convince her of his worth:

> The people who get hurt in the bloodbath generally're the ones who contributed to how bad things are. Or they're people who'll be better off out of there anyway. And the bloodbath and stabilizing stages lead to what I call the visionary stage. That's when you can really make things happen.... Revolutionary things. Sweeping changes that reach far beyond the corporation. You can change the course of every life you hold in your hands. You can change the course of a nation. You can completely alter history [25–26].

In his present turnaround project, Suits is trying to revitalize the Port of San Francisco. Since all the parties involved are supportive of his efforts, Sharon goes back into his previous ventures to find the culprit, who is indeed someone who had fallen victim to one of the bloodbaths. More importantly, however, through this case, Sharon enters the world of corporate capitalism. At the same time, it proves to be one of her first encounters with a bombing.

The bomb theme is picked up, again, in *A Wild and Lonely Place*, the novel that most conforms to the political thriller or adventure novel genre. Within this 1995 text, Sharon searches for "the individual who had bombed two Washington, D.C., embassies, two cars belonging to foreign diplomats, two homes of delegates to the United Nations, and two consular offices here in San Francisco. In the past five years, the bomber had killed three people and badly injured three others. Pressure for his capture from both our own government and foreign powers was enormous" (8). A hint of the cultural anxieties to come in a few short years is apparent in Sharon's unease:

> Somewhere in this city was a person who methodically plotted and carried out monstrous crimes. A person who'd gotten away with them time and again. He could be any nationality, could come from any walk of life. Could look as ordinary and harmless as the wrappings that concealed the bombs. Could kill or maim again at any moment. The thought of such a creature walking the same streets as the people I cared about chilled me through and through [13–14].

Coupled with McCone Investigations' interest in the Diplobomber is that of RKI's. When Renshaw discovers that Sharon has inside information (from a police friend working the case), he asks for a meeting, at which she discovers that RKI has been hired to guard the Azad consulate, which had received (unpublicized) warnings from the bomber.

A bombing attempt at the Embassy takes Sharon to the consulate, where she meets the consul general's granddaughter, Habiba. Because of the child, Sharon agrees to help RKI, although she disapproves of the firm's refusal to go public with the bomber's communications. Then, when Habiba is kidnapped, Sharon learns another secret: the child's father, Dawud, has gotten away with a crime by eluding police and fleeing to a remote Caribbean island. McCone believes that he has taken his daughter there, and she flies to St. Maarten to try to retrieve the little girl. She is successful in rescuing Habiba, but, before she can return her to her grandmother, the Azad consulate is blown up, killing the consul general and several others. Sharon comes to learn that the bombings are a "statement ... on the evils of diplomatic immunity" (268), and that Azad is the primary target because of Habiba's father and his unlawful behavior. When Sharon confronts the Diplobomber, he kills Dawud, and then she kills him in turn. Again, McCone commits murder, but in self-defense. This is an act the old Sharon would avoid at all costs, but one in which the new 1990s Sharon engages more frequently.

The Broken Promise Land covers ground more familiar to readers of the early series, as it points to the problems of corporate greed, if through a more local venue. In this novel, Sharon's country music star brother-in-law, Ricky Savage, is being stalked by a former lover. As his marriage to her sister crumbles, Sharon needs to discern who among his entourage is responsible for allowing the woman to get close enough to Ricky to terrorize him and his family. Although the case, the first one Sharon takes after moving into her new offices at Pier 24½, is largely personal in scope, its depiction of the music business conforms to the themes of the 1990s novels. For instance, Sharon learns of the contemporary music scene through Ricky, "and what he'd said about his associates had reinforced my image of him at the center of a school of parasitic fish, each eager to attach its suckers and hang on for a fast and profitable ride" (245). Savage is well aware of the downside of his profession, as he admits: "'It's a weird existence .... Here I am, caught up in the middle of all this cut-throat game playing.... And my songs — all they are is stories about my life, ... But I lay them down on tape and suddenly they're *product*, and there're hundreds of people trying to cash in on them. And I don't know these people, any more than they know me'" (246).

Through Ricky's descriptions, Sharon realizes how little she has understood her sister's life: "I imagined how lonely she must have felt all these years, how much at the mercy of a huge power- and greed-fueled industry that considered her, her children, and even her talented husband objects to be used and thrown away" (234–35). The case is resolved, and Sharon comes to a new appreciation of her sister. She also learns that the music industry, now a huge corporate conglomerate, is quite capable of ruthless and cold-blooded behavior in its greedy pursuit of profit.

Muller's next novel fits more with the "adventure" trend. In *Both Ends of the Night*, Sharon becomes involved in the murder of an old friend, Matty, an ordeal that brings her into uncomfortable proximity with the witness protection program, whistle-blowers, and corporate fraud. She discovers that Matty's lover was a whistle-blower about to testify about illegal activities taking place in an aviation firm, when the firm's friends in high political places worked to free a corporate officer:

> The Justice Department moved swiftly, securing a series of indictments against Stirling and his associates, ranging from conspiracy to distribute controlled substances to capital murder. But the day after the indictments were handed down, a federal judge in Fort Smith — who had been appointed by a former governor whose campaign fund had benefited substantially from David Stirling's contributions — decided that Duncan Stirling, in spite of his access to aircraft and large amounts of cash, posed no significant risk of flight [216].

The whistle-blower, whose real name is Ash Walker, entered the witness protection program, but after his wife fell victim to a shooting, he disappeared until he thought he was safe, at which point he resurfaced and met Matty, inadvertently causing her death.

Sharon and Hy track down Ash, only to find that he has killed the corporate officer he believes is in charge of the fraud (and, thus, of his wife's murder), and both investigators choose to ignore his crime. It looks as though the other corporate officers, one of whom is in line to become a U.S. senator, will go free, until Sharon finds and then turns over information to a colleague, in order that it might "fall into the right hands at the FBI — by a trail so long and convoluted that their origin will never be traced" (340). She thus brings closure to the case, but, again, is herself complicit in obstructing justice by helping Ash avoid murder charges.

Both Ends of the Night is the last of the hybridized texts I have been outlining. In the following five novels, identity, selfhood, the nature of relationships, and other personal issues dominate the plots. To summarize, *While Other People Sleep* concentrates on identity theft; *A Walk Through the Fire* focuses on the depth of Sharon's relationship with Hy; *Listen to the Silence* traces Sharon's search for her own identity; *Dead Midnight* explores Sharon's relationship with her brother, as well as familial efforts to cope with suicide; *The Dangerous Hour* evolves around the identity of one of Sharon's employees; and, finally, *Vanishing Point* (2006), Muller's latest novel, delves into the complexities of marriage, compromise, and closure. All these texts are more in line with the early series than with the hybridized 1990s works, for they return to the personal themes, leaving behind the international issues addressed by the five novels under study here. For whatever reason, Muller chooses to abandon the hybridized form she has devised, and her character revisits the more familiar ground of the earlier books.

If the five 1990s texts I have identified share more similarities with political thrillers and adventure novels than the earlier works in the McCone series, they do not simply adapt that genre's formula, but transform it. For example, while in a more traditional political thriller/adventure novel, as Cawelti observed, the "the hero frequently receives, as a kind of side benefit, the favors of one or more attractive young ladies," this facet of the genre becomes a site for translation and revision. To some degree, the hybridization of the series can be attributed to Sharon's new boyfriend, Hy Ripinsky, and this, in itself, marks a crucial shift in the McCone character, whose previous partners have little if any impact on her job. Even so, Sharon and Hy's relationship is atypical of the political thriller, since Sharon is the character with agency — not her bad-boy lover.

Sharon meets Hy in *Where Echoes Live*, in an environmentally based case, which takes a detour through a 1956 murder. He is an aggressive activist with a shady past, and Sharon frequently comments on the danger he exudes. *Wolf in the Shadows* offers a characterization of Hy, when Sharon notes that he is: "a gentle passionate man, but a man whom I'd also heard described as dangerous, perhaps violent" (9). *Till the Butchers Cut Him Down* provides the following analysis: "He was also frequently secretive, occasionally violent, and sometimes emotionally stingy" (103). Hy is a man with a past, as Sharon recalls in *A Wild and Lonely Place*: "Those were dangerous times, violent times. A lot of people got rich, and everybody else — including Hy — profited nicely" (77). Again, in *The Broken Promise Land*, Hy is described as "a stranger who harbored nightmares and recriminations enough to outlast a long period of reclusiveness, a marriage, and the untimely death of his wife" (66). And, finally, in *Both Ends of the Night*, it is their mutual friend, Matty, who sums up Hy's character: "'It's pure Ripinsky all right: tough as nails, with a bleeding heart the size of Texas'" (12). It is Hy who inspires Sharon to learn to fly, who involves her with the shady RKI, and who encourages her in her effort to open her own agency.

Indeed, where it is Hy who most conforms to the political thriller/adventure story protagonist mold, intriguingly, he is either absent or sick, when push comes to shove for Sharon. In *Wolf in the Shadows*, Hy is missing and wounded when Sharon finds him. In *Till the Butchers Cut Him Down*, Hy is away on some mysterious business; in *A Wild and Lonely Place*, Hy is too ill to help her pilot a plane, forcing Sharon to take the controls, as she also takes control of the situation; in *The Broken Promise Land*, Hy helps with Ricky's security, but he is angry with Sharon, closes up emotionally, and eventually leaves her and the case; and, in *Both Ends of the Night*, Hy sleeps through most of Sharon's encounter with a killer. In effect, therefore, while Sharon's new strong and dangerous lover is supportive of her emotionally (at least sometimes), he is never available to rescue her, to help her, or to assist her physically on her cases. Quite the contrary, Sharon has the agency, and it is she who more often helps him. No young women (or men) in brief clothing dominate this landscape. Rather, Sharon and only Sharon solves the crime, brings the culprit to justice, and closes her cases.

As a result, Muller breaks the mold of the adventure genre. While she retreats from the hybridized form, and, hence, does not quite break into the political thriller market, only a few women have ever ventured there. Now she is one of them. Unquestionably, the political thriller/adventure story is a terrain largely dominated by men, and it remains a space waiting to be settled by women. Muller may not pursue the hybridized form she invents, but she does dare to move onto this male turf, and, if nothing else, she has made an effort to place a female character in a male venue, and that, in itself, is no small accomplishment.

Works Cited

Ames, Katrine, and Ray Sawhill. "Murder Most Foul and Fair." *Newsweek*, (May 14, 1990?): 66–69.

Cawelti, John G. *Adventure, Mystery, and Romance: Formula Stories as Art and Popular Culture.* Chicago: Chicago University Press, 1976.

Eco, Umberto. "The Narrative Structure in Fleming." In *Popular Culture: Past and Present*, ed. Gernard Waites, Tony Bennett, and Graham Martin, 242–262. London: The Open University Press, 1982.

Mandel, Ernest. *Delightful Murder: A Social History of the Crime Story.* London: Pluto Press, 1984.

Muller, Marcia. *Both Ends of the Night.* New York: Mysterious Press, 1997.

_____. *The Broken Promise Land.* New York: Mysterious Press, 1996.

_____. *The Dangerous Hour.* New York: Warner Books, 2004.

_____. *Dead Midnight.* New York: Mysterious Press, 2002.

_____. *Listen to the Silence.* New York: Mysterious Press, 2000.

_____. *Till the Butchers Cut Him Down.* New York: Mysterious Press, 1994.

_____. *Vanishing Point.* New York: Mysterious Press, 2006.

_____. *A Walk Through the Fire.* New York: Warner Books, 1999.

_____. *Where Echoes Live.* New York: Mysterious Press, 1991.

_____. *While Other People Sleep.* New York: Mysterious Press, 1998.

_____. *A Wild and Lonely Place.* New York: Mysterious Press, 1995.

_____. *A Wolf in the Shadows.* New York: Mysterious Press, 1993.

7

Searching for the Past:
Nostalgia in the
McCone Novels

KELLY C. CONNELLY

Whether in the form of Miss Marple bemoaning the rise of a new housing development in St. Mary Mead or Philip Marlowe gazing in subdued awe at a stained glass representation of knights errant, nostalgia has long been a significant element in detective fiction. In the Sharon McCone series, Marcia Muller refines the nostalgic impulse of the detective novel, using it to explore questions of identity and society in a post-modern world. Early in the series, McCone uses nostalgia to avoid answering questions about herself and the increasing complexity of the world around her. Once she is forced to confront her past, in the form of her birth parents' Native American heritage, McCone is able to move beyond simplistic nostalgia and into a full appreciation of the values and traditions as a means of maintaining stability in her own chaotic times.

In documenting McCone's changing attitude, Muller demonstrates the multiple uses and forms of nostalgia. Nostalgia has often been described in critical terms, as an artificial means of avoiding the complications inherent in one's own times. However, nostalgia need not have only negative implications. In *Shifting World: Social Change and Nostalgia in the American Novel*, David C. Stineback defines nostalgia as "the individual's recognition of and reaction to history as an irresistible, ongoing process of loss, and disappointment" (14). It is the individual's response to "the incoherence of his social situation" that leads him to "an insistent sense that the present is somehow morally or spiritually inferior to an earlier period in history" (15). Nostalgia, then, can be read as a reaction to and critique of the individual's present environment, rather than as an inflexible and illusory attachment to the past. John J. Su reaches a similar conclusion in *Ethics and Nostalgia in the Contemporary Novel*, arguing that "nostalgia, in other words, encourages an imaginative exploration of how present systems of social relations fail to address human needs, and the specific objects of nostalgia ... represent efforts to articulate alternatives" (5). Nostalgia can be viewed as a means of seeking an alternative solution to, rather than simply escaping from, the problems of the present. It can be "more than a simple and romantic reminiscence; it is also *retrospection*, a movement towards the past from the present, and back again — another kind of return" (Munt 141). Nostalgia can reflect, as Muller realizes, an idealizing of the past but with an eye toward how lessons from the past can be applied in the present.

Incorporating the concept of nostalgia into the McCone novels, Muller places herself firmly within the tradition of detective fiction. Nostalgia is an inherent part of the detective story formula in large part because the detective's search for the truth inherently involves a search into the past. In the detective story, the primary impulse is one of nostalgia in the sense of recovery. The detective's role is to investigate the past, to seek solutions to explain what has happened. Among others, Tzvetan Todorov has explained that the detective narrative is comprised of two stories; the first is the story of "what really happened," and the second is the story of the investigation, or how the reader comes to know what has happened (45). Because of its focus on an action completed in the near or remote past of the first story, "[t]he detective story is much more concerned than narratives normally are with the elucidation of a series of events which closed either before or only shortly after its own starting point" (Kermode 180). In seeking to explain this series of events, the detective is engaged in "an act of recovery, moving forward in order to move back" (Porter 329). The detective novel encourages its heroes to take a historical perspective, to view the past as holding the solution, in a sense, and to view the past through the lens of nostalgia.

Significantly, the detective must not only explore the past, but he must also recreate it. Catherine Kinney asserts that "[f]rom Oedipus forward, the greatest mysteries suggest a ritual reenactment of the Fall" (77). More particularly, these mysteries begin with a Fall and reflect the detective's attempt to recreate the Edenic world by identifying and containing the threat that has led to the Fall. The detective story, then, relies on the "convention of Eden disturbed by chaos, loss, and conflict," with its primary goal being "the reinstatement of that paradisical [*sic*] unity" (Munt 134). In traditional detective stories, the detective must restore society to its pre-criminal state by ridding the community of the immediate threat of further criminal activity. This restoration, "while not annulling the deed (the body is still dead), gives the reader a sense of intellectual control over it" (DeFino 74). While this return to the pre-criminal state may be only partial or temporary, it must reflect the removal of any immediate threat and a return, if not to peace, then at least to the status quo.

Because of this focus on the past, both as a source of enlightenment and as an ideal for recreation, the traditional detective story, in all its forms, has been permeated by nostalgia for bygone times. In the British mystery puzzles of Agatha Christie, for example, nostalgia emerges primarily in the form of the characters' comments on numerous changes as they move forward into the modern age. For example, in *The A.B.C. Murders* (1935), Lady Clarke speculates that murder has increased due to "all the noise and speed nowadays — people can't stand it" (106). Miss Marple also bemoans the changing nature of perhaps the most superficially idyllic village in Christie's novels, St. Mary Mead:

> One had to face the fact: St. Mary Mead was not the place it had been. In a sense, of course, nothing was what it had been. You could blame the war (both the wars), or the younger generation, or women going out to work, or the atom bomb, or just the Government — but what one really meant was the simple fact that one was growing old [*Mirror Crack'd* 10].

This nostalgic impulse toward a simpler past is widespread in Christie's novels. The popularity of Bertram's Hotel, for example, is attributed not to its present state but to its ability to transport the customer to "a vanished world," to return him or her to Edwardian England (10). Christie recognizes that the nostalgic impulse may be based on an illusion; Hercule Poirot reminds his associate Captain Hastings that perhaps the "good old days ... were not so happy as you think" (*Curtain* 17). Nonetheless, nostalgia permeates the atmosphere of Christie's novels, as her characters attempt to retain the values and established traditions of a time now on the brink of extinction.

In Christie, it is generally the effects of the First World War that trigger the characters' impulses toward nostalgia. This nostalgia is rarely personal and instead reflects a discomfort with the general postwar atmosphere. Mrs. Price Ridley, in *Murder at the Vicarage* (1930), complains of "a loosening of moral fiber" since World War I (92). While Mrs. Price Ridley is herself a somewhat anachronistic figure, her complaints are reflected in the thoughts of Christie's more contemporary characters. Colonel Hastings, for example, describes the "world depression" of 1935 that affected him as far away as South America (*A.B.C.* 1). Lynn Marchmont, returning from a stint with the Wrens in 1946, similarly notes the "aftermath of war": "Ill will. Ill feeling. It's everywhere. On railways and buses and in shops and among workers and clerks and even agricultural laborers. And I suppose worse in mines and factories. Ill will" (*There Is a Tide* 44). "All the world is mad" (*They Came to Baghdad* 8), and in these "far-fetched times ... incredible things happen" (*By the Pricking of My Thumbs* 138). This nostalgic view of the past as a simpler and superior time may be illusory, but it ultimately reflects a discomfort with the modern condition and a desire to find an alternative solution to the problems of modernity.

American authors writing in the hard-boiled style of the 1930s would retain the nostalgic impulse of detective fiction, turning the impulse inward, as detectives began to question their ability to make any real difference in a world of global war, political corruption, and widespread economic depression. As the source of justice in an uncertain and dangerous world, the detective hero of the hard-boiled novels is a nostalgic reminder of heroes past. In particular, "critics have often pointed out that Philip Marlowe and other detectives in modern mystery fiction are updated versions of the chivalric, heroic knights who do their best to uphold a trace of justice in a chaotic, unjust world" (De Los Santos 77). As such, even the earliest detectives were anachronistic, having values associated with "an earlier, more heroic past" (Geherin 201). These modern-day knights errant were nostalgic figures; their mere presence was a reminder of presumably better times when justice was a more widely accepted value. Throughout the tradition of the detective novel, but most specifically in the hard-boiled detective novels from the 1930s through the 1950s, the detective hero was already an anachronism, a figure out of step with his own times, who was willing to sacrifice himself for the greater interest of justice.

In *The Big Sleep*, Raymond Chandler explored the anachronistic nature of the detective figure in a modern world. Like Christie's characters before him, Marlowe is attempting to call upon "a legendary past, not to retrieve an object of great value, but to rescue a personal code of honor made pointless by the Great War's impersonal violence and the vulgar self-interest of the succeeding years" (Rzepka 202). While calling upon General Sternwood, a wealthy potential client, Philip Marlowe is confronted with a stained glass depiction of "a knight in dark armor rescuing a lady who was tied to a tree and didn't have any clothes on but some very long and convenient hair" (*Big Sleep* 589). Marlowe's description of the scene reflects his sense of frustration with his own role as a servant of justice in the modern world. As Marlowe sees it, the knight "was fiddling with the ropes that tied the lady to the tree and not getting anywhere" (589). Marlowe again reflects on the frustrating job of the knight in the modern world while re-enacting a game of chess: "Knights had no meaning in this game. It wasn't a game for knights" (707). As Chandler explains in "The Simple Art of Murder," Marlowe must walk down the mean streets of the modern world without becoming mean, tarnished, or afraid (991–92). As a detective, he must be "the best man in his world and a good enough man for any world" (992). However, the world is no longer good enough to fully appreciate his value as a hero.

By the novel's end, Marlowe has solved the mystery, but he cannot restore order or see that justice is done. As in many of his other cases, "all of Marlowe's perseverance and effort is wasted in the final discovery of a long-dead victim" and a perpetrator who will go unpunished (Routledge 96). The murderer of Rusty Regan will go free, and the corrupt world of the rich will remain unchanged. Marlowe's view of the knight has been confirmed: "the knight in the stained-glass window still wasn't getting anywhere untying the naked damsel from the tree" (747). Captain Gregory, with whom Marlowe reluctantly cooperates on a missing person's case, explains that it is the world that has made it nearly impossible to make any permanent difference. As he explains to Marlowe, he is "'[a]s honest as you could expect a man to be in a world where it's out of style'" (743). Marlowe will not be deterred, though. Instead, he "embraces his knightly role in a hopeless gesture of defiance toward a post-war world that cannot countenance it and refuses to be made meaningful by it" (Rzepka 202). The reader is perhaps the only person who fully appreciates Marlowe's anachronistic dedication to the justice and honesty of an earlier time in a world in which he could just as easily give in to the lure of corruption.

Marcia Muller's Sharon McCone was born into this tradition of nostalgic detectives, frustrated by their inability to stem the tide of time and return the world to a simpler condition. Like many California private investigators before her, Sharon McCone watches with disappointment as the landscape around her changes, becoming more modern and losing its connection with the past. McCone remembers fondly that Port San Marco "had once been a great fishing port" (*Games* 27). On the other hand, the Port San Marco of McCone's childhood was a transitional village, with its "roller coaster and pinball parlors, hot dog stands and beer halls" (27). Although McCone is not old enough to remember the port from its earliest days, she assumes that she "would have loved the rough-and-tumble fishing port of yesteryear" (27). As a result of the change from individual fisheries to large automated companies, the town made "the transition to the modern age, and now so-called smogless industries and expensive housing tracts dotted the hills west of the port" (27). These changes brought not deterioration, but expansion, with new luxurious tourist accommodations and a performing arts center (27). Despite this appearance of progress, McCone is resistant to modernization, seeking out the one spot in the town that has not changed — the wharf with its charter fishing boats, souvenir shops, and restaurants (29). She expresses a similar resistance to modernization in *Wolf in the Shadows*, noting that the Baja she loved as a child has disappeared, only to be replaced by posh hotels and condominiums (238). Her nostalgia reflects not a generalized concern for the decline of a community, but her personal desire to reverse time and to recapture a past she may never even have experienced.

McCone's geographical nostalgia reflects a larger sense of her discomfort with her own role in a changing world. As she did in Port San Marco, McCone often haunts the establishments most likely to retain some connection with the California of the past. Her love for Ellen T's arises from its ability to "preserve a bit of the fading tradition of the San Francisco neighborhood tavern" (*Ask* 51). McCone's affection for Miranda's, "an ordinary waterfront dive" threatened by plans for development, similarly arises from its nature as a throwback to times past (*Dead* 87). To McCone, Miranda's is "a relic of the days when our piers actually catered to ships and cargo, and the longshoreman was king of the waterfront" (*Broken* 34). These times pre-date McCone, who is nostalgic not for her own past but for the superficial simplicity of a past she has never experienced. By remaining faithful to these traditional establishments, McCone attempts to stop time and stay suspended in the safety of her imagined past.

Most significantly, McCone's dedication to All Souls Legal Cooperative reflects a dedication to an ethical tradition being displaced by the corporate greed and corruption permeating society during her own time. Marcia Muller explains that the decline of All Souls was, in essence, a reality dictated by the progression of time: In the 1990s, All Souls was simply "an outmoded institution" ("Partners" 56). McCone reflects on the changes in All Souls that rendered it incompatible with its initial virtues: "In the old days All Souls had possessed a certain laid-back ambience as well as an excitement about the challenge we were presenting to the legal establishment. Now we *were* establishment" (*Wolf* 23). As All Souls becomes more corporate, and more consistent with the standard operating procedures of its own time, McCone becomes detached and disillusioned. Unable to find her place in a legal services corporation as it changes with the times, and unable to envision herself as an agent for the ruthless and successful security firm of RKI, McCone decides to remain an independent operative, taking with her those relics of the past that will remind her of the seeming simplicity of an earlier value system no longer in place.

Desperate to retain some sense of security in a changing world, McCone attempts to use her possessions to sustain her connection to the past. Rae Kelleher, one of McCone's operatives, reminds McCone of man's need to use possessions to protect himself, noting "that things like table linens, china, and silver are how we keep the big bad world at bay" (*Both Ends* 196). McCone, in particular, uses her possessions to keep the "big bad world" of progress at bay. McCone's attachment to her "ancient armchair," with its "worn upholstery and bleeding stuffing," reflects her desire to maintain a connection with the past, despite any inconvenience (*While* 203). McCone was originally drawn to the chair by its already worn appearance: "The chair was old and ill treated when I found it in the cubbyhole under the stairs that was my first office at All Souls Legal Cooperative" (203). Again, her sense of nostalgia does not reflect a longing for her own past but for a past that she has never experienced. Clinging to this imaginary simpler time, when McCone moves, "a fit of sentimentality" motivates her to bring the chair with her (203). She views the chair through the lens of nostalgia, imagining that by retaining possessions from the past, she can resist the complications of her own present.

McCone's references to her chair as well as to her favorite restaurant as relics (*Dead* 95) reflect a significant attachment to something lost. A relic is "a survivor or remnant left after decay, disintegration, or disappearance" or "a trace of some past or outmoded practice, custom, or belief" (*Merriam-Webster* online). McCone's need to surround herself with relics is a reminder, then, of her misplaced status in the contemporary world. She is a figure from the past, a heroine out of her own time, and her attachment to her battered chair reflects her own knowledge that she is attempting to hold onto something that cannot be retained. McCone's attachment to possessions, including her attachment to her MG, which she refuses to trade for a more practical car, and her Citabria, which she reluctantly agrees to replace only with an older model plane, suggests an attempt to use possessions to retain some semblance of a life that is no longer viable. If she can surround herself with the trappings of security, she can ignore the greater changes in the world around her: "The world might be veering out of control, but [our home] was a refuge that connected us to a saner past" (*Listen* 136).

McCone cannot completely ignore the changes around her and, like Agatha Christie's characters, she is distraught at the changes that have made her a relic in her own society. McCone is constantly reminded of the limited security available in a modern world. Hank Zahn, McCone's former employer and trusted friend, bemoans the fate of the "good guys" in the modern world: "'It's an ugly, scary world these days, and the good guys all too often don't have enough legal tools on their side to protect them'" (*While* 70). McCone's lover, Hy Ripinsky, similarly reminds her that "'It's pretty goddamn wild and lonely out there nowadays'" (*Wild* 35). In the face of urban life, which is "too often chilled by indifference, hostility, and crime" (*Ask* 5), McCone questions her ability to make a difference or to act heroically.

Faced with her fear of inadequacy, McCone imagines a simpler past, nostalgically recalling the apparent simplicity of her earliest cases. When McCone finds herself entangled in the complicated world of corporate corruption in *Dead Midnight*, she reflects wistfully on the "simple" investigation of theft and murder she began in *Leave a Message for Willie* (173). McCone's memory of "simpler" crimes is typically illusory nostalgia; she has been dealing with complicated murder, sabotage, and blackmail cases since the beginning. What has changed is the nature of the atmosphere in which she conducts her investigations. McCone notes that the proliferation of crime novels, television shows, and movies has made her job significantly more difficult, as "the average individual has become as savvy in ways of avoiding detection as your typical street criminal" (*While* 36). Adding to the complication is the changing nature of society, with its "justified" paranoia resulting in more cases involving "the tricky maze of human relationships" (*While* 16). Finally, as the number of McCone's cases has increased, so has the body count she has witnessed. McCone notes that as she has gotten older, she has seen more violence and been witness to more deaths (*Games* 71). Given the violent and chaotic nature of her own society, McCone wistfully longs for the "master criminals" she has grown up reading about, the "Professor Moriartys, the Fu Manchus, the Goldfingers" (*Walk* 276). As usual, McCone is most nostalgic not for the cases of her early days, but for the cases she has never seen herself—those of a fictional era before her own.

At least superficially, McCone attempts to adapt to the changing world by accepting the developing technology. In 1994's *Till the Butchers Cut Him Down*, McCone accepts a car-phone, "hurtling into the twenty-first century faster than the speed of light" (274). She then reluctantly begins to accept advances in investigatory techniques, "relying on sophisticated equipment, technical assistance, and experts of all sorts" (*Dead Midnight* 173). The last of McCone's futile attempts at resistance sees her succumbing to the lure of the computer, which she had earlier dismissed as "a creation of the devil" (*Walk* 9). Despite her protests against the "unnatural" relationship between her nephew and his computer, McCone can appreciate the results (*Both Ends* 43). On the surface, McCone is adapting to the modern world by overcoming her fear and aversion to technology; below the surface, however, she is discovering that the advances she has made in her investigatory practices have brought her closer to the world of corruption that she attempts to change.

By the time McCone appears in her tenth novel, *The Shape of Dread* (1989), she has already suffered the wearying effects of being a detective in the modern world. As explained earlier, detectives like Philip Marlowe, when faced with the chaos and violence of the modern world, experienced "a larger sense of fear, an undefined malaise that hangs over events before they happen, a fear the more terrifying because, he suggests, sudden death lies as much in the familiar as in the unknown" (Margolies 41). Rather than confining chaos, the hard-boiled detective story became the study of chaos, "the corruption, the degradation, the violence—and the illusions that grow out of it" (DeFino 75). As an inheritor of this tradition, McCone becomes frustrated with her inability to change the larger society around her. McCone explains that she has been forever changed by "a decade [of] uncovering secrets of people's lives that literally made one's flesh creep... the havoc and destruction caused by human greed, carelessness, and stupidity" (*Shape* 239). As a result, McCone begins to lose sympathy, faith, and enthusiasm for her chosen profession.

McCone's enthusiasm continues to wane, as she finds herself unable to remain unaffected by the horrors she has uncovered. She finds herself becoming more cynical and suspicious (*There's Nothing* 125), as her faith is "repeatedly shattered as ugly truths were revealed" (*Pennies* 184). Even more troubling to McCone is the rapid erosion of her previously sharp distinction between the ethical and the unethical. The once seemingly insurmountable distance between herself and the unethical investigators of large corporations like RKI has become non-existent in her eyes: "Lately, though, I'd had a sense that the distance was shrinking, as if I stood on the edge of a cliff whose ground was eroding beneath my feet, forcing me to repeatedly step forward" (*Broken* 46). McCone relates this erosion of her strong morality to the "constant battering from a world in which nobody really gave a damn" (*Both Ends* 73). In the face of a violent and indifferent world, McCone fears a permanent change in herself, becoming more like the world around her rather than resisting it.

McCone's response to this feeling of a loss of morality and faith is to again indulge in nostalgia. Her nostalgia is, for a change, personal — that is, it concerns her own past. In *Trophies and Dead Things*, McCone feels a sharp pang of nostalgia for the self she was during her own times at Berkeley (138). McCone's brother realizes, though, that McCone is also experiencing nostalgia for a time other than her own. Like Marlowe envisioning himself as a frustrated chivalric knight, McCone is a "throwback to an earlier generation" (*Listen* 24). McCone recognizes this herself, reasoning that she "didn't belong in this world of the nineteen-eighties, where things counted more than people" (*There's Nothing* 20). McCone's insistence on identifying with the codes of a time now past marks her as an individual in her own era and as a reminder of the hard-boiled detectives/knights errant who have come before her.

In attempting to delve below the surface in her depiction of her heroine's turmoil, Muller moves beyond the tradition of the British puzzle mystery or the American hard-boiled story. Muller explains that "Sharon McCone ... was to be as close to a real person as possible" ("Partners" 51). In order to give McCone depth as a person, Muller began with the creation of a history, of a detailed past beginning with McCone's childhood ("Partners" 52). This thoroughly envisioned personal history allows Muller to move beyond the limitations of her predecessors and explore the personal nostalgia that accompanies a search not just for the solution to a criminal mystery but for one's own identity.

McCone acknowledges that "very often ... the key to a person's present lies in the past" (*Both Ends* 144). However, she has often felt detached from her own past, finding herself incapable of tracing the development of her identity. This is true even of her memory of her superficially idyllic teenage years (*Both Ends* 152). McCone has been marked as different from her own family by her visible Native American heritage, which has been explained as a throwback to her part-Shoshone heritage. At first, McCone feels no nostalgia for this cultural or ethnic heritage, "no pull from her culture, only a mild curiosity as to why [Mary McCone] had left her own people to become the deeply religious Catholic wife of a much older white man" (*Walk* 129). Although McCone asserts that she will be searching for the answers to this question until the day she dies (*Till the Butchers* 142), she actually makes no attempt, despite her skills in investigation, to trace the mystery of her own past. Muller, in 1983, went so far as to claim that McCone's Native American heritage was not "likely to make a difference in any of the future books" (Isaac 23). In 1990, Muller explained that because McCone did not "really identify with her ethnic heritage, there are some books in the series where it is not mentioned at all" (Taylor 263). McCone's family history, particularly her Native American ancestry, is irrelevant to her, until she is finally confronted with the truth about her connection to a past with which she has previously had no contact.

In *Listen to the Silence* (2000), Sharon McCone is confronted with the fact that she was adopted. For an investigator, who realizes the importance of the past, her lack of knowledge of who she is and where she came from is the worst fate she can imagine (36). In order to find the truth of her heritage, McCone embraces both the past and the future in methods of investigation. She allows herself to rely on the intuitive methods and the insight of dreams practiced by her Shoshone ancestors, but she also, for the first time, embraces the technology of the computer. By combining these methods, she discovers that her biological parents are both Native Americans. As McCone begins to accept the truth about her past, she experiences a new connection to her heritage and a stronger sense of her own identity. She will begin to find a balance between past and present, between her nostalgic idealization of a past with which she has had no real connection and the future that she has forcefully resisted.

McCone's attitude toward nostalgia changes significantly after she has begun to accept her own past and its effect on her present. In *Dead Midnight* (2002), McCone makes her first appearance since discovering her Native American heritage in *Listen to the Silence*. McCone's tone in observing alterations in the geography of San Francisco has changed significantly, as her nostalgia is now balanced by a realistic impression of both past and present. When viewing evidence of the "revitalization" of the waterfront, McCone briefly notes the costs of progress, but she is now able to appreciate for the first time the beauty of what has come into being (15–16). Rather than focusing on McCone's traditional rants against modernization, Muller shifts the focus to Glenn Solomon's complaints of the sharp have/have-not division that has arisen as a result of "progress." McCone does not respond to or join in Glenn's nostalgic view of the past as superior. Rather than dwelling on the past as a means of avoiding the future, McCone can now appreciate what has been, while also appreciating what her hometown has become.

McCone also develops a keener ability to use the techniques associated with both the past and the future in *Dead Midnight*. In *Shaman or Sherlock? The Native American Detective*, Gina and Andrew MacDonald explain that a key difference between Native American detectives and Anglo detectives is their reliance on intuition rather than reason (27–28). In *Dead Midnight*, McCone attempts to use the methods of her ancestry, of her past, by allowing herself to rely in significant part on her intuition in solving the mystery at hand. This reliance on intuition is not new; she has relied on the revelations brought to her by dreams (*Pennies* 140; *While* 298) and has trusted her instincts (*Wolf* 42–43) in the past. However, in *Dead Midnight*, McCone unashamedly puts to use the technique of "listening to the silence" taught to her by her father (78). McCone is no longer bound by methods of the past, though, as she also uses the computer as an investigatory tool with ease (30). Traditionally, nostalgia has been viewed as a paralyzing impulse: "By clinging to established habits or chosen illusions in opposition to the actuality of social change, ... alienated and nostalgic characters ... frequently become inflexible in their thinking, as if they were, in fact, members of a more stable, less democratic order" (Stineback 18). Unlike these rigidly nostalgic characters, McCone will overcome this paralyzing influence; she has accepted the value of a time past but has blended the methods of the past with those of the present to maximize her investigatory abilities.

More significantly, McCone's newfound ability to maneuver between the past and the present will allow her to deal more fully with her own personal tragedies. Before *Dead Midnight* begins, McCone's brother Joey has committed suicide. McCone's initial instinct is to view the past in a slanted manner, in this case to remember only the negative moments she has shared with her brother (180). Ultimately, she is once again able to transcend her limited view of the past, and positive memories begin to fill in a complete picture of her relationship with her estranged brother (181). By viewing the past through a more realistic lens, McCone is able to move into the present and to view a possible future. She still recalls the "evil deeds done as the result of greed, cowardice, or just plain stupidity" to which her job as a private investigator has exposed her (268). However, she will not let these memories prevent her from moving forward. In the end, she will let go of the past, in particular of the deaths of two people with whom she has been close, in order to move forward.

McCone continues her forward momentum in the next novel in the series, *The Dangerous Hour* (2005). McCone's nostalgic impulses have not disappeared; she is nostalgic for a time when she could wear jeans all the time (55), and at times she misses the idealistic days of her early work at All Souls (4). However, McCone is now more aware of the need to balance the past and the present and to use her nostalgia not as a crutch, but as an impetus to make changes in her current life. When McCone's nostalgia leads her to examine old files, she now puts her improved techniques and knowledge to use, solving a previously unsolved case (153). She is also now able to view her time at All Souls more objectively, realizing that even if she has not changed the world, she had improved the lives of many individuals within the world (156). She is even able to realize that while she misses her brother, his death has freed her from the restraint of worrying about him all the time (117). McCone is now able to view the past through clearer, less nostalgic eyes. She has moved on in her professional life and is finally willing to take a forward step in her personal life, agreeing to marry long-time lover Hy Ripinsky (304–05). McCone continues to keep one foot in the past, but she has become willing to use her view of the past as a means of coping with, rather than avoiding, the complications of her own present.

In *Vanishing Point* (2006), McCone not only remains free from the paralyzing effects of her own nostalgia, but she is able to use her professional skills to help a client realize the truth about illusory notions of an idyllic past. Rather than searching for her own past, real or imagined, McCone begins the search for a client's mother, who disappeared twenty-two years earlier (10). Jennifer Aldin is much like McCone before her; she is desperate to find the truth about her own past and to reclaim this past as a means of avoiding the discomfort and unhappiness of her current life. What McCone finds is not what Jennifer has imagined; in the end, Laurel Greenwood is simply "a mother who cold-bloodedly abandons her children" to avoid taking responsibility for her own actions (317). The past does not hold any real solutions for Jennifer, and McCone must watch as her client suffers through a realization that what she has imagined about her past has been a fantasy. McCone now fully realizes the potential dangers of nostalgia, with its ability to blind us to reality by sanitizing the past (62).

McCone's mature image toward nostalgia, her ability to appreciate both the seeming simplicity of the past and the promise of the future, continues to be reflected in her attitude toward geography and her possessions, two of the foci of her nostalgia in the past. With respect to geography, McCone recognizes the increasing wine industry and tourism in Paso Robles as a step forward after the San Simeon earthquake (25). Although she notes that the town was once a "little town where people led quiet, ordinary existences" (25), her overall tone is no longer one of wistful nostalgia for the past and resentment of the modernization of the present. Even more significantly, in describing the furnishings of her office, McCone fails, for the first time, to mention the historical significance of her beloved armchair (40). Later, when she finds Derek Ford (one of the computer assistants at McCone Investigations) lounging in her armchair, she comments that it is "not sacrosanct ... it's not even that comfortable" (277). McCone can now view the chair as a part of the present rather than as a treasured attachment to her imagined past. Similarly, when McCone mentions Miranda's in *Vanishing Point*, Muller omits any discussion of the threat of progress or the nature of Miranda's as a "relic" of times long gone (42). While trying to get a sense of the lives that were lived in her client's former home, McCone is unable to reconnect with the past; "too much time had passed" (56). She has moved beyond her romantic attachment to all things past and can more effectively view and maneuver within the world as it stands today.

McCone has not abandoned her attachment to the past, but she has realized that there are compromises that may allow her to visit the past while living in the present. She will retain her MG, but she is already "lusting after a Blackberry" (318). Most significantly, she will retain her house, which has been in the past an object of nostalgia. In *Vanishing Point*, McCone recalls lovingly the past of her home, remembering the early days of her remodeling (30–31). However, she does not view the object solely as a relic. Rather, she also values the house for its current value, for its location in an enclave of security and friendliness seemingly rare in her modern world (31). Hy, realizing McCone's attachment to her house, agrees to a compromise; rather than buying a new home, they will construct an underground extension of the old one. Through a final act of recovery, McCone and Ripinsky will literally dig through the dirt of past generations to build a new future.

Marcia Muller follows the pattern of her predecessors, recognizing that the detective novel's primary focus is the effect of the past on present events. The central theme of her work addresses "how a past event can trigger a present explosion" (Taylor 263). McCone experiences this explosion herself, when her sense of identity is threatened by the realization that she is not who she has thought herself to be. When McCone is forced to confront her own past, her true heritage, she is freed from the weight of her own nostalgia. She realizes that the past is no simpler than the present, and the illusory attraction of nostalgia is broken. While McCone initially uses the past as a means of rejecting the complexities of the modern world, she comes to realize that the past is simply a source of strength that can be used to cope with, rather than to avoid, the chaos and violence of her own environment. McCone's nostalgia is now fluid, allowing her to move forward and backward in time and increasing her abilities as a detective as a result.

Works Cited

Chandler, Raymond. *Raymond Chandler: Stories and Early Novels: Pulp Storeis/The Big Sleep/ Farewell, My Lovely/The High Window*. New York: Literary Classics of the United States, 1995.

_____. "The Simple Art of Murder." In *Raymond Chandler: Stories and Early Novels: Pulp Storeis/The Big Sleep/Farewell, My Lovely/The High Window*, 977–992. New York: Literary Classics of the United States, 1995.

Christie, Agatha. *The A.B.C. Murders*. New York: Berkley Books, 1935.

_____. *At Bertram's Hotel*. New York: Pocket Books, 1965.

_____. *By the Pricking of My Thumbs*. New York: Pocket Books, 1969.
_____. *Curtain*. New York: Pocket Books, 1975.
_____. *The Mirror Crack'd. Miss Marple Meets Murder*. Garden City, NY: Doubleday, 1980.
_____. *The Murder at the Vicarage*. New York: Dell, 1930.
_____. *There Is a Tide*. New York: Dell, 1948.
_____. *They Came to Baghdad*. New York: Berkley Books, 1951.
DeFino, Dean. "Lead Birds and Falling Beams." *Journal of Modern Literature* 27, no. 4 (Summer 2004): 73–81.
De Los Santos, Oscar. "Auster vs. Chandler or: Cracking the Case of the Postmodern Mystery." *Connecticut Review* 16 (1994): 75–80.
Geherin, David. *The American Private Eye*. New York: Frederick Ungar, 1985.
Isaac, Frederick. "Situation, Motivation, Resolution: An Afternoon with Marcia Muller." *Clues* 5, no. 2 (1984): 20–34.
Kermode, Frank. "Novel and Narrative." In *The Poetics of Murder: Detective Fiction and Literary Theory*, eds. Glenn W. Most and William W. Stowe, 175–195. New York: Harcourt Brace, 1983.
Kinney, Catherine. *The Remarkable Case of Dorothy L. Sayers*. Kent, OH: Kent State University Press, 1990.
Merriam-Webster Dictionary Online. www.m-w.com (accessed July 13, 2006).
Muller, Marcia. *Ask the Cards a Question*. New York: Warner Books, 1982.
_____. *Both Ends of the Night*. New York: Warner Books, 1997.
_____. *The Broken Promise Land*. New York: Warner Books, 1996.
_____. *The Dangerous Hour*. New York: Warner Books, 2004.
_____. *Dead Midnight*. New York: Warner Books, 2002.
_____. *Games to Keep the Dark Away*. New York: St. Martin's Press, 1984.
_____. *Leave a Message for Willie*. New York: Warner Books, 1984.
_____. *Listen to the Silence*. New York: Warner Books, 2000.
_____. "Partners in Crime: Developing a Series Character." In *They Wrote the Book: Thirteen Women Mystery Writers Tell All*, 49–58. Duluth, MN: Spinsters Ink, 2000.
_____. *Pennies on a Dead Woman's Eyes*. New York: Warner Books, 1992.
_____. *The Shape of Dread*. New York: Warner Books, 1989.
_____. *There's Nothing to Be Afraid Of*. New York: Warner Books, 1985.
_____. *Till the Butchers Cut Him Down*. New York: Warner Books, 1994.
_____. *Trophies and Dead Things*. New York: Warner Books, 1990.
_____. *Vanishing Point*. New York: Warner Books, 2006.
_____. *A Walk Through the Fire*. New York: Warner Books, 1999.
_____. *While Other People Sleep*. New York: Warner Books, 1998.
_____. *A Wild and Lonely Place*. New York: Warner Books, 1995.
_____. *Wolf in the Shadows*. New York: Warner Books, 1993.
Munt, Sally R. "Grief, Doubt and Nostalgia in Detective Fiction; or 'Death and the Detective Novel': A Return." *College Literature* 25, no. 3 (Fall 1998): 133–144.
Porter, Dennis. "Backward Construction and the Art of Suspense." In *The Poetics of Murder: Detective Fiction and Literary Theory*, eds. Glenn W. Most and William W. Stowe, 327–340. New York: Harcourt Brace, 1983.
Rzepka, Charles J. *Detective Fiction*. Malden, MA: Polity Press, 2005.
Routledge, Christopher. "A Matter of Disguise: Locating the Self in Raymond Chandler's *The Big Sleep* and *The Long Good-Bye*." *Studies in the Novel* 29, no. 1 (Spring. 1997): 94–107.
Rzepka, Charles J. *Detective Fiction*. Malden, MA: Polity Press, 2005.
Stineback, David C. *Shifting World: Social Change and Nostalgia in the American Novel*. Cranbury, NJ: Associated University Press, 1976.
Su, John J. *Ethics and Nostalgia in the Contemporary Novel*. New York: Cambridge University Press, 2005.
Taylor, Bruce. "The Real McCone." *Armchair Detective* 23, no. 3 (1990): 260–269.
Todorov, Tzvetan. "The Typology of Detective Fiction." In *The Poetics of Prose.*, Trans. Richard Howard, 42–52. Ithaca, NY: Cornell University Press, 1977.

8

The Journey of Sharon McCone, Private Investigator

PATRICIA L. MAIDA

Do fictional PIs grow up, mature, and change like real people? Sometimes. Some authors produce characters who seem ageless; others use a slow-aging process; still others portray characters who never seem to change or evolve. Marcia Muller paints Sharon McCone, her private detective, in true colors — as a PI who lives in the real world and is matured by the reality she lives. I would like to explore Sharon McCone's evolution, as an existential journey, examining along the way the factors that create identity, especially at the intersections of circumstance and choice.

Marcia Muller created a persona for Sharon McCone determined largely by her career choice — a private investigator operating in a field usually populated by men. An independent woman who uses her brains to outwit opponents, McCone is not a femme fatale; she is an attractive woman who has the characteristics of a feminist. (How could she have spent the 1970s at Berkeley without being affected by women's issues?) Muller never wastes a line describing McCone putting on make-up or assessing her wardrobe — she appears never to shop for clothing. When McCone begins her career, she describes herself as petite, with long black hair her most outstanding feature. Years later when she tries to disguise herself, she realizes that a change is needed: "I saw it [my hair] for what it was and wondered why I kept it this way. With it flowing down my back I looked like one of those people who are trying to make time stand still" (*Wolf* 195). She now has her hair cut shoulder length in a becoming style, still maintaining a natural look.

When Sharon McCone makes her debut in *Edwin of the Iron Shoes* in 1977 as a young investigator working for All Souls Legal Cooperative, she proves to be a tough, modern woman who can hold her own in a man's profession. She is one of the new wave of female detectives. Glenwood Irons notes that "women detectives created in the past thirty years are outgoing, aggressive, self-sufficient sleuths who have transcended generic codes and virtually rewritten the archetypal male detective from a female perspective" (xii). Sue Grafton considers Muller the "founding mother" of this new breed of female detective that is sometimes tied to the hard-boiled detective school (Irons xx). The new female detective is influenced by feminism and realistic fiction; she is smart but also physically able to endure beyond what was asked of her older sisters in crime. She may get roughed up. She may also have to carry a weapon and use it when threatened.

The voice of the empowered female detective comes through as she speaks directly to the reader. Scott Christianson points out that in hard-boiled detective fiction the first-person point of view prevails: "The narrator is the hard-boiled detective him/herself, who talks all the time to the reader in direct, evocative, colloquial language that represents the hard-boiled hallmark of the genre" (129). McCone is a straight-talker who knows when to keep quiet and when to assert herself. Unlike her male counterparts, she does not reinforce her words with obscenities, but instead chooses a stern look to speak for her. Occasionally, she is given to telling obnoxious people off, with a brisk "Go to hell."

"Stoic" is the definitive term one might use to describe her. Not just tough-minded, McCone is intelligent, ambitious, and well adjusted; she also has the capacity to remain cool and contained under pressure. It is this enduring trait that Muller builds on as she shapes Sharon's character. When the series opens, a youthful Sharon is a recent graduate of the University of California at Berkeley where she was a sociology major with an interest in social justice. The middle child in a family of five, she is the only one of her siblings to finish college. Although raised in San Diego, she chooses to make San Francisco her home, joining her Berkeley friends in the newly created All Souls Legal Cooperative as an investigator. Readers learn early on that Sharon, dark haired with Native American features, looks different from her blond brothers and sisters. She is told that she resembles her grandmother, Mary McCone, who is part Shoshone. Not only does Sharon look different, but she behaves differently, turning her back on the laid back southern California lifestyle. While her younger sister, Charlene, plays the ingénue, gets pregnant and becomes a teen bride, and her oldest brother, Joey, becomes a drug addict, Sharon works her way through college as a security guard. Her mother does not approve of Sharon's unconventional occupation and lifestyle, yet Sharon maintains contact with her. However, Sharon is closer to her father, who is less judgmental. As the series evolves, however, family and friends' roles change.

As McCone's character develops from 1977 through 2004, personal and communal events involve her in investigations that change her life. The maturation of her character can be seen in the contrast between the young Sharon in *Edwin of the Iron Shoes* (1977) and the poised professional in *The Dan-*

gerous Hour (2004). As an investigator for All Souls Legal Cooperative, Sharon takes on her first murder investigation with the murder of antique dealer Joan Albritton. She tells the reader, "I felt a stirring of excitement. Murder cases didn't come along every day, and I did feel a personal commitment to this one" (*Edwin* 11). But as her friend and supervisor Hank Zahn points out, the police are not happy to have a PI interfering, especially one that Lieutenant Greg Marcus considers "a pretty little girl" (14). Although Marcus tolerates Sharon, she shows her mettle in solving the case but not before she has to stand up to several powerful men. Frank Harmon, a tough bail bondsman, rankled by her persistent questions, counters with, "I don't like being badgered by little girls playing detective" (109). References to gender and age reflect the uphill climb for a young woman in a man's field. Although she is aware of her inexperience, Sharon is also confident in her strengths as she tells one of her adversaries "I don't know about being what you call a 'super sleuth.' I'm competent. I'd say my strong point is knowing how to ask the right questions" (26). She also knows when to be quiet. However, she does speak up for her social values. We see this when socialite Cara Ingalls spews forth a venomous attack on low-income people. Sharon, though shocked, is "matter of fact" in replying, "Where do you suggest they go?" (130). Sharon contends, "I try to hang on to my ideals" (130), something that Ingalls, who turns out to be Albritton's killer, has abandoned. Though the novel is filled with tough men presenting themselves as suspects, it takes a woman to find the real killer — another woman. The subtext here emphasizes the positive and negative powers of women. Sharon's commitment to people that society often overlooks is clear in this case and is consistent throughout her career.

Sharon's relationship with Greg Marcus, begun in *Edwin*, reveals her youth and immaturity. Tall, blond, muscular, older — Marcus is attractive. He treats Sharon like a precocious child, feeding her chocolates and calling her by the pet name papoose. (Unsurprisingly, his pet name for her eventually begins to wear thin.) In fact, in her study, Ann Wilson argues that the hypocorism is doubly offensive as if "papoose" slights McCone's race and gender (151). This slight is unwarranted, as it is Sharon who traps the murderer, a woman who has had a romantic history with Marcus. Clearly, he underestimates her.

An important rite of passage occurs in her second caper, *Ask the Cards a Question* (1982), as Sharon deals with a murder that occurs in her own apartment building in the Mission District on Guerrero Street. In this case, we see her close ties to the community and her capacity for friendship. Although she lives in a small studio apartment, Sharon has allowed Linnea, a friend from her high school days, to stay with her while she comes to grips with a recent divorce. Ultimately, Sharon saves Linnea's life, shooting a man who is about to kill her. This is the first occasion where Sharon has used her .38 Special to kill someone who poses a threat. The appropriate use of the weapon is a rite of passage for Sharon; she chooses one life over another in making a judicious decision to use her gun. However, she regrets having to take a life. A positive outcome of the case is the monetary reward she earns from the owner of Circle Wharf and Warehouse for discovering who has been stealing their merchandise. With this money Sharon is able to buy a home. From the beginning of her career, we see that she is not materialistic — her house is small; her little red MG provides transport for years to come; her clothes are nondescript. Her focus is totally on her profession.

In contrast to the early Sharon McCone, when we meet her again in *The Dangerous Hour* (2004), she is a mature CEO of a growing investigation business. We learn that she made the decision to go out on her own after All Souls expanded. Once again coming to the aid of a friend and protégée, Sharon deals with credit card fraud and a personal vendetta that threatens to close her business. Hy Ripinsky, her lover, remains in the background, allowing her to proceed unimpeded with her work. His character is in sharp contrast to that of Lieutenant Greg Marcus. Ripinsky sends Sharon one rose every Tuesday, the color having changed over time from yellow to deep red — quite different from Marcus's gifts of chocolates. Mick Savage, her teenage nephew, now works for her as a computer sleuth, along with other employees, including Ted Smalley, the former paralegal from All Souls who has become her office manager. No longer squeezed into a converted closet at All Souls, she has a modern set of offices in the South of Market area (SoMa) overlooking the Bay Bridge. She *has* come a long way.

Sharon's voice matures over the years, from that of a girlish, inexperienced twenty-something adventurer to a professional who runs her own business. We hear her "trying on" the role of a PI in *The Cheshire Cat's Eye* (1983), where Sharon is faced with Nick Dettman, an attorney who tries to give her a hard time. After trying various approaches and chatting up Dettmann at length, she confides to the reader: "I smiled, covering my nervousness" (55). Her opponent eventually admits that she is "a forceful young woman" (55). When an African American café owner closes off communication because he believes she's been "jiving" him, Sharon tries on the smile again, keeps talking, and pleads inexperience and *hunger*— this works and she gets information along with a helping of ribs and fries (35–36). She uses her youth and physical attributes to charm both men and women, but she lets the reader know that she's often scared and unsure of how to proceed. By the time we hear her voice years later in *The Dangerous Hour* (2004), she is confident, speaking in no-nonsense brief directives. Roles are reversed as McCone is in charge of a staff that needs her wisdom and experience. When her new-hire, Julia Rafael, is arrested for credit card theft, McCone warns the arresting officers not to manhandle Julia: "Careful. You've got witnesses" (5). She does not waste words, but just firmly states, "I trust my employees" (7).

Although she shares the common characteristic among fictional sleuths of being independent, she is not a true "loner." This is what makes her unique and interesting. She has a large family, has a tight circle of friends, and is involved in the life of her community. Family is a value for McCone. When we first meet her, her parents are still married to each other and living in the family home in San Diego. Her two older brothers and younger sisters lead disparate lives. Joey — the eldest — gets into drugs and goes from job to job, not able to maintain steady relationships, eventually committing suicide. John marries, has children, starts a business as a painting contractor; then his wife leaves him and he is bereft for a time. Patsy marries and divorces. Charlene — the youngest — gets pregnant at seventeen, marries singer Rick Savage, and has five children before they divorce. But the life-changes her siblings experience affect Sharon's life as is evident with each ensuing novel. And the reader connects with the McCone family — ready to tune in again to hear how each of these characters continues to grow. When her parents divorce, Sharon is shocked to learn that her mother has a lover whom she soon marries. Her father, at loose ends at first, develops a relationship of his own. Each novel is enriched as these characters change their lifestyles but remain constant in Sharon's life.

Especially life-altering is Sharon's father's unexpected death, and the subsequent discovery of her adoption papers among his effects. This event opens up a whole new dimension to her life as she searches for her birth parents. She finally understands why she looks so different from her siblings — she is in fact a full-blooded Shoshone. Her birth mother, Saskia, now a lawyer, gave her up for adoption. Her birth father, Elwood Farmer, an artist, was unaware that he had a daughter until Sharon traced him and revealed the facts of her birth. The reader sees that Sharon not only looks like her birth mother, but shares her tenacity and strength as well. From her birth father, the reader sees common intuitive flashes, a kind of understanding that informs Sharon when she is solving a puzzle.

The events in her family have an impact on Sharon's view of marriage. Her parents have divorced, her brother John is divorced, and now Patty and Charlene are divorced. Despite the differences in age and lifestyle, Sharon remains close to her youngest sister, Charlene. When Charlene and Rick Savage's marriage comes apart, Sharon is drawn into the conflict. The story of the breakup is the nub of the plot in *The Broken Promise Land* (1996). While divorce changes the players, it also expands Sharon's connections as new people join her family, notably her assistant Rae Kelleher as Rick's new wife. One can also see that the impact of these divorces among family and friends affects Sharon's own reluctance to commit to a lasting relationship.

Sharon is an accepting person. When Mick Savage, Charlene and Rick's precocious son, leaves San Diego and asks to stay with her, she shows unusual wisdom in directing his energies. Mick has been suspended from high school for getting into the school's computer system and changing data. He is so adept at computers that she hires him as her tech person at the office. When he finds romance with Charlotte Keim, the firm's financial analyst, Sharon is at first shocked, but keeps an open mind as their relationship develops. This experience gives her some insight into the emerging youth culture. Her relationship with Rae Kelleher also shows an evolving understanding. Rae, who starts out at All Souls as the abused wife of a doctoral student, finds the strength to leave the marriage — especially with the encouragement of the All Souls community. As she matures, Sharon hires her to become part of McCone Investigations. However, when Rae becomes the lover and then wife of her former brother-in-law, Rick Savage, Sharon accepts Rae in her new role.

Friends are extremely important to Sharon, especially the founders of the All Souls Legal Cooperative whom she has known since her Berkeley days: Hank Zahn, attorney, and Anne-Marie Altman, Hank's wife. She considers Hank and Anne-Marie her closest friends (*Wolf* 24). She tells us, "All Souls was, in truth, the closest thing that many of us had to a home and an extended family, and I couldn't imagine life without it" (*Pennies* 19). Sharon plays a critical role in helping Hank and Anne-Marie's adopted daughter, Habiba Hamid, with whom she develops a close relationship. The bond between Hank and Anne-Marie Altman remains even after Sharon leaves All Souls to set up McCone Investigations. New people on the scene include Charlotte Keim (financial advisor), Mick Savage (technology expert), Craig Morland (former FBI agent/ investigator), and Julia Rafael (trainee). These people become the mainstays in her new business.

Sharon's romantic relationships are perhaps the most revealing measure of her character. In her youth, she is attracted to Lieutenant Greg Marcus, head of the San Francisco Homicide Division. Divorced and forty-one years old, Marcus is still in good shape and shares Sharon's interests in classical music and art — but he is overly protective of her, at times treating her like a child. Obviously something of a father figure, Marcus is helpful at connecting Sharon to people in the San Francisco Police Department. His brusque, assured professional style provides an appropriate foil to Sharon's youth and inexperience at the beginning of her career. But she quickly outgrows him and the need to be protected by an older man.

As her career becomes established, Sharon falls for disk jockey Don Del Boccio. They share a love of music and food, but he does not seem to be her intellectual equal. He is also put off by the chances she takes and the danger she can bring to those she loves — his self-protective stance makes him seem weak next to her. Thinking back on her relationship with Don, Sharon admits,

"Don and I had proved to be too different. His upbeat attitude began to seem shallow; it grated, just as my cynicism and jealous guarding of my privacy irritated him" (*There's Something* 21).

When we meet up with her again in 2004 (*The Dangerous Hour*), Sharon is hooked up with a daring man, Hy (Heino) Ripinsky, a partner in an international corporation that handles dangerous assignments — hostage negotiations, kidnappings, terrorism. (The two first meet in *Where Echoes Live* [1991].) A man with his own mystery, Ripinsky is a widower who owns a sheep ranch up in Mono County on the shore of Tufa Lake, but there is a nine-year gap in his life that he refuses to discuss. McCone keeps a "file" on him, collecting details of his life but she does not fully uncover his past. She admits that he is "a gentle, passionate man" but that others had characterized him as dangerous, perhaps violent" (*Wolf* 9). Unlike Marcus, Ripinski supports Sharon in her work and trusts her to pursue her best instincts. He does not interfere, but will help if asked. For example, in *A Walk Through the Fire* (1999), Sharon is attracted to Russ Tanner, who owns a helicopter service in Kauai. As Sharon works on uncovering saboteurs at a filming site, she and Tanner almost become lovers. Ripinsky notices the chemistry between them and leaves the island, telling Sharon to contact him when she has made her decision. Typically, Ripinsky gives her distance; Sharon ultimately chooses him over Tanner. McCone and Ripinsky are well matched: he goes off on dangerous assignments, the details of which he cannot reveal, and Sharon pursues her own cases. Both survive life-threatening situations, most often working alone. It seems as if Muller is showing how completely independent and capable Sharon McCone is to the extent that she does not need Hy Ripinsky or any man to lean on. But Hy does propose marriage and Sharon accepts. We see them functioning as a newly married couple in *Vanishing Point* (2006).

McCone, like many fictional private investigators, lives alone (with her cats). Even though her lovers spend periods of time staying with her, she maintains her own place — although most recently she shares Touchstone, a getaway cottage, with Hy Ripinsky. When she first moves to the city, Sharon rents a studio apartment in the Mission District of San Francisco. As she becomes more solvent, she buys an "earthquake house" on Church Street, on the fringe of her old neighborhood, an area that developed "out of a blend of races and social classes that lived there in peaceable and friendly proximity" (*Leave* 21). She makes this small house, originally built as temporary shelter to house the homeless after the 1906 earthquake, into a comfortable, if modest, home. She and Hy engage an architect to design a new home they will share.

Intuition is the personal trait that continues to develop as Sharon ages. She is often completely stumped by a puzzling case only to find the answer when she least expects it — through a startling insight, a dream, or an irrepressible feeling. For example, in *Pennies on a Dead Woman's Eyes* (1992), Sharon senses how an earlier crime was committed: "Call it a morbid preoccupation with the crime; call it a weird psychic link, even.... I'd sensed what might have gone on there. I knew, and yet I didn't know" (104). Although women's intuition is something of a cliché, Muller gives McCone's gift added credibility through her Native American genes. We see this when Sharon is particularly anxious about a situation and telephones her birth father, Elwood Farmer, who tells her to trust herself and she will then know the answer. He says, "The answer is within you" (*Dead Midnight* 21). And she admits that she is a "truth-seeker" who will continue to search (21).

Gratuitous violence is not a trait that McCone shares with the hard-boiled school. Her cases do not contain multiple murders or gory scenes. The focus is always on people and the puzzle she seeks to solve — the motivation for the crime, the whereabouts of a suspect, and the unmasking of the perpetrators. Although McCone is frequently harassed, shot at, or physically injured in the pursuit, she stands up for herself and does not back down. Her small size puts her at a disadvantage, but she uses her wits to compensate. Although she owns guns, McCone is reluctant to use them. She confides to a client: "I own two, and know how to use them. But no, I don't carry one unless I'm going into a very dangerous situation" (*Leave* 73). When she admits that she once killed someone to save a friend, she says that it was "nothing to be proud of ... just something I had to do" (74).

McCone's investigative methods are typical of the hard-boiled school: she is tenacious in pursuing a case, undaunted by threatening circumstances, willing to endure duress, armed and ready to fire when a life is at stake. Men, like the deadly duo in *Leave a Message for Willie*, challenge her authority: "You women should know better than to force your way into professions you're not suited for" (185). Playing the compliant woman role, McCone manages to catch the men off guard and overpower them. Highly analytical, she plans her moves — often using her trained employees to assist. She has her contacts, like Adah Joselyn with SFPD, but she also develops her own operatives who use technology to speed up the process of the old fashioned "gumshoe." Computers, airplanes, and the resources of an international high-tech agency (RKI) are now at her disposal.

Learning how to fly puts Sharon ahead of her peers and puts her in a position to work with Hy Ripinsky. Flying also gives McCone an edge among her sisters and brothers in crime. Marcia Muller reports that she herself decided to learn how to fly so that she could portray the fictional McCone's efforts accurately ("Interview"). The Citabria Decathlon that Hy Ripinsky owns allows them to fly together for business and pleasure. In *Both Ends of the Night* (1997), Sharon recalls the advice she received from her aviation instructor, Matty Wildress: "You know, McCone, what flying is all about — the absolute essence of it — is good judgment. You make the best call you know how under the circumstances, and then you move on it — no hesitating.... You just do it, and don't let your pride get in your way." Sharon responds, "Are we talking flying here? Or are we talking life?" (100). Flying becomes a metaphor for life, or the way to live one's life — it aptly describes the philosophy that energizes Sharon McCone.

A detective who prefers to be *active* in the field rather than simply a supervisor, in *Wolf in the Shadows* (1993) Sharon turns down the offer from All Souls Legal Cooperative to take a "desk job" supervising operatives in the field; in fact, she is totally opposed to changing her career style. As computer technology develops, McCone sees the possibilities of the field and embraces the opportunity for using computers as a tool for detection. Although personally she prefers to be out in the field interviewing people and following tracks, she relies on Mick Savage, who has become a computer super sleuth. He is so proficient that Sharon ultimately expands her company, with Mick's assistance, to include cyberspace protection for her clients.

On the path to success, Sharon has had to deal with the circumstances that life brings to her and has made life-altering choices. Thinking back on when her career interests took root, McCone reminisces about reading detective novels while working the nightshift as a security officer. "I'd devour them, one or two a shift, and there'd still be time left over, so I'd dream. And what I'd dream about was going into the night, strong and unafraid, on a mission to right wrongs" (*Wolf* 81).

Being offered a position at All Souls gave Sharon the opportunity to pursue that dream. Her Berkeley cohorts were of a similar bent with aspirations to make legal assistance affordable to everyone. Sharon recalls: "We were still a young energetic firm that cared more for its clients than its profit and was committed to the principle of affordable high-quality legal representation for low and middle-income people" (*Pennies* 19). Opportunities arise that allow her to take cases on the basis of their social merits. Ames points out that because many female writers of detective fiction "came of age in a period of political activism ... the political ideology of these novels tends towards a liberal humanism that is deeply concerned with the plight of the socially disenfranchised" (qtd. in Wilson 156). Money is a subsistence issue at the beginning of her career, but Sharon often works without pay if she thinks it's the right thing to do. As life moves on, so do the kinds of challenges she meets: crimes against gays and the homeless, gentrification of the inner city, credit card fraud, stolen identity, kidnapping, fraud in the biotech industry, or immigration abuses.

When an acquaintance from her Berkeley days asks Sharon to help him, she cannot turn him down. T. J. Gordon, also known as "Suitcase" Gordon or "Suits," is a true product of the '60s. He got his nickname from the suitcase he used to carry around, peddling "marijuana, term papers, ... amphet-amines, false identification, purloined copies of incoming exams" (*Till the Butchers* 10). Now a wealthy corporate turn-around specialist, Gordon is being harassed as he attempts to complete a lucrative business deal in the redevel-opment of the waterfront. Sharon is herself threatened during the investiga-tion but manages to escape unscathed. (A by-product of the case is the cottage, once owned by Suits, that Hy purchases with Sharon as joint tenant — a cot-tage that they rename "Touchstone.")

Concern for the underclass often motivates Sharon to take a case. We see this in *The Shape of Dread* (1989) when she strives to help an African American teenager who has been wrongfully accused and convicted of mur-der. The young man is set up by middle-class, wealthy individuals who know that he is powerless and not likely to have the money for a proper defense. In another novel, *There's Something in a Sunday* (1989), the plight of the homeless and disinherited gives Sharon cause to become involved in murder and the subterfuge of some of the city's activists. She discusses "NIMBYism," an acronym for "not in my backyard" (54), as she sees the results of the prac-tice in the Haight-Ashbury area when affluent investors try to keep undesir-able (poor) people out of the neighborhood.

In recent years, Muller has given McCone particularly timely issues to pursue. A stalker who steals Sharon's identity and threatens her life is the sub-ject of *While Other People Sleep* (1998). Lee DaSilva, a disturbed young woman, presents herself at significant social gatherings as Sharon McCone, invades Touchstone (Hy and Sharon's cottage) and attempts to burn it down, and then hijacks the Citabria. Although Sharon manages to help DaSilva land the plane, it is destroyed in the process, its "crumpled contours ... like an abstract sculpture" (323). In *A Dangerous Hour* (2004), another form of identity theft, this time in the form of credit card abuse, is the basis for the arrest of Julia Rafael. As Sharon soon discovers, the theft threatens her business since Rafael is an employee and her conviction will lead to McCone Investigations losing its license. In clearing Julia, Sharon unmasks a vengeful ex-convict who blames her for an earlier conviction; Sharon has to fight for her life in a confronta-tion with him.

The contemporary San Francisco "Dot Com" business becomes the focus of *Dead Midnight* (2002) as Sharon is asked to investigate the suicide of a young man employed by *InSite*, one of the many new online magazines. She is told that "the atmosphere at *InSite* was brutal. Sixteen, twenty-hour days, seven days a week, and no comp time. Low pay, and their promises of stock options went unfulfilled" (20). She infiltrates the business and finds herself pursuing a clever venture capitalist who will stop at nothing, not even mur-der, to protect her investment.

A kidnapping and the disappearance of her lover leads Sharon across the border to Mexico in *Wolf in the Shadows* (1993). She manages to clear Hy Ripinsky's name and rescue him from a band of kidnappers. At this intersection, Marcia Muller is actually crossing over from detective fiction into the "high tech thriller" genre. Ripinsky works with Gage Renshaw and Dan Kessell, former covert government agents who are now the principals of Renshaw Kessell International (RKI). A firm born in the age of terrorism, RKI handles sensitive international security issues for American companies and their affiliate offices overseas (*Wolf* 51). In tracing a kidnapping victim, Sharon contends with illegal Mexican border crossings, drugs, and the politics of a biotech company trying to avoid financial collapse. Ripinsky is missing and in danger, so Sharon takes off on her own across the Mexican border to find the place where the kidnappers are likely to be holding her client. On her own, she is able to accomplish what RKI agents are not able to do — find Ripinsky. Wounded and in need of help, Ripinsky recognizes Sharon's efforts, admitting, "I've always known you're good at what you do, but I didn't realize how good. I'm not sure I would've gotten this far if our positions had been reversed" (259).

With espionage, terrorism, and international crime on the rise, McCone rises to meet the challenges of a volatile, changing world. When she learns to fly, it is clear that McCone will move beyond borders and boundaries. Along with her heroine, Marcia Muller also crosses the genre borders of crime fiction and the thriller — but she avoids any taint of romance fiction or "chicklit," as the genre is often dubbed. Unlike her hard-boiled male brethren, Sharon does not boast of her romantic conquests; in fact, she closes the door to intimate details of her love affairs. Rae Kelleher, her office assistant, reads romance fiction and yearns to write a best-selling romance. Sharon chides her about reading "steamy, semi-pornographic novels," calling them "shop and fuck" novels (*Broken* 37–38).

From the start of the McCone series, Marcia Muller makes it clear that she is writing realistic mystery fiction. Her heroine, Sharon McCone, is a tough-minded, action-oriented individual guided by humanistic values. Changes that we observe in her persona over the years are the effects of growth and reactions to significant events. She may live alone for most of her career, but she is socially connected with and concerned about her community. In a recent hypothetical interview that McCone holds with author Marcia Muller, she asks Muller, "Did you know from the beginning that all these things were going to happen?" Muller responds, "No, I found out roughly at the same time you did, [but] ... the clues were there" ("Newsletter"). The core of Sharon McCone's personality does not change, but Sharon grows over the years, learning from her experiences and adapting to the opportunities that life presents. She remains an independent, successful woman detective.

Works Cited

Christianson, Scott. "Talkin' Trash and Kickin' Butt: Sue Grafton's Hard Boiled Feminism." In *Feminism in Women's Detective Fiction*, ed. Glenwood Irons, 127–147. Toronto: University of Toronto Press, 1995.

"Interview." www.twbookmark.com/authors/67/463/interview 8/85.html (accessed June 27, 2006).

Irons, Glenwood. "Gender and Genre: The Woman Detective and the Diffusion of Generic Voices." In *Feminism in Women's Detective Fiction*, ed. Glenwood Irons, ix — xxiv. Toronto: University of Toronto Press, 1995.

Muller, Marcia. *Ask the Cards a Question*. New York: St. Martin's Press, 1982.

_____. *Both Ends of the Night*. New York: Warner Books, 1997.

_____. *The Broken Promise Land*. New York: Warner Books, 1996.

_____. *The Cheshire Cat's Eye*. New York: St. Martin's Press, 1983.

_____. *The Dangerous Hour*. New York: Warner Books, 2004.

_____. *Dead Midnight*. New York: Warner Books, 2002.

_____. *Edwin of the Iron Shoes*. New York: Warner Books, 1977.

_____. *Leave a Message for Willie*. New York: Mysterious Press, 1984.

_____. *Pennies on a Dead Woman's Eyes*. New York: Mysterious Press, 1992.

_____. *The Shape of Dread*. New York: Mysterious Press, 1989.

_____. *There's Something in a Sunday*. New York: Mysterious Press, 1989.

_____. *Till the Butchers Cut Him Down*. New York: Mysterious Press, 1994.

_____. *Vanishing Point*. New York: Warner Books, 2006.

_____. *A Walk Through Fire*. New York: Warner Books, 1999.

_____. *While Other People Sleep*. New York: Warner Books, 1998.

_____. *A Wild and Lonely Place*. New York: Mysterious Press, 1995.

_____. *Wolf in the Shadows*. New York: Mysterious Press, 1993.

"Newsletter." www.marciamuller.com (accessed June 27, 2006).

Wilson, Ann. "The Female Dick and the Crisis of Heterosexuality." In *Feminism in Women's Detective Fiction*, ed. Glenwood Irons, 148–156. Toronto: University of Toronto Press, 1995.

Part III
TRAUMA

9

Anxious Authorship: The Detective Fiction of Marcia Muller and Gertrude Stein

JESSICA V. DATEMA

> It is very curious but the detective story which is you might say the only really modern novel form that has come into existence gets rid of human nature by having the man dead to begin with the hero is dead to begin with and so you have so to speak got rid of the event before the book begins.
>
> G. Stein, "What Are Master Pieces"

Gertrude Stein and Marcia Muller each use detective fiction to investigate their own writing habits through anxiety, which the psychoanalyst Jacques Lacan says does not deceive (*Television* 82). Both authors experienced this anxiety when readers limited them to their characters, as when audiences equated Sir Arthur Conan Doyle with Sherlock Holmes.[1] In general, anxiety signals possibility at the end of an era, but for the individual author it may also indicate a new potential for shifting out of serial writing and into a different, anxious investigation.

Although their novels are very different, Gertrude Stein's *Blood on the Dining Room Floor* (1948) [*BDRF*] and Marcia Muller's *Point Deception* (2001) [*PD*] both use detective fiction to examine the truth about their writing and get over blocked creativity. They use investigation instead of autobiography, which does not relate to truth except as subjective perception. These novels work through the "truth" of authorial inspiration with roundabout detective examinations.

The title *Blood on the Dining Room Floor* came from what Gertrude Stein was reading at the time—*Blood on the Common* by Anne Fuller and Marcus Allen. Additionally, the word "blood" in her novel's title refers to the way Stein wrote as a continual course. The daily exercise of writing was a process and flow where "writing was not really something that she [Stein] did. It was something that happened to her, like the visions of a Spanish saint," as seen in her opera, *Four Saints in Three Acts* (*BDRF* 84–85). More importantly, "blood" refers to the "truth" of Stein's writing beyond surface recognition, which was threatened by an intractable audience. Favoring "understanding" more than "knowledge," Stein's novel parodies any hope of real audience recognition and Enlightenment notions of truth.[2]

It was not until Stein was over sixty that the triumph of *The Autobiography of Alice B. Toklas* caused her anxiety about her reputation. For the first time, the mentor behind such hard-boiled precursors as Paul Bowles and Ernest Hemingway cared about her own characterization. *Everybody's Autobiography* describes how Stein felt: "Since the *Autobiography* [*of Alice B. Toklas*] I have not done any writing, I began writing something, I called it *Blood on the Dining Room Floor* but somehow if my writing was worth money then it was not what it had been" (84). To Stein, writing was a repeated habit of searching where you exist "as you are to be writing" (Bridgman 247–248). The writer that serves mammon generates words for society and popularity, while the real writer creates for the process itself. Anxiety arose when Stein's writing became worth money, and she felt pulled between pleasing the audience and her own idiosyncratic creativity.

The making of *PD* is also a critical "point" in Marcia Muller's career where she anxiously steps outside her alter ego, Sharon McCone. The title *Point Deception* indicates that the novel works through the "truth" about her detective fiction. This first Soledad County novel begins as a standalone break from the author's serial reputation and association with the detective Sharon McCone. In *Point Deception*, most of the psychological and linear plot revolves around a canyon, which has a murderous history of unsolved massacres.

The unresolved canyon murders allow Muller to take a break from her award-winning San Francisco series to analyze authorial "deceptions." Muller describes this investigation and departure as a moment of career anxiety: "Could I convincingly write such characters [other than McCone]? They were so unlike McCone and her associates, so unlike me. And it had been a long time since I'd lived within the mind and soul of anyone other than her" ("A Novelist's Life" 177).

The attempt at new characterizations ignites authorial anxiety in Muller who admits becoming too familiar with her main detective McCone. Embarking on new characterizations that unhinge the equation of author and serial detective, *Point Deception* includes more offbeat figures with circular or irresolvable histories.

With *Edwin of the Iron Shoes* (1977), Marcia Muller ushers in a "new Golden Age" of detective fiction and the Sharon McCone series. Marcia Muller, like Stein, is a pioneer rather than a perpetrator of the "Golden Age" in detective fiction. Allied with the hard-boiled form, the McCone series is part of a new era concerned with process more than resolution. Weisbard says that Muller is the "first of her breed and a departure from the gentle and genteel sleuths created by the Queens of the Golden Age.... She [Muller] paved the way for the new Golden Age, dominated by women authors and distinguished by a richly diverse set of series characters and situations" (39). Indeed the new age of detective writing emphasizes process, style, and structure more than resolution.

The Modernist author Gertrude Stein liked the hard-boiled form of the detective story, especially Dashiell Hammett's work. She emphasizes hard-boiled authors' innovative methods, and goes so far as to suggest that these writers produced "the only real modern novel form" ("What Are Master-Pieces," 358). While Stein certainly wrote within the tradition of Poe, she critiqued her Golden Age contemporaries, such as Agatha Christie and Dorothy Sayers. Due to her stylistic emphasis, Stein's work has more in common with later forms of hard-boiled fiction than Golden Age detection.

Blood entails a hard-boiled style of abstract and emotionless prose that contains neither detective nor solution. It unfolds as a process without *dénouement*, which undercuts developmental accounts. After asking the reader to take a more active role and not providing a plot, the novel ends by saying, "thank you for anxiously" to the reader (*BDRF* 81). It refuses to simply "explain everything" and asks the reader to anxiously search for clues. It even gets rid of the "Detective, [who] in their surveillance and search for truths, become implicated in this interpretation that is mere 'explanation'"(Chessman 148). In place of closure, the novel suggests a different kind of case. *Blood on the Dining Room Floor* stresses the search process itself.

In cases of anxiety, authors find it difficult to investigate the truth of their writing without an appeal to the senses and suffering. Authorial detection through anxiety is a process which is "quite vexing, [it] is a construction, search, *askesis*" (Lacan, *Television* 89).[3] Stein's writing utilizes the senses in a fashion not very different from the way a detective works through physical evidence to construct an account. When Stein wrote her only detective novel, *Blood on the Dining Room Floor* in 1933, she was at an anxious point in her career.

Blood was written right after the success of *The Autobiography of Alice B. Toklas*, when Stein could no longer continue her occupational writing habit. This marked an initial moment when her daily routine became worth some money and, consequently, blocked. Previous to this, Stein had written daily for almost four decades without recognition. Ironically, the sudden success meant an arrival and threw her *askesis* into question. Likewise, the writer's block Stein experienced helped her renew a process, as she mentions in *The Geographical History of America*: "Mostly in detecting anything being finished is begun" (119). In the stylistic tradition of modern hard-boiled fiction, Stein's writing employs a process of iteration and mystery.

"What Are Master-Pieces" describes the value of an end at the beginning, since the hero is liquidated and as Stein phrases it one has "got rid of the event" before the story begins (358). With the crime at the outset and an end at the beginning, detective writing avoids being caught up in human nature, and can engage what Stein called the "human mind."[4] This type of thinking takes the world not in terms of beginnings or ends but as a continuously present changing landscape.[5] One of the lines that *Blood* repeats is the fairy tale beginning that goes, "Once upon a time" (*BDRF* 78). Indeed this phrase is repeated many times in the book, including in the final chapter as a twist on linear narrative conventions. In placing this beginning at the end, *Blood* makes an open-ended mystery that avoids resolution.

Also beginning at the end of her McCone series, Muller goes outside the conventional hard-boiled locale of San Francisco. While set in the country, *Point Deception* contains some hard-boiled elements such as an atmosphere of fog, climactic vagaries, and shifty landscapes. The fog rolls in with the first victim, and Rhonda Swift, one of the main characters, reflects on the wayward path of the mind as well as the senselessness of the murder. These thoughts drift through her consciousness "like a cloud that she could use to blot out everything" (*PD* 74). Clouds on the coast usher in this new case, where Muller works through her own anxiety like an intoxicant. What threatens the hard-boiled cop Rhoda's steely calculations also constitutes the site of Muller's authorial anxiety.

Point Deception multiplies the main detective to include more promiscuous, psychotic, and unstable perspectives than that of Sharon McCone. As the total opposite of a city girl, Rhoda Swift is a small-town cop described as "very pretty: close cropped black hair; small, fine boned face; big momentarily horrified hazel eyes" (*PD* 17). Guy Newberry, another main character who lives and writes in New York City, gives the latter description. Chrystal is a call girl, Rhoda is struggling to get over her divorce, and Guy is a widower who still listens to the "voice" of his dead wife. These variable perspectives complicate Muller's usually consistent, reliable, and omniscient detective persona in the McCone novels. Moreover, Sharon has a relatively stable relationship with Hy Ripinsky, who may fly away but always eventually returns.

Instead of having one detective, *Point Deception* splits the narration between two very different characters. Guy Newberry realizes this variable connection while denying his attraction to Swift:

> East Coast, West Coast, Big city, small town.
>   Both truth-seekers by profession, though. No.
>   He: interpreter of hard facts. She: poet, even though she only wrote in her mind.

He: sophisticate, world traveler. She: impressionable, had seldom left her native state.

A loner, not family oriented. A woman with strong community ties and a love of children. A man who shunned pets. A dog lover.

No way. Absolutely not [*PD* 235].

Even while qualifying their differences, Guy's account actually ends up emphasizing their similarities. While Rhoda appears to be closer to the traditional detective role, it is the writer, Guy, who ultimately "solves" the case by figuring out how Bernard Ulrick, aka "Clay," never died (*PD* 324). Muller also plays with gender roles by displaying "Guy" as the more sensitive one, and "Swift" as more speedy, which their names represent.

Everything wanders back to the canyon in Muller's novel as a traumatic site where a family massacre occurred thirteen years earlier. As part of the landscape beyond San Francisco, Muller uses it to examine "dark places" not found on maps ("A Novelist's Life" 178). The victim's murder occurs at the novel's outset on the same date, October 12, of the earlier canyon murders. Bringing up a case that remains unsolved, Chrystal Ackerman's murder takes the whole "community" of Soledad County back into a spiral of fear, anger, and suspicion. The canyon is the novel's open center that figures a repressed, repeated, and returning "history" that haunts each of the characters differently.

When the mass murders took place, Rhoda Swift was a rookie cop and the first one to find the victims. A young child actually died in her arms. She did her best but, as Gregory Cordova, a resident of the canyon describes: "It's no wonder she made mistakes" (*PD* 61). Ironically, the biggest error Rhoda made was taking the fall for her colleague, Deputy Wayne Gilardi. This parallels situations of gender vulnerability in the workplace, where societal "secrets" are kept to maintain inequities of power.

In struggling with characters with side-lined careers and sketchy histories, Muller gives her investigation more depth. Using them to crawl in and out of the usual McCone habits or faults, Muller says that Swift began to "[reveal] hidden facets of herself," just as McCone had. Muller admits that many of these more sinister aspects came from her own experience, "the mistakes and losses and deprivations that make up the dark side of the human mind" ("A Novelist's Life" 178). Working through character flaws instead of the omniscient detective, *Point Deception* allows Muller to depart from the serial into a more meandering narrative.

While Sharon McCone's San Francisco is more conventional, Soledad County makes an unlikely hard-boiled setting. The McCone series depicts San Francisco but Alan Bairner says it leaves certain parts of the city out: "Just as we cannot rely on street maps to indicate the contours of San Francisco's hills, so we cannot place our faith in Muller's McCone novels to reveal the city's darker corners" (135). While McCone may not go into the darker realms of the hard-boiled city, Muller does move into "darker corners" with *Point Deception*. When the victim, Chrystal Ackerman, is stranded on an isolated winding highway that is an infinite stretch of Northern California, many cars pass, but no one stops, calls for help, or even makes an inquiry until it is too late. Although familiarity is a real feature of Soledad County, the town is hard-boiled, covering over murders and using coldness to repress its history.

Working in a French milieu, the mother of hard-boiled literature also sets her case in the countryside outside Paris, Poe's classic detective locale. Gertrude Stein lived for twenty-five years at 27 Rue de Fleurus, near Dupin's fictional residence. She hosted guests such as Paul Bowles, Picasso, and Hemingway. After the successful *Autobiography of Alice B. Toklas*, she moved to Bilignin in the French countryside outside Paris. She lived in a Louis XV chateau in the country with servants and guests for a good deal of her old age. Much of the action in *Blood on the Dining Room Floor* is set in Bilignin and includes the bucolic activities of Gertrude and Alice.[6] As if to counter assumptions about the lack of action in her post–Parisian lifestyle, Stein says: "Nothing happens in the city. Everything happens in the country. The city just tells what has happened in the country, it has already happened in the country" (*BDRF* 51). Countering assumptions that the country is cozy and feminine, *Blood* presents its gothic, masculine, and criminal aspects.

The victim of *Blood* and her husband live in a hotel, which is their home, since they have been in the business for some years. They reside in the hotel not just during vacations, and it has an uncanny permanence which "is not the same as a house in a country and a hotel in the country is not the same as a hotel" (*BDRF* 15). *Blood* suggests a "hotel" is different from a "country hotel," since it is a *most* uncanny home. This is where the victim "fell on the pavement of cement in the court and broke her back but did not die nor did she know why. In five days she was dead" (*BDRF* 14). Still, the mystery goes beyond this specific crime to indict more diffuse mental and physical domains.

The murder, although it could be suicide, is of an unnamed "hotel-keeper's wife" who was "sleepwalking" (*BDRF* 36). All fictional incidents are based on Stein's real-life friend Madame Pernollet and her husband, Monsieur Pernollet. In the book the husband is unfaithful, and "it was wonderful the way they covered it up and went on. This was due to three strong wills, so the horticulturist said. The will of the hotel-keeper's father, the will of the hotel keeper's oldest son who was not yet twenty and was studying to be a lawyer and the will of the horticulturist's sister who was employed there and who admired everybody, so she said and was the one certainly helped to admire the hotel-keeper" (26). The "horticulturist's sister" indeed admires Monsieur Pernollet and the text suggests that she is his lover. Stein's other detective

pieces — "A Waterfall and A Piano," "Is Dead," and "The Horticulturist" —
were all part of *Blood* and sometime later made into separate stories (Dydo
564). They wander between real-life incidents and Stein's imagination to work
a real mystery.

In truth, Stein may have willed her own detective novel a failure after
the "success" of *The Autobiography of Alice B. Toklas*. The novel's "failure"
comes from its exposure of real societal inabilities to impart law and justice.
Intimating institutionalized criminality,[7] *Blood* challenges a community of
consensus based on gossip to "read the beginning again" (60). Appealing to
the reader as criminal, the narrator repeatedly asks, "Lizzie do you understand," but not as a question, more a demand (*BDRF* 60, 79, 20). Lizzie may
be a reference to Lizzie Borden, and the family murder in Massachusetts where
Lizzie was blamed but later evidence showed that the housekeeper may have
been the murderer. *Blood*, like Borden's case, was never fully explained, and
the name may also be a reference to Alice B. Toklas herself. Regardless, *Blood*
uses "Lizzie" to convey the complexity of real events in the French countryside and Stein's anti-climactic brush with murder.

"Wandering" occurs in *Blood* as a way of textually and affectively working through Stein's writer's block. While suspicion falls on Alexander, his
guilt is not certain but only suggested. Some critics suggest Stein herself may
be "Alexander," the criminal or unfaithful husband. Another backdrop of
Blood is Stein's affair with May Bookstaver (1901–1903), which caused much
anxiety in the "marriage" of Gertrude and Alice. Harriet Scott Chessman suggests: "Stein herself is the possible criminal on trial in *Blood*; she becomes associated with the hotel-keeper who was unfaithful to his wife, a betrayal that
begins her downward slide" (Chessman 153). This infidelity disrupts the couple's chateau, which provides the locale and routine of creating itself.

Sometime prior to the writing of *Blood*, Alice found out about May
Bookstaver, whom Stein called Mary, May Mary, and M. M. in this and other
works. *Blood on the Dining Room Floor* includes this name in a different way,
this time as "The confessions of Mary in this case" (*BDRF* 34). Gertrude's
infidelity soured Alice's daily habit of editing Stein's manuscript, which she
avoided doing herself. Even though Alice ran their country house and policed
all Stein's company, Virgil Thompson describes her surveillance as a kind of
subservience: "Alice had decided long before that 'Gertrude was always right,'
that she was to have whatever she wanted when she wanted it, and that the
way to keep herself always wanted was to keep Gertrude's writing always and
forever unhindered, unopposed" (*Mothering the Mind* 138). When functioning well, their relationship entailed strict roles and rules where Stein's "writing" was above everything else.[8] When anxiety disturbed their creative routine,
Stein was forced to change her wayward habits.

Sympathizing with the more human and vulnerable Swift, Muller also changes the detective's perspective to renew her hard-boiled realism. In a retrospective interview after her first novel, Muller discusses how the detective genre changes with real women's lives. "Mystery fiction has caught up with women's lives as they actually live them in the modern world," and this has allowed her and others to achieve their goal of writing about women characters "who felt no need to apologize for their jobs and who were brave and tough enough to get those jobs done, while still retaining their humanity and vulnerability" (James 58). While Muller writes McCone as an ideal feminine figure — a "taller, thinner, younger, braver woman who looks as though she has Indian blood" (59) — in *Point Deception* the heroine's characterization entails more faults. The character of Rhoda doesn't hide any faults and meshes with what Chandler says about the importance of realism in hard-boiled fiction (13). Rhoda Swift's rookie cop attitude is real and not ideal, a perspective which Muller develops to complement the principal serial detective.

Muller, like Stein, engaged in forays to investigate the truth about her own fiction. Her research entailed real-life excursions to flesh out characters. Calling up her fictional doppelganger, she took flying lessons to write McCone's adventures as a pilot. Engaging in pursuits beside the upper class, *Point Deception* is Muller's descent into less elevated personas. It figures real-life situations of sexual violence, alcoholism, and political crimes, which remain unresolved. In addition, the canyon relates to undocumented casualties, like Guy Newberry's wife who died in a complicated political situation.

In the novel, Rhoda Swift encourages Guy to seek justice regarding his wife's murder and bring this unrecorded event to legal notice. Guy confides the tangled details of this traumatic incident in Djakarta since she is a cop who "still believed in justice," although he worried that "the lack of it would break her" (PD 284).

Ironically, Guy finds justice in the provincial setting of Soledad County and realizes Rhoda is the first representative of the law to listen. Still, evidence is suppressed or delayed. Even after six months when Diana's camera is sent, it takes the writer a year to develop the film and even longer to formulate an account.

Repression of reality is also mimed in Stein's text to convey the significance of what is not culturally allowed to appear. *Blood* gives us enough information to suspect foul play. It uses fragmentary connections to hint that Alexander secretly seduces or rapes women. It is also suggested that Alexander had other "sisters" whose "gardens" he tended: "Anyway they all started to live in their way and Alexander the horticulturist knew their way and hoped some day that they would have a garden and he would do what he would for their garden. Of course he will. That is what happens in the country" (*BDRF* 49). The passage says Alexander's profession is "horticulture," which phonetically suggests a cultivation of whores and cultures. He tends the girls' gardens (i.e. has sexual relations with them) and then sends them away to marriage and silence somewhere else. In addition to figuring female sexuality, this garden brings up *the* garden, an undocumented or pre-historic setting. Ultimately the novel does an alternate type of detective investigation to reveal what falls out of linear history (Chessman 156). Given the garden sometimes refers to Alexander's "sisters," *Blood* also comments on incest and the taboo.[9]

Stein critiques the common view that a crime has not occurred if it does not appear in the paper or in plain view. In her estimation, realism is not given by the news, which "has no feeling of movement and has in its way no feeling for events.... Newspapers excite people very little. Sometimes a personality breaks through the newspapers — Lindbergh, Dillinger — when the personality has vitality. It wasn't what Dillinger did that excited anybody. The feeling is perfectly simple. You can see it in my *Four Saints*. Saints shouldn't do anything. The fact that a saint is there is enough for anybody" (*How Writing is Written* 151). Personalities appearing in the paper like Dillinger are an exception and not the rule. This criminal is noteworthy not for his crime, but because he lived fully in the moment, activating what Stein calls the "continuous present." In this sense he shows the reader what it means to exist, like the saints emitting a presence beyond their own perspective.

This "presence" is Stein's focus in the autobiographies, but also is the main theme of *Blood*. Her autobiographical works make an unconventional attempt to write the drives behind "anybody's" personality. Instead of recording a linear history of her own subjective viewpoint, *Blood*, like Stein's autobiographies, displays extra-symbolic life moments, as seen best in the lives of criminals, artists, and saints.

In her only detective work, Stein writes a veiled autobiography to anonymously grapple with the paradoxical parts of identity — "that everyone is the same and everyone is different" (BDRF 86). Indeed, the detective form itself (i.e., its situation, pattern of action, characters, setting) is constructed as similar and different since "the classical story involves, like any successful literary formula, a combination of interests of a rather divergent sort" (Cawelti 106). As with the structural configuration in detective fiction, the autobiographical subject is an inflexible representation while its characters and details may change.

In her most famous autobiography Stein veils herself in the third person as Alice until the end. Contrarily, *Blood on the Dining Room Floor* calls the narrator "everybody" and is not in a first-person perspective (38, 52). In this text, Stein uses "everybody" to refer to cultural rituals, societies, and tribes that are universal but often overlooked. *Blood* is a transition point between *The Autobiography of Alice B. Toklas* and *Everybody's Autobiography* where the narrator is not just an individual, but a cultural examination of "everybody." As halfway between the early and late autobiographies, it is an investigation at the edge of Stein's own renown.

Likewise, Muller's *Point Deception* is a case that plays upon rifts, both in the setting and in characters' lives. To negotiate these gaps, she goes beyond a symbolic detective's perspective into more fragmented passages. The Soledad County case does not unfold in the city and, for a time, manages to evade the press. Its canyon murders highlight the unresolved holes in Muller's fictional reputation that fix the author to her detective McCone. Forgoing audience approval, *Point Deception* wanders outside the McCone identification and audience familiarization.

To investigate non-public parts of identity contrary to their reputation, Gertrude Stein and Marcia Muller turn to detective fiction. With *Blood on the Dining Room Floor*, Stein contemplates if this will be her "last" work. Likewise after the twenty-first novel of her series, *Listen to the Silence*, Muller wonders if Sharon McCone is over. Their authorial anxiety is a result of an audience that is too close and an author that is strictly associated with her popular character. They stop this unbearable notoriety by redirecting style and a new writing practice.

As hard-boiled authors departing from the "Golden Age," Gertrude Stein and Marcia Muller use detective fiction to investigate their own career anxiety. Instead of becoming fictional casualties, they go beyond the spectacle of subjectivity—as Stein mentions in one of the last works she ever wrote: "I like to read detective and mystery stories, I never get enough of them but whenever one of them is or was about death rays and atomic bombs I never could read them. What is the use if they are really as destructive as all that.... It's the living that are interesting not the way of killing them" (*Reflections on the Atomic Bomb* 161). Using anxiety to stylistically transition, both authors avoid becoming a *cause célébre* through modern forms of detective fiction.

Notes

1. Authorial anxiety regarding audience also struck Sir Arthur Conan Doyle in 1894 when he wrote "The Final Problem." Sick of being called Sherlock Holmes, Doyle wrote this short story to end the equation with his famous character. Readers of *The Strand* were outraged and more than 20,000 cancelled their subscriptions. In a paternalistic society relying on the enlightened detective to protect and order reality, the audience considered Doyle a criminal for killing off Holmes. It would be years before he worked through his following which hounded him in *The Hound of the Baskervilles* (1902) and later "The Empty House" (1905).

2. Stein departs from her mentor's epistemological views, as well as his views on "stream of consciousness." Unlike William James, Stein did not believe in conformity to common knowledge. In James' view, if the cultural, common, and continuously growing "knowledge" of a community were to cease, all systems of truth would be lost. Stein, however, believes that "deviation from the consensus or the undermining of consensus itself becomes a clear gain" (Chessman 158). One of *Blood's* main themes is the ineffectiveness of communal knowledge and certainty, or the importance of deviating from consensus "beliefs."

3. An *askesis* is a process, search, and mystical practice through an analytic investigation that is not measured calculation. It is the way Gertrude Stein cared for herself and others, in the sense that Michel Foucault describes in *The Care of the Self.*

4. In *The Geographical History of America*, Stein explains the "human mind" as a search for real Other recognition. This is in contrast to "human nature," which seeks other recognition. While "autobiographies have nothing to do with human mind," in "What Are Master-Pieces," Stein claims detective fiction does (*Geographical History* 81). The "human mind" is not an essential or fixed mental capacity but the kind of narrative investigation that Stein associates with detective fiction. It entails a notion of "mastery" that cannot be measured except as an on-going search.

5. Stein modeled her "landscapes" after Cezanne's method of painting. They were not imitations of space, but presentations of movements such as breathing, fighting, walking, or bullfighting. Cultivating an *askesis* around representative figuration, Stein tries to write "the way Cézanne paints apples, [as a search] for the relation to the real as it is renewed in art at that moment" (Lacan, *Ethics* 141). Her landscapes are less a display of representational reality and more a display of the continuous present.

6. *Blood* was written after World War I when anxiety about World War II was building (1933). It prefigures Stein's later autobiography, *Wars I Have Seen*, where everyone suspects Nazi monolithic criminality but cannot say or speak of it with any free certainty.

7. Anxiety about sexuality, incest, and shadowy sexual relations appears in Stein's work, including the early journals, now published as the *Radcliffe Manuscripts*. Some sketchy and disturbing scenes appear to be referencing her own personal experience. Lisa Ruddick suggests, "We have no way of knowing whether Daniel Stein, like the father in the vignette [*The Making of Americans*] abused his daughter sexually; but Stein, by writing the episode, was at least discharging anger at her father" (Ruddick 112). Even if there were no incestuous incidents with the father, incest is a feature of Stein's work.

Works Cited

Bairner, Alan. "Sharon McCone's San Francisco: The Role of the City in the Work of Marcia Muller." *Irish Journal of American Studies* 6 (1997): 117–138.

Bridgman, Richard. *Gertrude Stein in Pieces*. New York: Oxford University Press, 1971.

Cawelti, John G. *Adventure, Mystery, and Romance: Formula Stories as Art and Popular Culture*. Chicago: University of Chicago Press, 1976.

Chessman, Harriet Scott. *The Public Is Invited to Dance: Representation, the Body, and Dialogue in Gertrude Stein*. Stanford, CA: Stanford University Press, 1989.

Dydo, Ulla E., and William Rice. *Gertrude Stein : The Language That Rises: 1923–1934*. Evanston, IL: Northwestern University Press, 2003.

James, Dean. "Marcia Muller Interview." *Mystery Scene* 45 (1994): 24.

Lacan, Jacques. *The Four Fundamental Concepts of Psycho-Analysis*. 1st American ed. New York: Norton, 1978.

_____. *The Ethics of Psychoanalysis (1959–1960). The Seminar of Jacques Lacan, Book VII*. Ed. Jacques-Alain Miller. Trans. Dennis Porter. New York: W.W. Norton, New York: 1992.

_____. *Television: A Challenge to the Psychoanalytic Establishment*, ed. Joan Copjec. New York: Norton, 1990.

Muller, Marcia. "A Novelist's Life Is Altered by Her Alter Ego." In *Writers on Writing: Collected Essays from the "New York Times,"* 175–179. New York: Times Books, 2001.

_____. *Point Deception*. New York: Warner Books, 2001.

Perry, Ruth, and Martine Watson Brownley. *Mothering the Mind: Twelve Studies of Writers and Their Silent Partners*. New York: Holmes & Meier, 1984.

Ruddick, Lisa Cole. *Reading Gertrude Stein: Body, Text, Gnosis*. Ithaca, NY: Cornell University Press, 1990.

Stein, Gertrude. *Everybody's Autobiography*. New York: Vintage Books, 1973.

_____. *Four in America*. Freeport, NY: Books for Libraries Press, 1969.

_____. *The Geographical History of America; or, the Relation of Human Nature to the Human Mind*. New York: Vintage Books, 1973.

_____. *How Writing Is Written*. Los Angeles: Black Sparrow Press, 1974.

_____. *Reflection on the Atomic Bomb*. Los Angeles: Black Sparrow Press, 1973.

_____. "What Are Master-Pieces and Why Are There So Few of Them?" In *Writings, 1932–1946*, 353–364. New York: Penguin Putnam, 1998.

Stein, Gertrude, and John Herbert Gill. *Blood on the Dining Room Floor*. Berkeley, CA: Creative Arts Book Co., 1982.

Weisbard, Phyllis Holman. "Mysteries." *Feminist Collections*. 16, no. 2 (1995): 39.

10

The Lost Child: Haunting
Motif in the McCone Novels

HARRIETTE C. BUCHANAN

The popularity of the series detective story depends on readers becoming attached to the main characters and avidly following their adventures from story to story. The masters of the genre not only tell compelling stories that feature interesting and believable characters, but also depict characters who grow and develop over the course of the stories. The series thus becomes a supertext[1] that can be viewed as one large novel, gradually unfolding the life of the main character as well as developing the supporting characters.

Marcia Muller has created a highly engaging series in her novels about Sharon McCone, one of the first fictional female private investigators. In addition to the development of McCone and of her relationships with the recurring supporting characters, Muller also moves several thematic motifs through the stories. Intimately connected to the ongoing images of the functions and dysfunctions of the family unit is the development of the motif of the lost child.

This lost child is variously a victim, a villain, or a victor. As Muller explores the lost child, we see victims who remain victims, villains who turn the misery of their victimhood toward victimizing others, and victors who overcome their victimhood to emerge as fully integrated, functional personalities. This latter motif sometimes occurs within the context of a single novel, but other times emerging personality development of a recurring character works through the course of several novels. Sharon McCone faces the lost child within herself in several of the series' most recent installments. This chapter explores Muller's presentation of the lost child as victim, villain, and victor, beginning with a general discussion of the archetypal nature of this motif, and continuing with a detailed discussion of Muller's various lost children found throughout the Sharon McCone series.[2]

C. G. Jung first identified key psychological archetypes as being drawn

133

from the collective unconscious that underlies an individual's personal unconscious (3–4). Jung additionally identified the child archetype as being the core archetype from which the individual works. "The 'child' emerges as a symbolic content, manifestly separated or even isolated from its background (the mother), but sometimes including the mother in its perilous situation, threatened on the one hand by the negative attitude of the conscious mind and on the other by the *horror vacui* of the unconscious" (168). This suggestion of the "child" being torn between conscious and unconscious mind is carried further when Jung suggests that "it is a striking paradox in all child myths that the 'child' is on the one hand delivered helpless into the power of terrible enemies and in continual danger of extinction, while on the other he possesses powers far exceeding those of ordinary humanity" (170). Jung finally integrates these concepts by stating that "conscious and unconscious do not make a whole when one of them is suppressed and injured by the other"; rather the two should simultaneously exist in "open conflict and open collaboration" so that they can be "forged into an indestructible whole, an 'individual'" (288). Jung uses the concept of the archetype as a background from which to develop the particular examples of individuals struggling to reconcile opposing forces and thus to become "indestructible whole[s]."

Other theorists have developed concepts based on Jungian types in which a central focus is the struggle to balance opposing traits and come to individual wholeness. Joseph Campbell identifies this balancing act throughout the hero's journey in *The Hero with a Thousand Faces*. Campbell compares mythological stories to derive a monomyth in which the quest takes the hero through trials to achieve a boon or insight that he then brings back to his world. Campbell's hero must juggle trials and tests with sources of help in order to successfully complete his quest. In an effort to apply the hero story to women, Maureen Murdock, in *The Heroine's Journey*, identifies the journey for women as involving "an urgent need to heal what I call the *mother/daughter split*, the *deep feminine wound*. The return trip involved a redefinition and validation of feminine values and an integration of these with the masculine skills learned during the first half of the journey" (4). Describing her as "a spiritual warrior," Murdock says the heroine must integrate her masculine and feminine aspects so that she "can truly serve not only the needs of others but can value and be responsive to her own needs as well" (11). Carol S. Pearson develops a variation that identifies *The Hero Within: Six Archetypes We Live By*. These six archetypes are the Innocent, Orphan, Martyr, Wanderer, Warrior, and Magician. Each archetype has a goal, task, and fear that define the positive and negative aspects of the type, with the goal being to expand the strengths of each archetype within the self to help alleviate the fears.

Northrop Frye states the value of archetypes for analyzing literature by "suggesting the possibility of archetypal criticism ... [as] the possibility of extending the kind of comparative and morphological study now made of folk tales and ballads into the rest of literature" (104). Frye indicates that archetypal criticism is especially valuable in the study of popular literary forms. Muller uses the McCone stories to indicate ways the lost child motif can be central to the balancing act for characters who seek to overcome fears of victimhood. This plays out in one of three ways: The lost child victim can remain undeveloped to become a perpetually lost victim; the child can become an angry brat in whom the evil or psychopathic parts of the self turn the lost child into a villain; or the child can balance the fearful lost child with an outward-looking effort to accomplish good deeds and become a victor. Throughout, Muller presents Sharon McCone as a warrior heroine who relentlessly pursues truth, even at great personal risk.

Many of Muller's perpetual victims are bystanders suffering the effects of random crimes, while others are the victims of the crimes central to the stories. While this is terminal for many, others survive, diminished by their victimhood. Victims who survive in a diminished capacity are perhaps the most pitiable, since it seems unlikely they will find resolution for their suffering. In some of the stories, the lost child victim is literally a child, but in others this victim may be an adult who has failed to develop into a fully individualized person because of an inability to overcome the elements of his or her environment.

Many of the lost child victims in the McCone series are children who are neglected as a result of caretakers' misdeeds. In *There's Something in a Sunday* (1989), we encounter three innocent child victims: Lindy and Betsy Cushman and Susan Johnston. Lindy plays a more active role in the story when she calls McCone for help, but in the end she and her sister Betsy are unable to develop beyond being victims of their mother's madness and their father's failure. McCone says of Lindy, "She's seen so much in her short life, and she's probably had to fend for both herself and her little sister. It's made her capable of turning off her emotions like tapwater" (161). Susan is their friend whose mother, Irene, is a passive cause of much of the violence in the story. At story's end, McCone is sorry for most of the characters around whom the story has swirled, but mostly she feels sorry "for Susan and Betsy and Lindy, the innocent victims of it all" (206).

Another child victim whose future is uncertain at story's end is Zach Seabrook in *Both Ends of the Night* (1997). During the course of the story, Zach's father disappears, and McCone is hired by his father's girlfriend, Matty Wildress, McCone's flight instructor, who dies under suspicious circumstances at an aerobatic competition. After Matty's death, McCone feels sorry for the lonely boy. She temporarily places him with her friends Ricky and Rae, feeling it is the right thing to do. "Logically, since John Seabrook had no relatives that anyone knew of, Zach should be turned over to the juvenile authorities until his father could be located. But I wasn't about to inflict that kind of abandonment on a sensitive and grieving boy — especially now that I had full reason to believe his life was in danger" (102). McCone finds Zach's father, but the disturbing circumstances of his story raise questions about the federal witness protection program that are part of the subtext of this story. We are left with questions about how Zach will deal with his father now that he realizes he never really knew him. These children are innocent victims whose futures remain unresolved by the ends of the stories.

Similarly uncertain are the futures of some of the adult lost child victims in Muller's McCone stories. One of the first of these is the hapless Neal Oliver, owner of the decrepit Appleby Island mansion at the center of *Eye of the Storm* (1988). The crimes of this novel swirl around Neal's dreams of turning this property into a marina/hotel, but he cannot cope with these crimes or their consequences. At novel's end, Neal's brother Sam plans to take him home to Michigan and place him under psychiatric care, but with little hope for a real recovery.

Later in the series, in *The Shape of Dread* (1989), we meet a similar victim, Lisa McIntyre. Wounded by the sharp mimicry of the murder victim, Lisa McIntyre flees San Francisco only to be found by McCone who had hopefully believed that the murder victim, Tracy Kostakos, has assumed McIntyre's identity. Shocked to see that the woman she has located is actually McIntyre, McCone notes her poor appearance. She "was painfully thin. The bone structure of her heart-shaped face was more prominent than two years before, her cheeks hollowed. Her curly light-brown hair seemed to drag under its own lifeless weight" (212). McCone's conversation with her opens avenues that will result in a successful conclusion to the investigation, but McIntyre's condition remains hopeless.

Like Neal Oliver from *Eye of the Storm*, Jillian Wellbright in *A Walk Through the Fire* (1999) is receiving psychiatric care at novel's end, but we are not at all certain that she will have the internal strength to benefit from this care since the other surviving members of the extraordinarily dysfunctional Wellbright family do not seem to be able to support her adequately. Equally victimized by family dysfunction is Harry Nagasawa in *Dead Midnight* (2002). A physician who has been fired from his residency because he illegally accessed confidential patient records for his brother Roger, Harry is equally doomed by his drug use. In the turmoil of the events surrounding McCone's unraveling the reasons precipitating Roger's suicide, Harry's plight is lost. The last we hear about Harry is when his other brother Eddie gives McCone this assessment. "Harry and I don't talk, hardly ever. He's got a mean streak, and it's gotten worse since he started doing drugs and drinking heavily.... He's smart, and he had the makings of a good surgeon, but he couldn't handle the pressure. Even if Rog hadn't put him in a position where he lost his job, he'd've crashed and burned sooner or later anyway" (206). While we are confident Eddie will be all right, we do not hold out any faith for Harry's recovery. These adult victims survive the mayhem of their various stories, but without any resources for growth beyond their victimhood.

Other perpetual victims are those lost children who become the victims of the violence of the McCone murder mysteries. One of these is D. A. Taylor, whose complicity in the crimes of *Trophies and Dead Things* (1990) causes him to commit suicide. A Native American (at least partly) whose focused anger during the 1960s has burned out, D. A. is bereft because his disillusionment has come from his disappointment that "there were no heroes" (255). McCone is unable to console him "because I suspected there had never been any heroes — not in the world he was longing for. That was a world all too often re-created not from fact but from wishful fantasy, and none of us could ever know where the truth left off and the lies began" (255–56). Another innocent victim who dies is Franny Silva in *Till the Butchers Cut Him Down* (1994). A young Native American woman, Silva dies when McCone's client's house is blown up, but her body is mistaken for that of "Suits" Gordon's wife, Anna. When McCone eventually finds Anna in hiding at the Ridge Reservation, they realize the body was that of Silva whose parents had reported her as missing. Anna says, "Franny. No one even told me she was missing; runaway teenagers are pretty commonplace up here" (330). With these two Native American characters, Muller has called our attention to a people who are in many ways the archetypal lost children of American history, persons displaced and abandoned during the nineteenth-century era of Manifest Destiny.

Another lost child adult victim is Mavis Hamid, a poet who has retreated into alcoholism in *A Wild and Lonely Place* (1995). Murdered when she resists being kidnapped along with her daughter Habiba, Mavis is found floating in a marina slip. McCone dives into the water to retrieve the body. Overwhelmed with emotion, McCone jerks herself to the surface just before becoming drowned by grief for the lost child-woman who was Mavis: "I'd been too late to save Mavis" (108).

Another victim who becomes lost in alcohol and drugs and whom McCone is unable to save is Dan Jeffers in *The Dangerous Hour* (2004). McCone first hears about Jeffers from a park attendant who describes him as a relic from the sixties who was obviously still battling drug addiction (91). Although McCone never finds Jeffers, she locates evidence that leads her to believe that the murderer in the story has killed Jeffers as well and likely hidden the body in some undetectable canyon on Sonoma Mountain (277). Jeffers is not only a lost child of the sixties, his corpse is lost as well. All of these lost child victims, whether literal or emotional children, remain lost, either because they are unable to pull their lives together or because they are dead.

Coming from similarly dysfunctional family backgrounds as many of the perpetually lost children in the McCone novels, Muller's villains are sometimes explained as being immature lost children who have lashed out at their world in anger and violence. Sometimes these villains act out of passions thwarted and sometimes out of evil greed. Muller presents the passionately angry lost child villains as being, to some extent, understandable. These are the characters for whom Muller allows McCone to feel some sympathy. One of these is Josh Haddon in *Till the Butchers Cut Him Down*. Haddon has been responsible for the problems that "Suits" Gordon has hired McCone to solve. He also is responsible for the explosion that killed Franny Silva, although he did not intend for anyone to die. Haddon had been desperately in love with Anna, and when he thought he was responsible for her death in the explosion that actually killed Silva, he becomes lost in grief. McCone prevents Gordon from shooting Haddon's helicopter down but cannot prevent Haddon's anguished grief from causing his self-destruction. Although she cannot approve of what he has done, McCone does understand the love and grief that have motivated Haddon's actions.

Another villain who acts out of grief is Langley "Fig" Newton in *A Wild and Lonely Place*. McCone has been brought into the so-called Diplo-Bomber investigation to discover the identity of the person who has been bombing consulate offices and homes. As the tale unravels, McCone figures out that the bomber is motivated by rage over the fact that members of ambassadors' and consuls' families have diplomatic immunity and can literally get away with murder. McCone's friend and San Francisco police officer Adah Joslyn is kidnapped during the story, and McCone realizes that it is the Diplo-Bomber who is responsible. Red herrings abound and only at the very end do McCone and the reader realize that the pathetic-seeming Newton is the villain. Because Dawud Hamid had murdered a woman Newton loved, even though the woman was unaware of his feelings, Newton has conducted his deadly campaign. In order to save herself and Joslyn, McCone kills Newton but feels remorse. Joslyn talks with McCone about the experience later. "It's gonna take you a lot of time to get over that [the death of Newton]. Some ways, you never will." When McCone asks if Newton said anything about what he did, Joslyn offers this assessment. "He was a very withdrawn guy, McCone. He just didn't connect with other people, especially at the end" (273). Victimized by personal grief over lost love that neither had the ability to express, both Haddon and Newton commit crimes that make them villains.

Other lost children are less victims of grief than of their own inability to understand the neglect or abuse that they suffered in childhood. Perhaps the worst and most personally threatening of these are Lee D'Silva and Bud Larsen in *While Other People Sleep* (1998). In parallel stories, both McCone and her office manager, Ted Smalley, are being harassed by stalkers. McCone's stalker is trying to usurp her life by impersonating her while Smalley's stalker is acting out a hate crime against Smalley and his partner, Neal Osborn. Slowly McCone uncovers the clues that reveal her stalker/impersonator to be Lee D'Silva and Smalley's and Osborn's harasser to be Bud Larsen. McCone learns that D'Silva is the only child of an alcoholic mother and a distant father. Growing up, D'Silva tried desperately to hide the shame of her mother's alcoholism and to live a perfect life. D'Silva had apparently read a magazine article about McCone and began working to become just like her. One of D'Silva's childhood friends tries to explain her behavior: "I couldn't blame her for taking the money and running [her behavior after her mother's suspicious death]. She tried so hard, she gave so much, but nothing was ever enough. The more she did, the more Hal and Marge [her parents] demanded. I guess she just finally snapped…. Poor kid" (269). McCone echoes the friend's "poor kid" and continues with this train of thought. "So I should feel sorry for her? Yes, she had a terrible life, but lots of people have terrible lives, and they don't use them as an excuse to embezzle from their own fathers. They don't use them as an excuse to invade and destroy someone else's life. Not if they're decent human beings" (269). D'Silva's experience is obviously regrettable, but this hardly pardons her actions.

At the end of the novel, after D'Silva has wrecked Hy Ripinsky's beloved Citabria, she tries once more to manipulate McCone by accusing McCone of betraying her and causing the wreck. She also tries to implicate her father in her mother's death. McCone sees through her game and calls her on it. "You'll do anything to get sympathy won't you? … Anything, including framing your own father for something you did. You're a very sick woman, and I hope that in prison you'll get the help you need to come to terms with your past and cope with your future" (341–2). When she hears this, D'Silva's response is telling and casts doubt on McCone's hope. "'Prison!' The little-girl mask fell away, and her eyes flared. 'You fucking bitch!' she exclaimed" (342). In the parallel plot, Smalley's and Osborn's home is invaded when gruesome objects are delivered that carry notes accusing the two men of being faggots and perverts. When McCone finally catches Bud Larsen and confronts him, Larsen snaps. He accuses Smalley and Osborn by saying, "You're still filthy perverts," and adds the information that, perhaps, explains his hatred. "I know your kind, all right. Uncle Nick, the nicest man on the block, took care of kids so their folks could get away. Always punched them on the arm and called them buddy—just like you, Osborn" (333). Although his attorney tries to quiet him, Larsen reveals that Uncle Nick had sexually abused him and other children in his care and threatened their safety if they told. While this abused childhood may in part explain Larsen's behavior, it cannot exonerate him. Smalley wins this exchange when he says: "No, Bud, … you're wrong. Uncle Nick was sick; he preyed on children. Men like that *are* called perverts. Neal and I are healthy men who love each other. *We're* called gays" (334). Both D'Silva and Larsen have stalked and violated the sense of identity and sanctity of McCone and Smalley, but McCone, while understanding the abused, neglected, and lost children that they were, cannot, in the end, forgive their villainy.

The lost children whose anger turns into a greedy thirst for power or material goods are perhaps the most reprehensible of the villains of the series. Greed and jealousy make Neal Oliver, in *Eye of the Storm*, the victim of a woman who is an illegitimate descendant of a daughter who was driven out by the family who had originally owned Appleby Island. McCone pieces the identity of the killer together from letters she finds in the mansion that recount the story of the rejected daughter, from what she knows of the troubled background of Stephanie Jorgenson, and from the age-old motive of crimes committed from a misguided sense of disinheritance. Believing she has a right to Appleby Island, Jorgenson first tried unsuccessfully to buy the property and then resorted to terrorizing the inhabitants and finally to committing murder. An unhappy child of an unhappy marriage, Jorgenson has no knowledge of how to live a positive life.

The villain who victimized Lisa McIntyre in *The Shape of Dread* is Tracy Kostakos.[3] Tracy is a talented comic whose routines consist of sketches that, sometimes cruelly, depict various character types. Victimized by Tracy in a sketch about a lesbian waitress, Lisa McIntyre is driven to run away from San Francisco. In Tracy's sketchbook, McCone finds what seems to be an autobiographical outline of her character: "What stands out is her greed — for material things, for life itself. Why such neediness? Easy to blame it on her family. The mother was cold. She never hugged her. She wanted to be a mentor. But there's no place for mentors in families. The girl needed a mother. The beloved father, for all his academic knowledge, was little better. Vague, fondly absent. Sometimes she thought him only half-alive" (101–2). Tracy's villainy lies in her manipulation of others for her own benefit and in the way in which her neediness sets off a chain of events that results in murders — Tracy's and those of several others.

A combination of greed and madness drives the members of the Wellbright family who are the villains of *A Walk Through the Fire*. The matriarch of the family, Celia, is proven to be crazy, accounting for earlier murders that she committed and for Jillian Wellbright's fear of having a female child who might inherit the family madness. Celia's son and Jillian's husband, Matthew Wellbright, has worked to conceal the murders Celia has committed and has caused the accidents that brought McCone to Hawaii to investigate. McCone unravels the complicated knots of the highly dysfunctional Wellbright family, including finding and helping to capture the apparently lost son, Andrew, who is currently running a drug ring that has been plaguing the Hawaiian

Islands. A mad mother and a missing father who spent their childhood years traveling in pursuit of his anthropological studies explain why the Wellbright children — with the possible exception of Peter who escaped to the mainland as soon as he could — are both lost and villainous in their greed for family position and wealth. Lost children who are warped by their victimhood into villains can be explained, perhaps pitied, but never forgiven in the world through which Marcia Muller moves Sharon McCone.

Not all of the lost children remain victims or become villains. Some of them find the individual strength and inherent human decency to overcome their sense of lostness and emerge as victors of their own lives. One of the first inklings we see of this is in Andrew McCone in *Eye of the Storm*. Called to Neal Oliver's mansion by her sister Patsy, mother of three illegitimate children, McCone finds her nephew Andrew the suspected source of some of the problems that seem, at first, to be of primary importance. McCone finds that Andrew is sulky and withdrawn. When she tries to draw his story out and to develop the first clues about what is really happening, McCone has difficulty breaking through Andrew's protective shell. As she comes to better understand the dynamics of Patsy's life, McCone realizes that Andrew's sulkiness is only a shell.

> He was the oldest of a single mother's brood: brother to the intellectually precocious Kelley and Jessamyn, the charmer. When Patsy didn't have a man around, Andrew was elevated to the position of man of the house, and probably a lot of responsibility for his sisters fell onto his bony shoulders. When Patsy did have a man, Andrew was demoted, and his mother's attention was drawn away from him and focused on the new love. And when that happened, the already introverted kid withdrew further [148].

Determined not to add to his problems, McCone relies on his drawings of a hand he had seen at his window to uncover the identity of the villain. McCone is encouraged when Patsy declares her loyalty to her new boyfriend Evans Newhouse and her belief that Andrew needs a father to avoid becoming "an insufferable little smart-ass" (241). McCone agrees but reminds Patsy that she really likes Andrew. In a rare moment of sisterly accord, she and Patsy agree with Patsy's proud "He's McCone all the way" (242). Although we do not meet Andrew in any of the subsequent stories, this assertion by Patsy and the promise of familial stability are borne out in later novels. We learn that Patsy has married Newhouse and become co-owner of a successful set of restaurants, which bodes well for Andrew's future.

One of the most engaging of the lost children who overcome potential victimhood is Habiba Hamid in *A Wild and Lonely Place*. When we first meet Habiba, described by one of the guards at the Azadian consulate as sly (18), we, like McCone, are charmed. McCone is leaving the consulate and sees the child's small head peer up from a large marble urn that serves as a hiding place.

The detective winks, and Habiba, with her "huge dark eyes" winks back, establishing an immediate connection with McCone (21).

This first encounter sets the pattern for the relationship between McCone and Habiba who develop a game in which the wink becomes a code for a secret meeting, a strategy used effectively when McCone rescues Habiba on a Caribbean island after her father kidnaps her. Habiba is lost because her mother, Mavis, has retreated into an alcoholic haze, and her father, Dawud, has left the country to avoid the problems caused when he murdered a woman. Habiba's personal intelligence and strength enable her to survive and triumph over these problems. At the novel's end when she has been orphaned by the murders of her parents and grandmother, Habiba will be taken as a foster child by McCone's friends Hank Zahn and Anne-Marie Altman. When McCone asks Habiba if she is happy with Hank and Anne-Marie, who have no experience with children, Habiba says, "The child-rearing stuff? They don't know anything about it, either. But that's okay. My ... nanny Aisha and my Grams already taught me table manners and things like that. Besides, I like Anne-Marie and Hank, and ... if I stay in San Francisco, I can see you and Hy, too. If you want to" (275–6). Habiba has triumphed over her condition of being a lost, lonely child and becomes one of the ongoing characters in the McCone stories, gaining strength as we see her time and again.

A final adult lost child who triumphs over adversity to emerge a victor in her own life is Julia Rafael. First introduced in *Dead Midnight*, Rafael is presented as a young woman with a very troubled past whom McCone is convinced is turning her life around. When McCone first hires her to train as an investigator, she gives the following description: "A tall, strongly built Latina with a haughty profile and spiky hair, Julia had dragged herself up from one of the worst personal histories I'd ever encountered in a job applicant. I'd taken a chance on her because I figured that anyone with so much guts and determination to improve her lot in life couldn't help but succeed as an investigator" (42). McCone's faith in Julia is shaken in *The Dangerous Hour* when Rafael is arrested for identity theft and credit card fraud.

Working to clear Rafael and later her own firm (brought under official scrutiny by a complaint from the individual whose identity Rafael had apparently stolen), McCone sees Rafael retreat once more into a lost child persona. Julia reemerges from that condition because McCone's restored faith and investigative skills clear Rafael and McCone Investigations. Julia Rafael, like Habiba Hamid, overcomes being a lost child and becomes integrated into the extended McCone family.

Over the course of the McCone novels, Muller introduces us to her extended family. Over the early novels we slowly learn that Sharon is the middle of five children in the somewhat dysfunctional McCone family. At family gatherings Ma hovers in the kitchen, fussing that everyone do as she asks, and Pa hides in his garage, tinkering and singing bawdy ballads. All through these early novels, McCone wonders why she is so different from her siblings who lead troubled and troubling lives.

Her oldest brother, John, when we first meet him in *Double* (1984), is dealing poorly with his divorce. We never meet the next brother, Joey, whose suicide at the beginning of *Dead Midnight* means that neither McCone nor we will ever gain insights into his troubled history. The two younger siblings are sisters Charlene and Patsy. We first meet Charlene in *Double*, and her rocky marriage to country musician Ricky Savage flickers through the background of several other stories before coming to the center in *The Broken Promise Land* (1996). The youngest McCone is Patsy, whose story figured prominently in *Eye of the Storm*. Although in the early stories all of the McCone siblings lead troubled lives, by the most recent installments of the series, they have — with the exception of Joey whose suicide marks him as permanently lost — built solid lives for themselves. In *Wolf in the Shadows* (1993), John, who proves helpful in McCone's quest to locate the missing Hy Ripinsky, has established himself as Mr. Paint, a successful painting contractor, and is no longer one of the dysfunctional McCones. After breaking up with Ricky Savage, Charlene marries her lover, Vic, and settles into a comfortable life in which she and Ricky amicably share custody of their six children. Patsy has settled into a happy marriage in the recent stories. Except for Sharon, whose career will be discussed later, the McCones are well established.

McCone also develops an extended family with the staff and attorneys at All Souls, the legal cooperative where she works as an investigator in the early novels. This is particularly true of Sharon's assistant at All Souls, Rae Kelleher. We are introduced to Kelleher in *There's Something in a Sunday*. Rae also integrates into the All Souls family after leaving her manipulative, immature husband, Doug. We learn that after Rae's parents died when she was a child she was raised by a grandmother who resented being saddled with her. Rae tells us that when she was a young woman she tried to fill the lost loneliness by sleeping with a range of men before marrying Doug. Although she has escaped from Doug, Rae is not in the clear yet. Over the course of the novels, she moves into All Souls and dates Willie Whelan, the somewhat shady flea market king of *Leave a Message for Willie* (1984), who has become a legitimate jewelry dealer and whose television ads have catapulted him to a kind of stardom. At the end of *Pennies on a Dead Woman's Eyes* (1992), Rae has broken up with Willie over her resentment of his insistence that she sign a prenuptial agreement.

When *Wolf in the Shadows* begins, only a week after the conclusion of *Pennies*, Rae is once more a lost child. McCone comments that "Rae herself seemed ... uncared for; her curly auburn hair needed washing, and her jeans and sweater looked as if she'd slept in them" (18). By the end of *Wolf*, Muller shows the revival of Rae's strength in a sampler she has needlepointed that says "A rule with no exception: If it has tires or testicles, you're going to have trouble with it" (296). Finally when Rae meets Ricky Savage in *The Broken Promise Land*, both of them experience a kind of "love at first date" that develops into the close relationship for each that neither could achieve in their first marriages. Both Rae and Ricky have emerged from being lost children to become integrated beings. The need that they recognize in each other and that is met in their relationship is captured in Ricky's song "The Empty Place." In the audio journal that she keeps, Rae describes the way in which Ricky's description of the empty place resonates closely with her history: "It was the kind of place that starts out as a bubble in a little girl who knows she's not loved, and gradually expands into a huge vacuum that threatens to turn her inside out and swallow her whole" (292). Fortunately, Rae and Ricky have filled each other's empty places and form the close unit that gives Rae the confidence to write the novel that meets with acclaim during *The Dangerous Hour*.

Although McCone's toughness defies any sympathy from us, she is in many ways also a lost child who slowly gains strength and confidence over the course of the 23 novels published through 2004. From the first we have learned that Sharon McCone feels set apart from the rest of her family. In each of the novels she finds occasion to comment on being one-eighth Shoshone, accounting for her dark looks as a throw back to her great-grandmother, Mary McCone. She contrasts her behavior to that of her siblings, commenting that she alone has avoided the kind of trouble in which they are constantly embroiled. While John and Joey were getting in trouble during their high school years, she was a cheerleader dating the football captain. While Charlene and Patsy were rebelling and becoming pregnant out of wedlock, she was working and putting herself through college.

When we first meet McCone in *Edwin of the Iron Shoes* (1977), she is singularly unattached. Hank Zahn is boss and friend, but she has no close ties to anyone. Gradually we see that the All Souls group forms a surrogate family since her relationship with her own family is, at best, strained. McCone continually puts off returning her mother's frequent phone calls. When she attends an investigators' conference in *Double*, she stays with her family in San Diego, but the relationships are uneasy. McCone is the go-between for her mother and John, who just separated from his wife. She is also a go-between for her parents whose strained relationship is already visible. During *Where Echoes Live* (1991), Ma tells McCone that she is leaving Pa to live with a new man with whom she has fallen in love. In this novel, McCone also meets Hy Ripinsky, the first man with whom she can be totally honest.

Prior to *Where Echoes Live*, McCone has had and discarded two lovers.

Greg Marcus, a police officer, resented her career and her intrusion into some of his investigations. Don Del Boccio, a disk jockey, became too domestic for her. In *Where Echoes Live*, Sharon's third lover, George Kostakos, proposed marriage, but McCone is acutely aware that, as with the other men in her life, she has hidden a dark side of her personality from him, a dark side that Hy Ripinsky immediately recognizes. "Hy understood the darker side of me, the one I'd never dared reveal to George. Understood it, and neither approved nor disapproved. Accepted my violent urges and dangerous impulses because at some time in his past he had been a victim of the same" (*Where Echoes* 300–1). The course of this romance, is not, however, totally smooth. Its ups and downs cause McCone to doubt what she knows and to push to learn more about the mysterious Ripinsky.

Before the romance can smooth out, however, McCone has to face the problem of her own identity. At the beginning of *Listen to the Silence* (2000), Pa has died. In going through his papers, McCone finds documents that indicate that she is adopted. Shocked to discover this secret, a secret that she learns has been the wedge between her adoptive parents, McCone goes in quest of her birth parents. After dealing with a few red herrings that indicate that Austin DeCarlo is her father, McCone discovers that her birth mother gave her up for adoption in an effort to protect her from the rage of Austin's bigoted father and also to pursue her own dreams of a college education. McCone's birth mother, Saskia Blackhawk, is a successful attorney in Boise, Idaho, and her birth father is not Austin DeCarlo, but Elwood Farmer, an artist who has retired to the Flathead Reservation in Montana. By the end of *Listen*, McCone is beginning to sort through her feelings about her heritage and to accept the new family arrangement in which she finds herself. Coming to a new understanding of her adoptive mother, McCone tells her, "Ma, the family's intact. Elwood feels like a father to me, and that's good because I miss Pa a lot. But Kia will be more like a friend or a favorite relative. I already have a mother" (334). The next novels deepen these connections, with McCone staying in telephone contact with Farmer and both mothers, as well as enjoying the addition of half-sister Robin and half-brother Darcy to her extended family.

McCone has slowly grown from being truly alone to becoming integrated into all of her families: her adoptive family, her birth family, and the family that has grown out of the friendships that began at All Souls. The ghosts of the past, of her lost child, will always haunt her, however. During the course of the investigation in *Dead Midnight*, she has occasion to note a personal similarity with Roger Nagasawa when she considers the issue of placement in birth order. "The middle child, even in the family portrait. A difficult place in the birth order. I'd been the middle child in my adoptive family, and it had made me feel set apart from my older brothers and younger sisters, turned me into something of a loner" (55). While haunted to some extent by this past, McCone cannot remain a true loner.

Over the course of the novels following their first meeting, McCone's and Ripinsky's relationship has grown. In *The Dangerous Hour*, McCone has been fretting because she is uncomfortable with the knowledge that Ripinsky wants a deeper level of commitment from her. At a book signing for Rae, McCone talks with former lover turned good friend Greg Marcus. After telling her that he plans to marry, he senses that she is anxious because Ripinsky wants to marry her. She tells Marcus, "In case you haven't noticed, marriage isn't what the McCone family does best" citing the examples of her parents' divorce and the assorted relationship troubles of her siblings (173). Marcus reminds her that her mother, Charlene, and Patsy are now happily married and asks about her birth parents. When McCone indicates that both of them had happy marriages before their respective spouses died, Marcus tells her, "Heredity's as important as environment. So what are you afraid of?" (173). By the end of the novel, McCone has overcome her fears and is ready to accept Ripinsky's proposal. As she tells herself: "You've risked your safety time and again. You've risked your life, too. Why not risk happiness?" (290).

When we first meet Sharon McCone, she is like many of the characters in her stories. She is a lost child, a loner, but, to her credit, she refuses to become a victim. Like the other lost children in the series of novels who have faced their loneliness and lostness and found the inner strength not to be overwhelmed, she has emerged a victor. Other members of the extended McCone family are also victors, having overcome problems that interfered with their abilities to form positive relationships. Their successful integration into nuclear and extended family units is underscored by the presence of lost children who have remained perpetual victims, or who have repressed their anxieties into the activities that have driven them to commit the crimes that turn them into villains.

Over the course of the Sharon McCone novels, Marcia Muller has used the motif of the lost child to add depth to stories that might otherwise be mere genre entertainments. The lost child motif, like other important unifying themes, has added layers of richness and complexity to the McCone novels, raising them to a literary level that many mystery novels fail to attain. The twenty-sixth McCone novel is soon to be published, with many others promised. Those of us who have joined the extended McCone family eagerly look forward to the new problems that Sharon will solve — along with the assistance of her various family members.

Notes

1. In "Sigrid's Saga: Text, Subtext, and Supertext in Margaret Maron's Sigrid Harald Novels," I have developed more fully the concept of the text, or main individual plot of the story; the subtext, or social issue around which the text focuses; and the supertext, or the psychological elements of the characters' development over the novels.

2. An earlier version of this paper was more inclusive, but it soon became too long and unwieldy. The motif of the lost child plays out much more fully than space allows here. I invite readers of this essay to find other examples that I do not have space to include here.

3. One of the ironies here is that McCone is attracted to Tracy's father, George, with whom she has an affair beginning in this story and extending through the two subsequent novels.

Works Cited

Buchanan, Harriette C. "Sigrid's Saga: Text, Subtext, and Supertext in Margaret Maron's Sigrid Harald Novels." *Clues: A Journal of Detection.* 17, no. 2 (Fall/Winter 1996): 33–42.

Campbell, Joseph. *The Hero with a Thousand Faces.* 2nd ed. Princeton: Princeton University Press, 1968.

Frye, Northrop. *Anatomy of Criticism: Four Essays.* New York: Atheneum, 1967.

Jung, C. G. *The Archetypes and the Collective Unconscious.* Trans. R. F. C. Hull. 2nd ed. Vol. 9, Part I of *The Collected Works of C. G. Jung.* Princeton: Princeton University Press, 1968.

Muller, Marcia. *Both Ends of the Night.* New York: Mysterious Press, 1997.

_____. *The Broken Promise Land.* New York: Mysterious Press, 1996.

_____. *The Dangerous Hour.* New York: Mysterious Press, 2004

_____. *Dead Midnight.* 2002. New York: Warner Books, 2003.

_____. *Edwin of the Iron Shoes.* New York: Mysterious Press, 1977.

_____. *Eye of the Storm.* New York: Mysterious Press, 1988.

_____. *Leave a Message for Willie.* New York: Mysterious Press, 1984.

_____. *Listen to the Silence.* 2000. New York: Warner Books, 2001.

_____. *Pennies on a Dead Woman's Eyes.* New York: Mysterious Press, 1992.

_____. *The Shape of Dread.* New York: Mysterious Press, 1989.

_____. *There's Something in a Sunday.* New York: Mysterious Press, 1989.

_____. *Till the Butchers Cut Him Down.* New York: Mysterious Press, 1994.

_____. *Trophies and Dead Things.* New York: Mysterious Press, 1990.

_____. *A Walk Through the Fire.* 1999. New York: Warner Books, 2000.

_____. *Where Echoes Live.* New York: Mysterious Press, 1991.

_____. *While Other People Sleep.* New York: Mysterious Press, 1998.

_____. *A Wild and Lonely Place.* New York: Mysterious Press, 1995.

_____. *Wolf in the Shadows.* New York: Mysterious Press, 1993.

Muller, Marcia, and Bill Pronzini. *Double.* New York: Mysterious Press, 1984.

Murdock, Maureen. *The Heroine's Journey.* Boston: Shambhala Publications, 1990.

Pearson, Carol S. *The Hero Within: Six Archetypes We Live By.* Expanded Edition. San Francisco: HarperCollins, 1989.

11

Muller Earth: Mythic Topography in the Soledad County Trilogy

Christine A. Jackson

With more than thirty novels to her credit in a career spanning three decades, Marcia Muller shows no sign of stopping. However, during her few hours of downtime from writing, her website informs us, she enjoys building "electrified miniature houses." Muller's website features pictures of rooms in two fully conceived residences of her fictional detective Sharon McCone (www.marciamuller.com). One tiny house purports to be McCone's on Bernal Street during the days with the All Souls Cooperative. The other structure stands as a replica of McCone's earthquake house on Church Street from McCone's more recent adventures. One room is the kitchen where Sharon and Hy concoct late-night snacks.

Muller's recent Soledad County trilogy moves out of the refurbished Victorian triple-deckers of McCone's neighborhood. Instead, Muller expands her passion for building and defining space by creating an entire region. With a "Google Earth"–like sweep, the Soledad County novels transport the reader from that foggy city by the bay to an imaginary terrain a few hours' drive north up the California coast and a few decades back through time. The three novels, named after topographical features, are *Point Deception* (2001), *Cyanide Wells* (2003), and *Cape Perdido* (2005). Set in different areas of Muller's imaginary territory, these works develop a complex mythic perspective that transcends the private eye subgenre.

Soledad, a region of stark beauty, is no paradise but a wild and lonely place. The "solitude" of its name is more consistent with "solitary confinement." Using a setting of fog, cliffs, the sea, and crumpled, ruined structures, Muller pries apart detective fiction conventions. Lead characters do not solve the mystery from the outside; their motives and memories *become* the mystery. The narratives twist both an Edenic landscape and the people who inhabit it into something broken and grotesque. Through this textured approach, Muller charges a traditional PI narrative with mythic time and space. Muller's change of strategy for her fiction could herald a seismic shift in the genre.

Over the past seven or eight years, Muller has moved closer to a de-personalized narrative, even in the McCone books. The titles reflect an increasingly self-destructive bent for our detective. Sharon has earned her pilot's license. With a more frequent aerial view, she is eager to "slip the surly bonds of earth." In *A Walk Through the Fire,* she escapes to Hawaii. In *Listen to the Silence,* her father dies, and she learns that her ethnic heritage is actually full Shoshone. After meeting a mother she never knew, she has to re-think her identity. In *The Dangerous Hour,* she is on a hit list, and in *Vanishing Point,* now married to Hy Ripinsky, she fears that she will disappear. The next murder victim may be McCone herself. The two most recent McCone books foreshadow Muller's need to give Sharon a makeover.

Throughout *The Dangerous Hour,* McCone is skittish and off her mark. Her frustrated exhaustion is palpable. An employee at McCone's agency is charged with credit card theft. The evidence against Julia looks damning, which causes McCone to question her initial faith in Julia's character. Of course, Julia has been framed. The true target of the set-up, somehow, is Sharon herself. A murdering drug dealer she had previously sent to prison is now free and out for her blood. Interestingly, Julia is the one who figures this out (DH 151). McCone is too scattered to put the information together.

Theft and a slashed convertible top on her parked MG during the "dangerous hours" keep Sharon on edge (DH 74). In a related development, Hy Ripinsky continues to pressure her to marry him. While reluctant to talk about what she calls "the 'C' word," or "commitment" (DH 111), Sharon is still miffed when Hy does not call her. She tries to reach him: "He didn't answer, and for some reason the machine wouldn't pick up. Monday. Fucking Monday" (DH 75). McCone feels rattled even while watching the TV news, preferring instead to wait until the next morning "when the events' sharp edges would be blunted" (DH 161). In a few sections, Muller gives McCone's voice a rest. Sharon abdicates authority as the narrator, giving the floor to typed transcripts of employees at the *Trabajo por Todos,* Work For All, Job Training Center (DH 56–58, 135–137). It is almost as if these other voices, non–McCone narrative perspectives, are in training for the Soledad County series.

In this book, McCone lacks her usual confidence. When she goes on a date undercover to pry out information, she takes a Shoshone name from her new ethnic identity. She is Robin Blackhawk, a double-bird name showing that she's ready to take flight (DH 126–131). Even as herself, she is filled with self-doubt and questions. How aggressive should she be? The old McCone would never have second thoughts about giving hell to a phone harasser, but

this Sharon wonders what's wrong with her (DH 157). She also questions if
she is a predator or prey (DH 255).

McCone is aware that she wants to run from Hy's marriage proposal.
She analyzes her reasons. She equates marriage with fear of loss (DH 186).
She also suffers from the loss of her brother, Joey. But a visit to a friend of
Joey takes her down memory lane, and she sees to the end of grief. "I was
smiling at the memories. Smiling at something that had to do with Joey. I
was healing" (DH 213).

The Dangerous Hour is partly about gender power struggles. Two murders involve men toppled, literally, from high places. However, Muller's artistic imagination is clearly moving away from the embodied "I" of the woman
detective toward disembodied myths and landscapes integral to the characters' emotional conflicts.

We see the beginning of this concept as Sharon visits a corrupt politico's
store. The shop sits at the top of a staircase overlooking San Francisco Bay.
In the store is a tree with a snake wrapped in it (DH 170). It is not clear if
the snake is real, but the tree is definitely not, as the tree branch falls off in
her hand. The image has no practical purpose except as a hint, perhaps ironic,
of a mythic dimension to McCone. Later climactic scenes of McCone in a
nocturnal battle royale with the villain continue the connection to myth.

> I crouched, panting on the floor of the little cave. The pain in my side radiated
> out and engulfed my entire body. I shuddered, fighting against it. When it sub-
> sided some, I edged forward and peered over the ledge [DH 286].

When urbanite Sharon treads the caves of Olompali National Park ground,
she is less Nevada Barr's protagonist Anna Pigeon, a National Park Service
ranger, and more Diana, huntress in a moonscape.

In the closing pages, Sharon's literal "dangerous hour" has passed, as the
villain is again behind bars. Still, Hy's marriage proposal awaits (DH 304).
There in the cockpit, she agrees to risk it, and he flies her to Reno before she
can change her mind.

Sometime between *The Dangerous Hour* and *Vanishing Point*, Hy and
Sharon are hitched. The now married Sharon takes the case of a missing
woman artist who runs away from her marriage and daughters, then reap-
pears two decades later, her personality grotesquely distorted. The case clearly
is emblematic of McCone's worst fears. She fears losing her autonomy when
sharing living space with Hy in the earthquake house on Church Street. The
theme unifying McCone's case with her personal conflict is the loss of self
through marriage or any close relationship. The fact that the missing mother
is an artist carries additional damages in terms of lost integrity of vision, independence, and self-reliance. To McCone, marriage is a kind of death.

In the novel's final pages, the ever intrepid Hy has the answer to McCone's fear of losing herself. The couple will have separate spaces, but he has begun construction on a neutral territory bedroom or as he calls it, a "playroom," with an adjoining bath (VP 322–323), accessible through an "interior stairway." McCone says, "I tried to picture where it would go. Couldn't" (VP 323). At this vanishing point, McCone shows an uncharacteristic lack of imagination.

Where the interior stairway leads Muller is upward to her own version of Yoknapatawpha County on the California coast. This new scene among the coastal pines comes partly from Muller's life. She and husband Bill Pronzini have a cottage on the Mendocino coast. At one point, Muller's car broke down along the coastal road, and with no cell phone, she had to wait by the side of the road. That image of a woman stranded on a dark, twisty road haunted Muller, and that scene begins *Point Deception* (PD 1–7).

In a 2001 interview with *Publisher's Weekly*, Muller explains another reason for her detour to a new setting and a different cast of characters. Creating her own county afforded "plenty of freedom to make up this place." She apparently needed to break away from McCone's life and clients, Hy, Hank, Mick, and the rest of the crew caught up in problems about kids, careers, partners, wrong choices, or divorces. Muller also knows early on that Soledad County is a place she wants to stay for a while. She says, "I think the county will become a series setting" (Koch 54). Matt Lindstrom may be speaking for Muller when he says in *Cyanide Wells* that San Francisco is "difficult to navigate — full of one-way streets and natural obstacles" (CW 183).

The frontispiece of each Soledad County novel is a map. Providing one kind of knowledge about Soledad, each map is marked with the snake-like roads, one-horse towns, and rocky promontories featured in the three novels. Only a few labels stake out known territory. Most of the map is blank. Margaret Kinsman assesses maps in an article on V.I. Warshawski's mean Chicago streets: "Maps, like cities, imply the possibility of choices: losing the way rather than gaining the way is always possible" (20). Kinsman emphasizes what a map fails to tell us — about "distances past and future, that are not found in the folds of the Rand-McNally" (21).

Losing the way in Soledad County is clearly the norm. In *Cyanide Wells*, Matt Lindstrom asks a friend, a California native, to tell him about Soledad:

> She closed her eyes, apparently conjuring a map. "Between Mendocino and Humboldt Counties, on the coast. Extends east beyond the edge of the Eel River National Forest" [CW 16].

Thus, the map evokes more than it defines. It pulls the reader upward into a literal and metaphoric aerial view of the land, its history, and people. Here the county defines a sweeping mythopoeic space vast enough to reflect and absorb human difficulties. In each book, the county's landscapes mirror psychological terrain. Recovery, redemption, and resumption of life characterize each book's narrative pattern.

In *Point Deception*, the fog cloaks past secrets. Rhoda Swift had been a rookie on the force thirteen years ago when she had to work a case in Cascada Canyon. Multiple murders occurred in a peaceful commune of hippie hold-overs from the seventies. Into the utopian settlement came meth-cooking drug dealers. The spree of violence ended in deaths, including those of several children. The killer or killers were never identified.

No one in the area speaks directly of Cascada Canyon, even though it sits between two well-traveled roads. It signifies the lost history of the town of Signal Port. Since the murders, the townspeople felt a malevolent undercurrent to Signal Port. Evil seemed to exude upward from the land to infect every citizen. "Like many of the descendants of Basques who had settled this part of the coast," the town residents have "a roundabout way of approaching a difficult subject" (PD 260).

Muller neatly conveys this emotional miasma with numerous references to the fog, which is both actual mist along the shore and internal confusion. "The fog was thick this morning, muffling the sound of the sea and cloaking the burned trees so they seemed gaunt figures holding a silent vigil" (PD 260).

Rhoda Swift's repression of what had happened keeps her in a subjective fog. She is unwilling to see clearly, both professionally and personally. After the murders, Rhoda's husband had an affair, and the couple divorced. Rhoda sank into alcoholism, which she now fights to keep at bay. Images from the night of the murders continue to haunt her.

Guy Newberry is an out-of-town reporter on a mission to dig up the truth about Cascada Canyon. As an outsider, he has nothing to fear from this dreaded site. He has his own roped-off past. Guy is a macho "guy," but his long-dead wife still talks to him. He has not yet accepted the reality that she is gone.

To thicken the fog of this haunted landscape, several present-day murders occur. The people in Signal Port avoid not only Guy, but each other. This is a town in trouble (PD 263).

Muller tells this story without a first-person narrator. Instead, sections alternate between Rhoda and Guy, each being the focus of a limited third-person POV. The reader, in a sense, floats between these two protagonists. Like tourists, we can appreciate the scenery as well as feel the tragedies upsetting Rhoda and Guy.

The entrance to Cascada Canyon is an eroded groove in the cliff face, with a narrow, almost hidden entrance. Its path takes the traveler toward that horrible past. By now, the reader, like area residents, has gone through so many veiled references and averted eyes about the mass murders that the Canyon walls fairly quiver with the charge of a mythic status. Rhoda and Guy travel the path together, bride and groom entering the past instead of the future. They encounter strange sights, a crumbling geodesic dome, and huge, twisted sculptures of ordinary items. One resembles an eggbeater. The sculptures represent how the ordinary daylight of life takes on a tortured appearance in the nighttime of repression.

This murder scene, with its connection to communal living, geodesic domes, do-it-yourself drug labs, and grubby life off the grid cuts through the rosy picture of the seventies. The past of the region was never the golden age it was supposed to be. People may recall it fondly, but Muller suggests a collective history prone to mistaken recollections.

By going to Cascada Canyon, Rhoda begins to remember and therefore wins her freedom from solitude:

> It's as if I'm coming alive again, she thought. As if facing the reality of what those murders did to me has set me free in all areas. I don't even want a drink tonight, because I'm no longer afraid to look inside myself and make peace with what I've done [PD 206–207].

Guy feels as if he's coming alive, too, and his dead wife's voice leaves him (PD 268). Without her presence, he expects to find grief, but sees only strength, a slight erosion against a cliff.

Soon Guy is strong enough to remember his wife's death in East Timor. As his wife, Diana, took a soldier's photograph, the soldier shot her in the head (PD 280–283). The story tells the risk of being an artist, but Guy the reporter goes his wife one better. The reader learns that Guy had recovered Diana's camera and kept this evidence of her murder in a safety deposit box. Hiding explosive information in an enclosed space is enough to shatter Guy's ability to cope.

To dispel their demons completely, Rhoda and Guy must leave the human community behind and enter a streaming, undifferentiated wilderness. A dramatic car chase re-enacts the traumas leading to their psychic wounds:

> Once they were into the forestland, the dripping trees compounded the rain. It was coming down so hard now that the wipers couldn't clear it fast enough. Mud oozed across the road from the eastern upslope; on one patch she [Rhoda] braked too sharply, skidded, and had to fight to bring the car out of it. Guy had momentarily closed his eyes — maybe praying for the first time in his life.... The tires started to slide on the blind curve above Point Deception, but she corrected and held them to the road. She leaned forward, trying to see the centerline [PD 327].

Reliving past disasters helps prevent the two from plunging into more deceptions. Later while walking toward Cascada Canyon, Rhoda cuts through her troubles as if with a machete. Once this couple faces the past, their way forward comes into focus.

> The day was clear and brilliantly blue, with not a trace of fog on the horizon. Even the skeletal trees couldn't detract from its loveliness, and the bright green secondary growth beneath them gave promise [PD 338].

In each book, the murderer never actually dies. He only goes underground for a time and returns, zombie-like, vowing to do more damage. This narrative pattern forms a perfect analogue for unresolved anger and guilt. To resume living, the damaged protagonists need to break away from repression, submerge themselves into the past, and confront the realities that harmed them in the first place. This imperative toward deep-down grieving overwhelms the "whodunit" storyline of these books. Muller has sentenced each character to Soledad to endure that necessary dark night of the soul. In each case, the real evil is the psychological damage the protagonist's repressed emotions inflict on the self.

In *Detective Agency*, Walton and Jones assess the functions of a first-person narrator.

> The women authors who appropriate the narrating "I" of the private eye novel modify it in the ways that are necessarily *self*-conscious. They evince an awareness that the body in question in the detective story is a gendered body; whether it is the body of the detective-narrator; the body of the victim; the generic corpus of texts; a body of stylistic, formal, and ideological practices that compose the hard-boiled detective novel; or the body of the reader [187].

By getting out from behind the eyes of Sharon McCone, Muller is free for a 360-degree view of human experience, regardless of gender. This quality is most obvious in *Cyanide Wells*.

This second book of the trilogy is also a limited third-person, switching between a male and female narrator. It takes place in a land-locked terrain, a landscape disfigured by mining and lumbering. The title refers to the town's name. In the past, a mining operation crucial to the region's economy used cyanide to reclaim gold ore from the mine tailings. The cyanide seeped into the land. The wells were eventually cleaned, but the idea of a poisoned water source remained. The citizens could use the town's name to keep away outsiders.

In many ways, *Cyanide Wells* digs the deepest of the three books. It received tepid critical notice when it first came out. True, it begins with a circuitous back-story, but the writing repays the reader's effort. Along with psychological resonance, Muller plants a string of startling revelations that up-end the narrative like successive landmines.

Matthew Lindstrom's ex-wife Gwen disappeared in 1988. He had already seen his marriage deteriorate. His wife was moody and unstable. He gradually realized that Gwen's psychological problems were serious, but before he could get help for her, she vanished. For a long while, the police suspected him of killing her, so he left his Michigan town, upset and conflicted. His attitude was that if Gwen were not dead, he might try to find her and kill her. "You know what you have to do," he mutters to himself (CW 58). Because Matt is not a reliable narrator, Muller leads the reader to wonder if Gwen left because of Matt's homicidal impulses. Feeling bereft, Matt travels, knowing that his journey is not geographical. He is traveling deep inside himself (CW 79). Eventually, he settles in Canada.

Back in the present, an anonymous phone caller informs Matt that Gwen is alive. She is living in Cyanide Wells as "Ardis Coleman," which Matt recognizes as her mother's maiden name. Matt travels to Cyanide Wells to learn that Gwen is an award-winning reporter. Her achievement had put the town on the map. She is now writing a book. Her current life is apparently a success, whereas his had been ruined. He is furious.

Unwilling to reveal too much about himself until he has a chance to approach Gwen/Ardis, Matt calls himself "John" and lands a job as a photographer for the local newspaper. Because Gwen/Ardis had been a reporter, Matt figures he can eventually find out about her by entering her world. His boss is Carly McGuire, the newspaper's "hell on wheels" editor.

Eventually Matt's undercover sleuthing reveals that the award won by Gwen/Ardis involved research of a double murder. Two gay men were shot to death in the home they shared. Their beautiful, upscale house falls under the shadow of a giant columnar rock cliff called The Knob. Muller is unambiguous about its associations, as Matt thinks about what the cliff looks like:

> Ahead, the Knob rose against the clear sky: tall, rounded on top, slightly atilt, eroded and polished by the elements. He couldn't help but smile. Perhaps it had resembled an upended doorknob to the settlers who named it, but to him it looked like a huge erect penis [CW 54].

Between Cyanide Wells, a poisoned female symbol, and The Knob, Muller obviously develops topographical analogues to both versions of the human body. The allusion also uses wasteland and fertility images to parallel barren emotional repression and fruitful resolution. The land is non-gendered, as are the troubles of the people who live there. Since the story takes place in May, the land is tender with green buds. This part of Soledad County is a wasteland coming to life.

Matt feels this sense of renewal and the possibility of a second chance with Gwen/Ardis. Their marriage wasn't all bad, he reasons. He dips into fond memories of Gwen gardening next to a gazebo, among the fragrances and rose blossoms of their home. As "John" the photographer, he finds that she now lives on Drinkwater Road, far from the toxic "Cyanide Wells" of the town. Outside the house at night, Matt peeps into the windows. "Around him the shadows were deepening. Scents drifted on the warmish air — freshly growing things, pungent eucalyptus, and something sweet that he had always associated with his first love" (CW 92). Matt initially wants Gwen back for a do-over of their life. Instead, his stalking changes into control. He wants to re-make the past into a version that suits him. With a shock, he realizes that Gwen/Ardis lives with someone else. From his stalker's hiding place, he is a voyeur to their evening life, watching through a lit window and casting himself as a player in the scene (CW 81–82). He takes surreptitious pictures.

Then, in a second bombshell, the camera lens shows that Matt's ex-wife is living with his current boss at the newspaper, Carly McGuire. In addition, the two women are sharing their domestic bliss by raising a mixed-race daughter.

Matt respects and likes Carly, so once he gets used to this idea of a lesbian relationship, he appreciates that Gwen/Ardis is moving on with her life. The women's relationship seems idyllic, noble even. He should move ahead as well. Then Gwen disappears again. Matt teams with Carly to find her, but the reader wonders: Has Matt killed her?

The town's history of poisoned water is central to the book's theme, as it works as a consistent metaphor for an undercurrent of poisoned relationships. In a brilliant balancing act, Muller shifts the point of view between Matt and Carly to control both meaning and form. We see his rage. We also see Carly's misery over losing her life's partner. "She pounded the mattress with her fists, twisted the comforter with vicious fingers and finally wept. *Why, Ard? Why?*" (CW 141). From Carly's flashbacks, we learn that Ardis treated her horribly. Then in a variation of "he said/she said," Muller provides a kind of "split screen," as the two of them argue over the truth about Gwen/Ardis (CW 110). Is she "despicable" (Matt) or "damaged" (Carly)? This is not quite *Rashomon*, but Muller sustains a double narration to explore a deeper truth about subjectivity and denial of human loss. The dual perspective also has a structural function. As suspense intensifies, each narrative section gets increasingly shorter for a rapid race toward the resolution.

Remember the "egg beater" sculpture in *Point Deception*? Muller continues the "bad artist" motif in this book. It is not a stretch for us to see Ardis's assumed name as "Artist," but "con artist" is a more likely label. Matt is amazed that work on her book for two years has produced only a short manuscript (CW 112). Ardis had been a gardener, but the only roses she maintains now are on her laptop's screensaver (CW 119). Preferring images of plants to people, Ardis has turned on the human community.

In *The Wilderness Within*, Kristina Groover analyzes the diversity of women writers' uses of the garden and wilderness themes in conjunction with spiritual quests. Toni Morrison's *The Bluest Eye,* Groover notes, uses blighted marigolds as a metaphor of incest. Groover reiterates that many writers deepen the spiritual struggle by going against the "safe at home" tradition. These writers "illuminate the limitations and even the dangers of home, community life, and storytelling" (126). By making gardening a part of Ardis's daily routine, Muller changes Matt's images of Gwen. The garden starts as a place for renewal and spiritual growth and ends in destruction. In the small community of Cyanide Wells, the well is poisoned, and all human and plant life coming from it has to fight its toxic effects.

Rhoda Swift makes a few cameo appearances in *Cyanide Wells*. She is still an authoritative cop, continuing on the force despite the problems from *Point Deception* (CW 85). Also, because she stops Matt on the highway in a traffic violation, she ends up revealing his true motivation to Carly. Apparently out of the fog, Rhoda now sheds light for those who need it.

"Perdido" means "lost" in Spanish. *Cape Perdido* asks if the Perdido River is a lost cause from the start. In the opening pages, Muller straightforwardly describes a literal river to let us know what is at stake as a corporation attempts to "grab" the water for profit. Later, her multi-layered, even radical, narration suggests an attempt to shift the river of literary convention.

Amid this conflict between environmentalists and business interests, four characters have dammed up their emotions over a past tragedy. For three of them, time stopped on the night of June 30, 1984, and the reader learns why in bits and pieces. Jessie Domingo is a young environmentalist with a grudge. Joseph Openshaw is a home-town boy who left Soledad for Berkeley, and is now returning to fight the corporate takeover of the river. Steph Pace owns the Blue Moon café where the locals hang out, but she is very weary of ordering vegetables. The family of old Timothy McNear had owned the lumber mill that used to support the town. Now it is in ruins. He appears to be on the side of the corporate profiteers, but he has qualms.

Jessie is the *naïf*, eventually realizing that life is never what it appears to be. Timothy is the embittered old man to balance Jessie. Eventually, we learn that Joseph and Steph had once been lovers, so they play a line of harmony among this quartet.

The characters are all under emotional pressure. The ostensible motivator in the present narrative is the incursion by a big corporation to make a "water grab." The company plans to float a huge water bag to collect water from the Perdido River and sell it. Since Muller and husband Bill Pronzini own a house in Mendocino County, she no doubt had this actual incident in mind. A plan to "bag" the Eel River occurred in Humboldt County in 2003, as reported in the *North Coast News*.

> In the long-term, district officials worried that if they didn't use the water, it could be transferred "out-of-basin" to another water district — putting a hard limit on growth in Humboldt County. In other words, use it or lose it…. Some of the customers that came forward were different, though. Instead of relocating their businesses in Humboldt County, they wanted to ship the water down to water-hungry Southern California. In giant bags [Rossi].

Muller transforms the actual events of the Humboldt County water bag issue into much more than a fight between pure environmentalists and greedy punks in pinstripes. "A high, elongated royal blue mass floated at the pier's end like the carcass of a giant sea creature, nearly filling the crescent-shaped harbor" (CP 52–53). Muller makes the bag a bright blue that "looks unnatural against the sea" (CP 53), a film on the water, like a suffocating algae. The bag becomes a metaphor of repression, as it dams up the natural flow of affection. In fact, a sniper shoots the water bag as if it were a thing that could be killed. Later, the thing becomes a murder weapon, as it nearly drowns Steph Pace.

The story itself is relatively conventional, but Muller's way of telling it is striking. We learn of the four characters' lives, past and present, from short narrations, almost sketches, of three or four pages. This approach conforms to Hélène Cixous' description of a feminist text that "starts on all sides, all at once, starts twenty times, thirty times, over" (Cixous 53). Despite some italicized dips into first-person interior monologues, Muller stays with limited third-person. Each chapter is labeled with the character's name. We do not hear that character's voice in words as in Faulkner's *As I Lay Dying*. We just discover how that character reacts to events. The third-person narrative decidedly separates teller from the text. Louise Erdrich uses this same strategy with the Kashpaws and Lamartines in *Love Medicine*, for instance. Muller places us high enough to view the land and its history. The reader essentially "follows" Steph as she ventures to the shore to find out new information:

> The cliffs curved ahead of her, dark and rugged, spilling down in huge, jagged slabs to meet the sand. At an outcropping that had always reminded her of a crouching prehistoric creature, she stopped [CP 38].

The land is ancient. Change is a constant from forces of nature. "The shore was lined with wind-warped cypress trees, and beyond them lay a sand beach" (CP 46). The reader's perch in the narrative affords a view of human change juxtaposed against the abiding land. The reader's point of view is not embodied in the character or disembodied through the narrative. Rather, we "hover" above the character and Soledad in a decidedly un-embodied, objectified state.

Combined, these persistent jumps in perspective have the effect of brushstrokes in a Cubist painting. We step back and ask, "What is it?" In places, the narrative leaves gaps; in others, the sequence continues as another character picks up the thread.

Frank Kermode offers a way to dispel this haze. He suggests that narrative, particularly of detection or psychological epiphany, often moves in uneven phases from deception to recognition. The changing perspectives set up false expectations that the reader follows. The non-linear story ends up "stimulating the reader to a fuller exercise of his imagination, to make him *read* in a more exalted sense" (Kermode 106).

Cape Perdido is not a fast read. Muller's narration alternates between being clear then obscure, like a view through the fog banks in *Point Deception*. Then, just as suddenly as Matt discovers his ex-wife in a lesbian relationship, the narration gives way to a revelation about the past and the sun shines through.

Before the sun appears, however, darkness falls. In a bizarre climactic scene, Steph Pace is tossed into the water under the huge water bag where she hangs suspended, fetus-like, in an air pocket. Horrifically, she encounters the corpse of a missing environmentalist. She shoves him aside like a rotted *in utero* twin. "Shuddering violently, she pushed Whiteside's body away. The motion of the waves returned it. She gave it a harder shove, fighting off nausea, and began dog-paddling as fast as she could toward the opening in the bag" (CP 290). She continues to have nightmares about the whole incident.

In his recent book *How to Read Literature Like a Professor*, Thomas C. Foster has a relevant guideline for this scene: "If she comes up, it's baptism" (Foster 152–162). Steph is an older woman redeemed by another chance for love long put on hold. In the closing pages, Joseph Openshaw tells her that a renewal of their long-deferred love is "very possible" (CP 302), and Steph Pace falls into a peaceful sleep over a map of Italy (CP 304). After many missed opportunities in the past, Steph eventually has the romance that Matt Lindstrom had dreamed about.

Of all the books, *Cape Perdido* has the most serious flaws. The unwieldy points of view leave little room for character to be revealed through action. Still it is clearly the most ambitious. Noir ecology blends with psychology for a thematic unity. Rhoda Swift makes another cameo appearance, and we learn that she is happy with her "Guy."

Muller uses the Soledad topography both to exemplify themes and represent internal struggles of characters searching for redemption. Two motifs unify the books: Muller's examination of the artist figure and metaphoric buildings.

Muller uses artist/reporter/photographer characters both to focus and distort events. Guy Newberry and Matthew Lindstrom provide a clear-eyed, if sometimes mistaken, view of events to balance the narrative. However, the creative impulses of Bernina, environmentalist and *faux* "earth mother," in *Cape Perdido* and of Gwen Ardis in *Cyanide Wells* are twisted and obsessive.

Horsley and Horsley analyze this noir concept of the "bad mother." Their article notes differences in how male and female noir authors depict the "murdering mother." Horace McCoy and Jim Thompson, for instance, use an objectified monster mother as an explanation for the psychological imbalance of the child. On the other hand, novels by women writers (Barbara Vine, P.D. James, or Patricia Highsmith are examples) work toward "reclaiming the subjectivity of the mother" through a close-up view of the evil mother's guilt for having distorted the child (370). In the framework of this discussion, Muller does not fall into either category. Instead, the characters reject guilt. Bernina's zeal for saving the environment leads her to actions that could destroy it (CP 244–245). Her attempts to justify her actions are silenced: "Bernina's mouth turned down but she didn't protest, just bowed her head and moved away into the parlor" (CP 245). The last we see of Bernina, she is loading suitcases into the trunk of her car (CP 248). She is sent packing.

The Horsley article mentions that "in the noir world, there is no possibility of a healing resolution" (374). Soledad does allow healing for its noir characters. Muller's creation of Gwen Ardis adds a distinctive twist to the "monster mother" concept by splicing artist and mother into one character. The journalistic vividness of the award-winning "Ardis" at first commands respect. Later, the failed wife/mother side of Gwen Ardis comes into horrific view. Like Bernina, Gwen Ardis has destroyed what she created. We also witness the effect of her instability on Matt, Carly, and Natalie, the adopted daughter. However, in Muller's topography, Carly learns from the mistakes of Ardis, and at the novel's end, Natalie is well on the way to healing:

"You know," Carly said, "you're really a good artist, honey. Maybe we should sign you up for some lessons."

"That'd be great. But will you stop calling me *honey*? You've been doing that all week, and I hate it. It sounds like you feel sorry for me. I don't like anybody to feel sorry for me — not even you" [CW 340].

Art is redemptive, and Natalie will be stronger by failing to feed Carly's guilt.

Each novel of the Soledad trilogy emphasizes emblematic architectural spaces. Against the natural terrain of soaring trees and immense cliffs, man-made structures sit humble and a bit pathetic, certainly fragile, against this backdrop. Gaston Bachelard in *The Poetics of Space* proposes that structures represent "psychological diagrams that guide writers and poets in their analysis of intimacy" (38). Muller's representation of most of these spaces finds human intimacy inadequate and tortured.

In *Boundaries of the Self,* Roberta Rubenstein considers "what kinds of meanings emerge from texts written by women in which the protagonist or central subject is male?" (4). Despite the imprisoned madwoman studied by Gilbert and Gubar, "the literary representation of spatial enclosure is not unique to the female gender" (4). Inside and outside are part of the common experience of both genders. Muller appears to agree, as she frames the male characters' deepest traumas in terms of space. Guy Newberry must escape the trap of his past, the filmed proof of his wife's murder that sits in a safety deposit box. When Matt Lindstrom watches Carly and Gwen through their living room window, he undergoes a similar experience of being outside the trauma of his own failed relationship. So does Joseph Openshaw, who refuses to enter his memory of that terrible night of death. Muller's depiction of splintered conflict rises above the limitation of gender through a transcendent point of view and non-engendered resolution.

The pain falls on woman and man alike. Architectural structures provide little shelter. In Muller's vision, buildings or human-built places cast doubt on human achievement. The towns are crumbling or flimsy storefronts "like a set in a Western movie" (CP 23). The geodesic dome in *Point Deception* illustrates hopes for the future, but these are curdled hopes, because of what happened there. The dome's "windows were filthy, and it resembled a deflating balloon, gradually caving in on itself" (PD 171). The building's ultramodern design connotes a communal, efficiently engineered utopia. Unfortunately, this ruined dome launches the blood-soaked rage causing multiple murders.

Mining and lumber interests also leave their ugly scars on the land. The gazebo surrounded by flowers in *Cyanide Wells* represents a vision of Paradise accessible to Carly and the young girl Natalie, if only the two can navigate around Gwen Ardis. The blooms are beautiful and tempting. Given the symbolic poisonous water nurturing them, Carly, Natalie, and Matt must proceed with caution.

In *Cape Perdido*, an old lumber mill represents the corporation's longtime death grip on the area. "The broken asphalt road led past a boarded up guard station between two of the mill's long buildings, which slumped under sagging roofs, their paint pitted, high windows broken" (CP 52). After an arsonist leaves the mill a smoking ruin, the townspeople meet instead in an old round barn. The structure serves as a "big tent," a civilized meeting place for environmentalists, the citizens, and representatives of the company purchasing the Perdido River water. Muller continues to create an aerial view of events, with the barn as a kind of *Axis Mundi*, center of the world, and resolution of the trilogy's structural motif.

Except for the comforting barn, the buildings all represent the characters' feeble attempts to set a human space under the sky, to gain shelter from destiny, and to shield themselves from the scrutiny of the gods. None of these places, curiously, are homes.

In *Fiction of the Home Place*, Helen Fiddyment Levy discusses the uses of the natural land in Jewett, Cather, Glasgow, Porter, Welty, and Naylor. "In summoning nothing less than a new homeland, the authors change the definition and uses of the American natural world. The often semi-divine protagonist encounters land as a midwife or as the mother who guards life and death" (Levy 9). With the Soledad County novels, Muller updates fictional uses of the natural world. Rhoda Swift is hardly a figure of sheer goodness and self-sacrifice like Alexandra Bergson in Cather's *O, Pioneers!* Still, Rhoda achieves a statuesque grace, having survived her past traumas. After emerging from her own troubles and wounds from the collective past, Rhoda Swift serves as a midwife to others, like Matt Lindstrom and Jessie Domingo, who need redemption.

During Rhoda's traffic stop of Matt Lindstrom, she discovers his real name, which she reveals to Carly McGuire (CW 85). Rhoda's information encourages Matt to come clean with Carly about his past and his real reason for being in Cyanide Wells. In *Cape Perdido*, Jessie Domingo, the idealistic environmentalist, gives her opinion of Rhoda: "Everything about Swift, her businesslike tone, her direct way of meeting one's eye, even her well-tailored woolen blazer — was making Jessie feel nervous and unsure of herself" (CP 212). Rhoda's no-nonsense presence is a wake-up call for Jessie, who later breaks out of her simpering, uncertain self to uncover and report a crucial clue to the past murder.

If the purpose of the Soledad County trilogy is for Muller to recharge her creative energies, the strategy apparently worked. In Muller's July 2006 newsletter, she unveils important news:

> As I'm writing this, Sharon is in the home stretch of her next adventure, THE EVER-RUNNING MAN, which you can expect out at this time next year. It's an explosive tale — literally — and because blowing things up fictionally is a great stress reliever, it's moving right along…. I made the decision last year to concentrate exclusively on the McCones. After all, she has so many more stories to tell [Newsletter, July 2006, www.marciamuller.com].

Judging from this title, we assume that in the new book McCone comes out swinging, a powerhouse of female authority that sends men packing. McCone has more rounds to fight, and Muller is seated ring-side.

Ultimately, the Soledad County trilogy is much more than Muller's vacation from the McCone series. These novels begin to blend conventions of detective fiction with a particularly American tradition of the mythic landscape.

Frederick Jackson Turner's appraisal of the frontier in the development of nineteenth-century America became crucial in understanding America's past. Turner defined "frontier" as "the meeting point between savagery and civilization." Muller's fiction provides a latter-day incarnation of Turner's frontier hypothesis relevant to the authors venturing into the frontier of writing and creating anew. In a sense, Sharon McCone is a frontier figure, both as first in the long line of women PIs and as a moral focus occupying that pivotal meeting point between the untamed and the tamed. In the Soledad County novels, Muller exercises the freedom to re-create a de-stabilized civilization, replete with the psychological savagery necessary for today's detective fiction.

The Sharon McCone and Soledad County novels represent Muller's unique take on the mean streets of Chandler and Hammett. By rooting her characters' conflicts in the land, she suffuses her work with an inspired regionalism similar to that of works by Cather and Faulkner. With the return to the McCone series, Muller pulls back. It remains for other writers, possibly Nevada Barr, Dennis Lehane, or Julia Spencer-Fleming, to continue blending noir detective fiction with topographic myth in all its stately progression. It also remains for future critics to evaluate Muller's place in the American literary tradition. When they do, they should make a special note of this complex psychological wilderness Muller has staked out for future writers to explore.

Works Cited

Bachelard, Gaston. *The Poetics of Space*, trans. Maria Jolas. New York: The Orion Press, 1964.

Cather, Willa. *O Pioneers!* Boston: Houghton Mifflin, 1941.

Cixous, Hélène. "Castration or Decapitation," trans. Annette Kuhn. *Signs*, Vol. 7, No. 1 (Autumn 1981): 53.

Erdrich, Louise. *Love Medicine*. New York. Harper Perennial, 1993.

Foster, Thomas C. *How to Read Literature Like a Professor: A Lively and Entertaining Guide to Reading Between the Lines*. New York: Quill-Harper Collins, 2003.

Gilbert, Sandra M., and Susan Gubar. *The Madwoman in the Attic: The Woman Writers and the Nineteenth-Century Literary Imagination.*, 2nd ed. New Haven: Yale University Press Nota Bene, 2000.

Groover, Kristina K. *The Wilderness Within: American Women Writers and Spiritual Quest*. Fayetteville: University of Arkansas Press, 1999.

Horsley, Katharine, and Lee Horsley. "*Mères Fatales*: Maternal Guilt in the Noir Crime Novel." *Modern Fiction Studies*, 45, no. 2 (1999): 369–402.

Kermode, Frank. "Novels: Recognition and Deception." *Critical Inquiry* 1, no. 1:1 (September 1974): 103–121.

Kinsman, Margaret. "A Question of Visibility: Paretsky and Chicago." In *Women Times Three:. Writers, Detectives, Readers*, ed. Kathleen Gregory Klein, 15–27. Bowling Green State University Popular Press, 1995.

Koch, Pat. "PW Talks with Marcia Muller." *Publishers Weekly* 248, no. 26 (New York: June 25, 2001).

Levy, Helen Fiddyment. *Fiction of the Home Place*. Jackson: University Press of Mississippi, 1992.

Muller, Marcia. *Cape Perdido*. New York: Warner Books, 2005.

_____. *Cyanide Wells*. New York: Warner Books, 2004.

_____. *The Dangerous Hour*. New York: Warner Books, 2004.

_____. *Point Deception*. New York: Warner Books, 2001.

_____. *Vanishing Point*. New York: Warner Books Mysterious Press, 2006.

Rossi, Jim. "Is the Water Bag Proposal a Trojan Horse?" *North Coast Journal*, February 6, 2003. http://www.northcoastjournal.com/020603/cover0206.html (accessed March 30, 2007).

Rubenstein, Roberta. *Boundaries of the Self:. Gender, Culture, Fiction*. Urbana and Chicago: University of Illinois Press, 1987.

Turner, Frederick Jackson. *The Frontier in American History*. Hypertext from New York: Henry Holt and Company, 1921 edition. http://xroads.virginia.edu/~Hyper/TURNER/ (accessed March 15, 2007).

Walton, Priscilla, L. and Manina Jones. *Detective Agency: Women Rewriting the Hard-Boiled Tradition*. Berkeley: University of California Press, 1999.

12

The Deafening Silence of the McCone Series

ALEXANDER N. HOWE

The female hard-boiled detective genre begins with an inquiry into the status of voice. Who speaks and by what authority? And, importantly, who remains silent?

The genre asks these questions at the same time that it demands that a new voice be heard — the voice of the female private eye. This gesture of "giving voice" is common enough in female hard-boiled fiction. However, in Marcia Muller's Sharon McCone series, the possibility of an active and effective voice is problematized to accommodate the author's strategy of epistemological critique at the heart of the series. Obviously, even a cursory glance at the various titles of the McCone books reveals an ongoing interest in listening to the haunting voices of the past, as well as a continued attention to a greater silence that cannot be articulated definitively. It is this "voice"— a voice of silence — that is the larger interest of the series, a point of fascination that offers a unique response to a variety of the criticisms that have dogged the female detective.

There is perhaps no greater thematic for dealing with literature than the voice, a fact that is highlighted from the very beginnings of detective fiction, despite the prominence given to the detective's perhaps more dazzling talent: seeing. Using Poe as a point of origin — a suspect genealogy, to be sure — we might view the detective genre as an attempt to amplify the human voice among the cacophony of the new metropolis. There among the din of the crowd, the detective places, of course, the voice of reason. To these ends, we are wise to remember that in Poe's "Murders in the Rue Morgue" (1841), the role of *hearing* is equal to that of *seeing*— that is, reading and deciphering. (Of course, Dupin relies on reported speech in his investigation; nevertheless, this emphasis on the power of listening still applies.) A careful "ear" allows Dupin to isolate distinct languages heard at the scene and thereby recognize that shrill, "very strange voice" responsible for the violence of the story, namely, the orangutan (Poe 149). Critical accounts of the story all too often find Dupin's solution — which results in the animal being safely contained within a local zoo — as an example of the formidable, and conservative, use of reason by the detective. However, I have always found the inhuman shriek of the orangutan not so easily dismissed. In support of this claim, I would call attention to the epigraph of the story taken from Sir Thomas Browne, which makes reference to the Sirens' song. While the details of this song — or the name Achilles assumed when in hiding — is "not beyond *all* conjecture" (Poe 141), I take Poe's emphasis as an indication that, despite all grand solutions to such enigmas, we remain within the realm of conjecture — despite the detective's adroitness. In other words, this infamous and lethal song suggests a more intransigent, haunting voice, a point that I will return to shortly.

This insistence of the voice within Poe is no doubt in keeping with the gothic elements so evident in his detective, characteristics frequently used to distinguish Dupin from his perhaps more famous successor, Sherlock Holmes. Without doubt, the "science of deduction" practiced by Holmes is a good deal more comprehensive than the ratiocination of Dupin, and, again without doubt, it is clear that sight is the privileged term of Holmes' *modus operandi*. The celebrated folios authored by Doyle's sleuth all pertain to physical evidence that can be quantified and catalogued (e.g., types of cigar ash, tracks left by various bicycle tires, etc.). Holmes frequently scolds Watson for incorrect leaps of logic and, just as often, for his inability to *see* evidence that is as clear as day — provided one knows what to look for. The "complete knowledge of London" (Doyle 185) that Holmes maintains requires that he see all, much like the panoptic gaze described by Foucault — a mechanism of penal technology contemporary with Doyle's stories.[1] As such, there remains a vital tie between Holmes' power of sight and his power of deduction, that is, between sight and knowledge. This is a well-trodden critical path, so I will simply pause to recall Virilio's pithy summation of the relay between science, sight, and power — that is, "I see" is always "I can" (Virilio 7). Of course, the point to be taken is that if something can be seen, it can be known, and thus dominated.

It is little wonder, then, that the intrusion of voice into the classical detective narrative always represents a moment of danger, or the loss of reason. As a model, we might take the example of Aristophanes' famous hiccups reported in Plato's *Symposium*. This interruption of voice — in this case, a bodily noise without meaning — disturbs the philosophical discussion of the assembled guests. Even the classical detective is not without his hiccups, as it were. Here, one recalls the use of voice as index in Poe's description of Dupin's Bi-Part Soul (Poe 144), as well as Doyle's discussion of music — sonority pushing beyond meaning — in the description of sleuth-hound Holmes

(Doyle 185). Tellingly, the irrational side of the detectives' personalities is inevitably marked by the interruption of the voice.[2] Naturally, the only elixir for this condition is the solution to mystery through which the classical detective will re-entrench his mastery. In this sense, in response to the voice as limit of meaning, we find a fetishization of the human voice utterly instrumentalized, as in the case of Holmes and his famous "More data!" Voice is reduced to an apparatus of the science of deduction, Watson's literary dalliances notwithstanding.

Of course, the hard-boiled genre is a criticism of the presumptions of such reason and the manner of its telling. It is little wonder, then, that Chandler privileges the question of spoken language in his hard-boiled manifesto "The Simple Art of Murder." As he suggests, Hammett and other early hard-boiled writers reclaim the possibilities of detective fiction from the English school by giving voice to the "common man," a rigidly gendered and frequently sexist rendering that is not without its problems. Nevertheless, in the work of Chandler and other hard-boiled writers, the corruption and injustice of the status quo are challenged, largely through this new modality of the voice. Not only is murder placed back in the hands of those who do it for more appropriate reasons, but the account of the crime is itself articulated in the "language they customarily used for these purposes" (Chandler 16). From the beginning, the hard-boiled voice is an empowered voice. "Speech makes the man" in these texts, as Porter has indicated (139). The first-person narration so frequently found in this fiction ensures that all is seen — and, obviously, known or ordered — from the detective's perspective. However, even before this ordering, the reader is confronted with the detective's voice — insofar as a reader can be "confronted" with the voice of literature.

While the power of the hard-boiled voice is undeniable, I suggest, not quite in passing, that Chandler's great brilliance as a writer was to script a detective who not only spoke in the language of his time, but a detective who did so only with great difficulty, and with a good deal of irony about the effects his words would have on the world. In other words, for Chandler, Marlowe is always split from his own voice. Undoubtedly, this divided voice often functions as a strategy for re-entrenching white, male authority, by way of invisibility or inaudibility, as it were. However, this notion of a voice split from itself is at the same time quite productive. Marcia Muller shows the way.

Marcia Muller is frequently acknowledged as "the founding 'mother' of the female hard-boiled private eye," a distinction famously granted by Sue Grafton. With the publication of *Edwin of the Iron Shoes* in 1977, Muller introduces a tough female detective compellingly cast — at least in part — in the mold of her male predecessors. Here, "speech makes the woman" as the reader comes to know Sharon McCone through her first-person narration that is marked by admirable perceptiveness, sensitivity, and wit. As Sharon quips during her first investigation, "I'm a mean shot with a .38, and I bake terrific bread" (187), an example of the detective's humor that dexterously negotiates the re-writing of gender categories inherent in the very notion of a female dick. This is hard going, to be sure, but time and again Sharon proves her mettle and the sharpness of her tongue, never shying from speaking out against prejudice, inequality, and injustice.

Given the thematic necessity of voice in the hard-boiled world, it is hardly surprising that the female hard-boiled detective fiction that follows Muller in the early 1980s is dominated by the metaphorics of the voice. Walton and Jones have suggested the necessity of reading the politics of the female private eye genre in terms of the idealism of the women's movement (and other activist programs) of the 60s and 70s (34). The demands for voice and representation were the watchwords of such politics — admittedly, a strategy with a vexed history — as became true of the female detective text. Sue Grafton has perhaps best expressed what is at stake in this entreaty: "Voice is a big issue. Until I found the right voice for Kinsey Millhone, I wasn't in business. Voice is about gettin' connected to your stuff. A sense of authenticity and truth. A writer's voice is that unique blend of viewpoint and language that echoes a writer's soul, if that doesn't sound too lofty or pretentious" (qtd. in Christianson 138). This notion of "authenticity and truth" is in keeping with Chandler's "simple art," as is this wonderfully articulated notion of "gettin' connected to your stuff," which takes up the hard-boiled, and feminist, mantra of "telling it like it is." As Christianson has argued, the power of this gesture is not to be underestimated. This new fiction (and here he is referring to Grafton specifically) "transforms the classic private eye genre into a place from which a woman can exercise language as power" (Christianson 129).

As the female hard-boiled detective began to find an audience, many detractors dismissed the political merit of the subgenre. Klein is perhaps the greatest representative of this perspective.[3] In her famous work *The Woman Detective: Gender and Genre* (1988), Klein claims: "The detective script and the woman script clash because the necessary condition for each are the inverse and contradiction of the other" (57). If a story succeeds at fulfilling the requirements of detective fiction, it cannot be a feminist narrative and vice versa. This assumes that the "detective script" is inevitably a conservative defense of the status quo that puts blind faith in the various institutions that support the diminished state of women in society. A defense of things as they are is necessarily an anti-feminist endorsement, as the "woman script" entails a critique of both gender stereotypes and the institutions that support the current inequity of these systems. In her reading of Muller's McCone, Klein finds the detective initially promising but finally disappointing, faulting her for "adopting individual solutions for societal problems" and having "no sense that both [the criminal and legal systems] are part of a larger, flawed system needing to be changed" (209). Unfortunately, neither the detective nor woman script proves fruitful in Klein's estimation.

Similarly, Munt has warned against politically retrograde solipsism that often plagues a female sleuth cast in the mold of liberal feminism, a discourse that speaks in the name of the right to self-determination (41). This position remains blind to institutional causes of oppression, and likewise neglects the female detective's connection with other women, family, friends, and loved ones. Munt's conclusion recalls the vexed history of activism and the issue of the voice, which might be typified by the blind spots of identity politics of the 80s and 90s. At its worst, identity politics forecloses the discussion of group formation and dynamics, frequently speaking in blank terms of individual rights, leaving the issue of group identity "spoken by those with the greatest resources, and the most powerful voice" (Munt 129). A voice given only to an individual (or only a single aspect of a group) is as good as silencing, an effect that unfortunately accompanies many of the apparent gains of female crime fiction, at least from the perspective of Munt's argument. As she concludes in a related discussion, "The promise that there is a 'self' to discover is problematic" (125), as is the promise of voice.

At the core of the argument between the two camps responding to the female private eye is the distinction between "voice" and "language." Christianson offers an excellent analysis of hard-boiled language, paying particular attention to the ways in which the detective uses tough talk, wise-cracks, and what he dubs "hard-boiled conceit," to order experience. While tough talk and wise-cracks promise violence should words fail, "hard-boiled conceit" (e.g., the strained metaphors and similes especially prevalent in Chandler) offers the possibility of creating new meaning within the chaotic hard-boiled milieu. In this instance, voice trumps language, we might say. This is not simply stylistic, but a "significant use of language as power" in that it introduces something new, as does all "serious" literature ("Tough Talk" 158). Understood in this way, hard-boiled language actually transcends genre fiction.

Elsewhere, in his discussion of Sue Grafton's work, Christianson modifies his terminology somewhat, suggesting that "hard-boiled language is a matter of *voice*" ("Talkin'" 138). As he writes, speaking of Grafton, "her hard-boiled style allows her to pursue 'possible routes and directions' in the production of a distinctive 'voice' that, in turn, transforms the style into something unique and feminist" (139). Grafton does not "transform" hard-boiled language for feminist purposes — nor is she herself in turn "spoken by" this discourse. Rather, "Grafton appropriates hard-boiled language for feminist purposes as an exercise of language as power" (136). This is important for Christianson who wishes to abandon the notion of "appropriation" when speaking of the female hard-boiled detective. Neither is it sufficient to read the female detective as "gender-bending," as this leaves the categories of gender merely displaced — and thus, in place. Rather, Christianson reads Grafton's detective, Kinsey Millhone, as "gender-busting," thereby thwarting the silencing that results from gendered categories (140–141). From this perspective, we might say that neither gender nor genre equal destiny, either for the individual or the formula character. The system of (hard-boiled) language is transformed by the uniqueness of voice.

While I am entirely amenable to this notion of "busting" the categories of gender and genre, I find that Marcia Muller provides a compelling alternative radical appropriation of hard-boiled voice, that is, the voice of silence. In so doing, Muller's fiction frustrates many of the complaints frequently encountered in criticism of the female detective, particularly surrounding the issues of essentialism and knowledge construction (and, naturally, gender and genre). Far from offering a specious voice of unity — of women, knowledge, and so on — Muller contends that there is always something uncanny about the voice, an excess that remains incapable of being accounted for by speaker (or critic), or reduced to the knowledge of the detective. Voice is inevitably haunted by its own utterance, saying both more and less than desired. This epistemological upheaval, or lack of definitive solution, by my estimation satisfies even the very rigid demands of Klein or Munt. The "reason" of the status quo, particularly regarding the construction of gender, is unfailingly revealed as an incomplete project, a schism that demands not reconciliation but mobilization. To these ends, Muller's work consistently addresses the question "what is a voice?"

This focus is apparent in the sheer number of voices that speak to McCone throughout her travels, but I am here especially interested in the "voices" McCone hears at crime scenes and within dreams. Readers of the series know that McCone is descended from Shoshone ancestry, the proportions of which change over time as the detective discovers the identity of her true parents in *Listen to the Silence* (2000).[4] This heritage, which is unmistakably written upon McCone's face, effectively doubles the female detective's position as other, or outsider, at the same time as it potentially doubles her skills at intuition. The apparent gesture is that McCone has the advantage of "native" and "female" intuition, although she always bristles at the suggestion of the latter. At first glance, this appears to be an integrative, quasi–New Age method of detection — Sharon will do her detective work in her sleep, as it were. While this formula might seem to uphold the complaints lodged by Klein and others regarding Sharon's lack of critical vision, McCone's *modus operandus* (and Muller's use of racial and gender stereotypes) is not so reductive as we might imagine.

Sharon's unique relation to place is perhaps best summarized in a comment made in *Where Echoes Live* (1991). As she affirms, "I don't believe in the supernatural, but I do believe that sometimes places can absorb the emotions surrounding events that have happened there. A house where people have been happy has a good feel. A place of misery never seems quite right. Crime scenes — especially those of homicides — are the worst of all, filled with the aura of rage and desperation and pain" (56). McCone tells us that she goes to crime scenes to get a "feel" for these motives and emotions, as these are indelibly written on the landscape. On these visits, the past does indeed "speak" to McCone. However, the voices she hears are not quite in keeping with the knowledge typically associated with the detective. Rather than looking for physical clues and unmistakable evidence — these sites are frequently visited long after a crime has taken place — Sharon often seeks a more ephemeral index at crime scenes, that is, the intricate relations of those surrounding a crime. Though she admits that the practice is "illogical and unscientific," McCone maintains, "just being there [at a crime scene] gives me a better sense of the individuals involved and their possible motivations" (*Trophies* 208).

This approach is not without its perils, and McCone frequently laments her tendency to become too involved in her cases. In *Pennies on a Dead Woman's Eyes* (1992), for example, she find herself haunted (even possessed) by dreams and visions of another individual involved in the murder of Cordy McKittridge. This "weird psychic link," as McCone describes it, while useful to the investigation, does not yield definitive answers to the crime. As she summarizes this partial knowledge after eerily having the dream (or nightmare) of another, "I knew, and yet I didn't know." (94).

Naturally, this intimate connection with place is evident in McCone's relation with the larger setting of the series, San Francisco. Muller is alternately celebrated and criticized for her presentation of this city. Complaints frequently cite the author's nostalgia for a San Francisco of the past that refuses to acknowledge the complexity of the modern city (Bairner 134–135). Similarly, others have indicated that Muller's representation of the city as a hub of vibrant and successful "multi-culturalism" diminishes the ongoing, local struggle of various factions, races, and ethnicities.[5] Bairner summarizes these criticisms well when he suggests that Muller's San Francisco is a "locale" but not a "locality" (135).

While I find these arguments sound in many respects, Muller's presentation of San Francisco, particularly as an object of nostalgia, is especially useful for my current purposes. In the author's work, no significant landmark is ever described without a reference to the historical significance of that site within the lived experience of people. While the sepia tint of memory does frequently intrude upon Muller's descriptions of places and landmarks, the author's goal is not a simple celebration of a bygone time that turns its back on the present and its concerns. On the contrary, Muller's descriptions frequently ask us to consider an object's difference from itself. As landmarks and larger "objects" of the landscape are powerful coordinates through which we order the narratives of ourselves, Muller asks us to question the "authenticity" of such stories, even while reminiscing at the contents of a "time capsule," such as a favorite neighborhood district, etc. Descriptions of Port San Marco in *Games to Keep the Dark Away* or the Embarcadero in *The Broken Promise Land* (1996) illustrate this well. The silence of the landscape, which remains incapable of being penetrated by the narrative voice, is all the more palpable in the ghost towns that McCone encounters — for example, Promiseville in *Where Echoes Live* (1991) and Cinder Cone in *Listen to the Silence* (2000).

Importantly, the voices that issue from these lost spaces cannot be appeased. They remain silent, yet demand recognition nevertheless. Here, one thinks of McCone's frequent conclusion: "The pain and anger and disillusionment of the past week fell away from me. Their vestiges would return, I knew. Bad memories would recur — probably for the rest of my life. But I would take comfort in moments like this, when I felt temporarily safe, warm, insulated" (*Trophies* 265). As this passage suggests, McCone will, as is typical at the end of the novels, take refuge from the larger trauma of the story with her friends and loved ones. However, these are passing moments, only briefly providing refuge. This attention to traumatic experience (both extraordinary and mundane), as well as the question of survival, keeps Muller's discourse from offering the sort of simple "solutions" for which she is often criticized. Indeed, trauma is the only guaranteed experience in McCone's San Francisco.

This reading of the greater, traumatic silence at the core of the McCone novels becomes all the more apparent with the development of Sharon's relationship with Hy Ripinsky, beginning in the novels of the 1990s. Importantly, an early gain won in this relationship concerns the issue of silence in the way I have been suggesting. McCone first meets Ripinsky in *Where Echoes Live*, in the remote area of Mono County near Tufa Lake, far away from San Francisco. McCone at first finds the vastness of the alkaline flats unnerving, and with good reason. Her "sensitivity" to voices of the past that inscribe themselves in physical places is here overwhelmed by the sheer magnitude of this natural expanse, which is barren and utterly inhuman. As the series progresses, Sharon is confronted more frequently with such places of sublime beauty, which remain eerily silent all the same, and therefore beyond the knowledge of the detective. Here one thinks of the Hawaiian mountains in *A Walk Through Fire* (1999), the mesa at the U.S.-Mexican border of *Wolf in the Shadows* (1993), the snow- and ice-covered Boundary Water Canoe Area of Northern Minnesota in *Both Ends of Night* (1997), and, of course, the area surrounding Touchstone, first encountered in *Till the Butchers Cut Him Down* (1994). These are just a few examples among many.

The issue of "echo" is crucial to the series as a whole, and, given its use in the title of the text in question, it demands further investigation. An echo is of necessity an odd coincidence of voice and silence, a pairing that is made all the more uncanny given the disembodiment of voice that an echo entails. When we hear our voice reflected in an echo, "the voice acquires an autonomy of its own and enters the dimension of the other; it becomes a deferred voice, and narcissism crumbles" (Dolar 40). The self-transparency of our own voices, which always seems audible as we speak, is shown to be illusory. In other words, in the echo, we are confronted with the fact that we are never equal to our own voices — that, in effect, we do not *have* a voice in the sense we normally ascribe to "having." With this in mind, it becomes all the more compelling when McCone describes Tufa Lake, a desolate desert landscape surrounding a dried-up lakebed, as "a place of great silence," "This is a place out of time — a place where echoes live" (*Echoes* 4). This figure is interesting as it suggests not simply the process of echo, but something like the (imagined) site of echoes themselves — that space where all disembodied voices reside.

The "echo" thus figures the way in which our voices, and all the stories we tell, are irrevocably split at the point of utterance. In the context of detective fiction, this break reads as a not-so-subtle criticism of knowledge construction, leaving all lost points of origin forever out of reach. The echo becomes a repetition of this missed encounter not simply with the voice, but with the "true" self. This "loss" of self is mentioned in a pivotal scene where Sharon tells Hy about the distance that has grown between her and her friends, something that has her questioning her own identity, as well. Like Tufa Lake, "There was also a place like that in the mind, where the past played and replayed" (107). This psychological repetition, which always marks a failure of representation, in turn is linked to the lived history of individuals tied to the specificity of place. This history reaches across generations. Walking through Earl Hopwood's makeshift museum of Promiseville, the abandoned mining town on the outskirts of the lake, McCone finds herself nearly lost among all the objects collected by Hopwood. The lived history of the town is linked unambiguously with the silence of the mesa. "Suddenly I became aware of the hush in this mausoleum of the past, was struck anew by the great silence of the valley" (287). With this thought in mind, Sharon has a strange image of her and Hy "walking along the deserted street in that pale, watery sunlight, insubstantial as figures in an overexposed photograph. As we walked, first the town and then the two of us faded to nothing" (287). Both the town and these two latecomers are themselves echoes of the greater silence that is figured by Tufa Lake. Just as an overexposed photograph is the result of a delay (of shutter speed), so too does the echo of this space ultimately reduce all experience — and history itself — to nothingness, to the lost voice that is an echo.

Sharon's thoughts recounted at the museum are no doubt a criticism of lack of life in "objects" and the prosopopeia (i.e., giving voice to inanimate objects or a deceased individual) that is always a component of the detective narrative — an ongoing interest in the McCone series that begins with the antiques collected in *Edwin*. These fetishes obviously make a very poor substitute for the living and a very meager memorial for the dead. (Here, one thinks of the ossification of all that falls within the classical detective's gaze.) Nevertheless, although the "vast emptiness and silence" of Tufa Lake threatens to overwhelm McCone (264), it is at the same time uncannily appealing.

A repetition of the "fading" (or subjective erasure) described in McCone's imaginary photograph occurs again near the end of the novel, as McCone and Ripinsky argue about going back into the mineshaft to rescue Earl Hopwood, who is bent on blowing up the mine. Without thinking, McCone insists on retrieving the crazed Earl Hopwood who had just attempted to take her life — Sharon's sympathy for others remains undaunted, even in this instance. When Hy accuses her of having a death wish, she is taken aback. She acknowledges that her self-described "addiction to danger" (342) — an admission she makes earlier in the novel — is itself a kind of death wish. In other words, she is tempted by that "fading" described earlier. Indeed, she is vivified by it.

This novel presents many such self-revelations — regarding herself, her profession, her family and friendships — and while Hy Ripinsky is there as a "sounding board," so to speak, Sharon arrives at these revelations very much on her own. The novel concludes with a sort of actualization of Sharon's metaphorical account of the lake area. Hopwood succeeds in blowing up the mineshaft, resulting in the apocalyptic fires that his interpretation of Revelation had promised — that is, a "burning mountain," an image that promises to haunt Sharon without respite (321). This emphasis of "traumatic repetition" is customary for the McCone files, a constant that certainly upholds the generic demand that a politically engaged crime novel provide no individual solution for social problems. As is also customary of Muller's conclusions, McCone finds herself rejoining the comfort of those close to her, in this case Hy Ripinsky. While the issues of mining pollution and ecological conservation spotlighted in *Echoes* are fairly specific to a given space, this area is, as Sharon reminds us, the place where echoes live. As such, it figures much larger impasses of knowledge, reminding us that our voices are but echoes lost there within that inhospitable expanse.

These notions of echo, silence, and traumatic repetition bring us to voice as it is understood in psychoanalysis. The voice — along with the perhaps more recognized object, the gaze — is used by Lacan to express the abyssal structure of the *objet a*, the cause of the subject's desire.[6] Though objects of fantasy may flesh out this aporia (i.e., "cause") at the core of the subject, the *objet a* is itself never equal to these guises, although it appears only through them. In a like way, the voice as object is never reducible to its sonorous qualities or to the sense speech would like to impart. It is, rather, the surplus of these operations. This excess no doubt owes to the fact that the voice always marks that place where language touches — indeed, emits from — the body. It is the evanescent articulation of flesh and blood, thereby defying reproduction or reduction to linguistic categories. I cannot pass over this point without a reference to the *femme fatale*, and, specifically, poor Carmen Sternwood who is so frequently described as emitting sounds from an unknown portion of her body, so to speak. Indeed, in this sense, she herself frequently embodies (or rather disembodies — the one operation begetting the other) the object voice for Marlowe.

With this insight in mind, I would make the following alteration to my initial thesis regarding the hard-boiled detective: From the first, hard-boiled detective fiction is an examination of the voice as it is eerily tied to the body. However, the great difficulty is that this connection remains forever receding. In other words, it is impossible to wholly embody a voice. As Dolar sums this difficulty: "There is no voice without a body, but yet again this relation is full of pitfalls: it seems that the voice pertains to the wrong body, or doesn't fit the body at all, or disjoints the body from which it emanates" (60). The voice, in this way, remains an extimate object there at the border of the body and meaning, as well as sound and sense.

The silence of Tufa Lake figures this all too well, particularly insofar as it absorbs the resonance of the death drive (or death wish) for McCone — a possibility that is perhaps glimpsed in the final conflagration of the mountain. Thus, Tufa Lake haunts the series generally, and certainly the events that transpire in *Echoes* are spoken of for some time. While the burning mountain is a unique figure, this greater silence "behind things" informs all of McCone's relations to place. Again, this is found in the voices heard by McCone even within the urban landscape of San Francisco. Though we come to know the city in detail through her eyes, the detective has the curious habit of not describing places, but describing a place's difference from itself— this from the perspective of time or affect. In this odd sort of reading, McCone does not endeavor to resurrect a lost image so much as she attempts to read the very gap that is opened between the images of her montage — she listens to the silence of this space. Though these voices from the past — like those heard in dreams — do offer guidance, McCone knows well that her interpretation ultimately misses the mark. Further, she knows that this missed relation is actually an act of great fidelity, insofar as it refuses the oppression of strict categories of experience (e.g., gender, genre, etc.).

I'll conclude with a difficult and necessary reference for any critic working with Muller, namely, *Listen to the Silence*. While there are numerous complications (perhaps even betrayals) that arise in this text, I would like to suggest that Muller's attentiveness to the traumatic aspects of the object voice inheres, at a certain level. To clarify this point, I'll begin with a negative example (i.e., silence rendered as knowledge) found in Hy Ripinsky's suggestion that Sharon "listen to the silence. It can tell you everything" (*Listen* 54). While this investigative approach is common to the series, McCone here needs reminding as the case at hand is so personal and disturbing. At the beginning of the novel, Sharon's father dies. As she is cleaning the scattered objects of his past from the garage, she happens across adoption papers indicating that she is not her parents' biological daughter. While the act of detection is always a process of identity construction, in *Listen to the Silence* this thematic is taken to the extreme. What Sharon must solve is the very question of her origins.

As the investigation begins, McCone finds various family members reticent on the topic of the adoption, and her mother goes so far as to plead with Sharon to abandon her search. At Hy's prompting, McCone adopts the counter-strategy of "listening to the silence," which is nothing more than an attentiveness to the gaps within an individual's narrative, a skill that is prerequisite for any act of detection. However, as should already be clear, silence understood in this way is not the silence of the "object voice" described above. Here one recalls the curious incident of the dog in the nighttime, that famous moment of reasoning (and a certain type of listening) found in the Sherlock Holmes' case "The Silver Blaze." In this episode, Holmes reduces even silence — effectively a lack of clue — to knowledge, or the silence of the voice to sense, an operation that proves pivotal to the investigation. By "listening to the silence" within the stories she is told during her search, McCone attempts the same maneuver. She will reduce silence to knowledge. The gesture of "unmasking" is especially dire, as she attempts to arrive at the "truth" about herself and her heritage, a promise that would seem to liquidate the silence and echoes previously invoked. However, I contend that this is not the only variety of listening, or silence, within this text.

The skill of "listening to the silence" is actually mentioned for the first time in an earlier work, *Wolf in the Shadows*. Sharon speaks fondly of her "newfound ability," something that Ripinsky teaches her on a camping trip just prior to the events of the novel. Not surprisingly, here again we find echoes of Tufa Lake when Sharon admits that "I'd found the echoing of vast open spaces oppressive and lonesome. But in a very few days he'd shown me how to be at peace with it; tonight, with only a faint sound of surf to break the stillness, I felt comforted" (267). This is not to say that she reads and conclusively interprets this stillness; rather she makes peace with her inability to do so. Admittedly, in contrast, for Sharon and Hy, silence is often reduced to meaning — much like the Sherlock Holmes example. This silent communication is typified in *Both Ends of Night* when Sharon speaks of her uncanny ability to communicate with Hy "without words, and often at great distances" (286). While this ideal communication is charming for a number of reasons, it would be easy to criticize Muller for staging a "perfect" union, with flawless communication, that refuses to acknowledge the unbridgeable difference that informs any relation.

However, again recalling the centrality of Tufa Lake to Hy's characterization, there remains a "silence" at the core of his nature, as well. This is often spoken of in the trappings of the adventure narratives that dominate the McCone series of the 1990s — that is, Hy has a mysterious and violent past, which includes possible affiliation with the CIA and various ecological terrorist organizations. These dramatic elements of character are supplemented with the more mundane silences that punctuate relationships, particularly those trying moments of the "What did she or he mean by that?!" variety. These items become especially maddening to Sharon during the months surrounding her marriage to Ripinsky, a time documented in *The Dangerous Hour* (2004) and *Vanishing Point* (2006). Nevertheless, McCone comes to accept this other variety of silence in their relationship as well, and here one recalls the conclusion of *Pennies on a Dead Woman's Eyes* with her throwing away the file she has opened on Ripinsky. Wald has written of the inverse relation between a murder mystery (particularly of the Golden Age) and a love story, claiming a "love story remains dangerous because unsolvable" (107). More so than any other contemporary mystery writer, Muller has elaborated upon this thesis through the various silences of Sharon's relation with Ripinsky.

Returning to *Listen to the Silence*, undoubtedly the very premise of the novel complicates my previous reading of the McCone series. Feminist crime fiction's basic demand to "tell it like it is" inevitably reveals the ways in which the categories of gender, race, and class are socially constructed, and therefore incomplete and finite. *Listen to the Silence* ostensibly betrays this from the outset, as Sharon sets off to find her biological parents and, thus, the definitive "truth" about herself. Predictably, McCone discovers that her parents were both full-blooded Shoshone Indians. Maureen Reddy's reading of this novel as problematic insofar as it reduces race to biology is no doubt correct, and I am frequently in agreement with her on the difficulties of the presentation of race within Muller's work (Reddy 174). That being said, I would like to offer an alternate reading of *Listen to the Silence* that is more in keeping with the insights of the object voice as I have been using the concept.

We find such insight in McCone's confrontation of her biological mother at the conclusion of the novel, an encounter punctuated with all the requisite silences and reproaches. At one point, McCone attempts to pull her hand from her mother's grasp, but she finds that she cannot move, her hand remaining "a limp, unfeeling lump of flesh and bone" (316). This symptomatic response of hysterical paralysis is the perfect figure for "family" relations as these are presented in *Listen to the Silence*. Crucially, this paralysis occurs during a moment of silence. Between mother and daughter there remains only an unformed mass of flesh and bone that exceeds either individual. Incapable of being named or accounted for — or excised, for that matter — this traumatic flesh is the bond of life itself, a connection that marks our uncanny relation to the other and history through the silence of the object voice. In this way, even the biological discourse that has informed McCone's quest for origins must prove to be a failed metaphor, inadequate to deliver on the detective's original hopes. McCone's relation with her biological father is a bit more difficult to rescue, I suspect, but I would just add that this "reunion" at the conclusion of the novel is rife with references to its own performance.

To conclude, in each of the instances mentioned above, McCone encounters a voice beyond reason, a voice that refuses to function as an interpretative tool on the way to a solution of any kind. Interestingly, though it remains traumatic, this encounter is not as assiduously avoided as it is in the case of her male colleagues; indeed, this voice repeats itself inevitably throughout McCone's detection. As Walton and Jones have claimed, listening is essential to the female detective (135), and the rewards of this skill might be just as great as those of hard-boiled tough talk. The object voice is a useful device for understanding this project, particularly insofar as it speaks to Muller's own critique of gender and genre. To these ends, Klein's pronouncement about gender and genre in the case of women's detective fiction might be modified as follows: In the Sharon McCone series, voice is irreducible to the categories of either gender or genre. If gender and genre fail — a certainty that is limited not simply to the female, hard-boiled detective — they do so because voice in this sense persists. It is a voice that cannot be "given" or "heard," yet it remains a ghostly presence demanding recognition. Hence Muller's unflagging interest in the spaces where echoes live and silence dwells.

Notes

1. See especially the "Panopticism" section of Michel Foucault's *Discipline and Punish: The Birth of the Prison* (New York: Vintage Books, 1977), 195–230.

2. While music is a perfect example of this sonorous escape from reason, as is Doyle's point, we find a more extreme instance of "hiccups" in "The Adventure of Charles Augustus Milverton," a pastiche that references, among other texts, Poe's "The Purloined Letter." As Holmes describes his distaste for Milverton, the king of all blackmailers, Watson tells the reader that he had "seldom heard [Holmes] speak with such intensity of feeling" (Doyle 573). What follows is perhaps the most atypical behavior of Holmes in all the stories, a departure introduced by a "loss," we might say, of voice.

3. Klein subsequently modified her position, at least to a certain extent, in "*Habeas Corpus.*"

4. While I often find this presentation of race to be problematic in the ways suggested by Maureen Reddy, I find Muller's characterization useful in a number of respects. See Reddy, *Traces, Codes, and Clues*, 172–175.

5. See Maureen Reddy's "Imagining the Margins: Muller's Explorations of Race" in the current volume.

6. Lacan speaks most explicitly about the "object voice" in the unpublished *Seminar X*. For a discussion of the "object cause," the reader is directed to Chapter 5 of Fink's *The Lacanian Subject*.

Works Cited

Bairner, Alan. "Sharon McCone's San Francisco: The Role of the City in the Work of Marcia Muller." *Irish Journal of American Studies* 6 (1997): 117–138.

Chandler, Raymond. *The Simple Art of Murder*. Boston, MA: Houghton, 1950.

Christianson, Scott R. "Talkin' Trash and Kickin' Butt: Sue Grafton's Hard-Boiled Feminism." In *Feminism in Women's Detective Fiction*, ed. Glenwood Irons, 157–170. Toronto and London: Toronto University Press, 1995.

_____. "Tough Talk and Wisecracks: Language as Power in American Detective Fiction," *Journal of Popular Culture* 23, no. 2 (1989): 151–162.

Dolar, Malden. *A Voice and Nothing More*. Cambridge, MA: MIT Press, 2006.

Doyle, Arthur Conan. *The Complete Sherlock Holmes*. New York: Barnes and Noble, 1992.

Fink, Bruce. *The Lacanian Subject: Between Language and Jouissance*. Princeton, NJ: Princeton University Press, 1995.

Klein, Kathleen. "*Habeas Corpus:* Feminism and Detective Fiction." In *Feminism in Women's Detective Fiction*, ed. Glenwood Irons, 171–190. Toronto: University of Toronto Press, 1995.

_____. *The Woman Detective: Gender and Genre*. Urbana and Chicago: Illinois University Press, 1988.

Muller, Marcia. *Both Ends of the Night*. New York: Warner Books, 1997.

_____. *Edwin of the Iron Shoes*. New York: Mysterious Press, 1977.

_____. *Listen to the Silence*. New York: Warner Books, 2000.

_____. *Pennies on a Dead Woman's Eyes*. London: The Women's Press, 1992.

_____. *Till the Butchers Cut Him Down*. New York: Warner Books, 1994.

_____. *Trophies and Dead Things*. London: Women's Press, 1990.

_____. *A Walk Through the Fire*. New York: Warner Books, 1999.

_____. *Where Echoes Live*. New York: Mysterious Press, 1991.

_____. *Wolf in the Shadows*. New York: Warner Books, 1993.

Munt, Sally. *Murder by the Book? Feminism and the Crime Novel*. New York and London: Routledge, 1994.

Poe, Edgar Allan. *The Complete Tales and Poems of Edgar Allen Allan Poe*. Vintage Edition. New York: Vintage Books, 1975.

Porter, Dennis. *The Pursuit of Crime: Art and Ideology in Detective Fiction*. New Haven, CT: Yale University Press, 1981.

Reddy, Maureen. *Traces, Codes, and Clues: Reading Race in Crime Fiction*. New York and London: Routledge, 2003.

Virilio, Paul. *The Vision Machine*. Trans. Julie Rose. Bloomington, IN: Indiana University Press, 1994.

Wald, Gayle. "Strong Poison: Love and the Novelistic in Dorothy Sayers." In *The Cunning Craft*, eds. Ronald Walker and June Frazer, 98–108. Macomb, IL: Western Illinois University Press, 1990.

Walton, Priscilla L., and Manina Jones. *Detective Agency: Women Rewriting the Hard-Boiled Tradition*. Berkeley: University of California Press, 1999.

Conclusion

Marcia Muller in the American Tradition: Still Breaching Our Insecurities

CHRISTINE A. JACKSON

Marcia Muller's thirty-plus years of writing stand like a literary Golden Gate, spanning the divide between popular and aesthetic literature. Since 1977 Muller's pioneering character, private investigator Sharon McCone, has stood on that bridge, casting a private and public eye on the turbulence of social, economic, and political change.

This current volume examines and evaluates the breadth of Muller's novelistic achievements. The essays overlap in some instances, addressing qualities and themes common to Muller's works. Although each essay touches on a range of subjects, three loosely defined categories emerge: expansion of gender roles and identity (Elliott, Chyan, Reddy, Bedore), elasticizing of the woman detective subgenre (Buckler, Walton, Connelly, Maida), and controlled development of thematic patterns illustrating trauma (Datema, Buchanan, Jackson, Howe). Because each critic's methodology offers a different lens for viewing Muller's work, the view from this bridge is clear and expansive. The essays bring together feminist, structural, historicist, mythic, psychoanalytic, behaviorist, and cultural approaches for a panoramic perspective.

Empowered women highlight most of Muller's work. The leading ladies in the series novels line a gallery wall with impressive portraits. Sharon McCone, Joanna Stark, Elena Oliverez, and Rhoda Swift all evince admirable qualities of ingenuity. Muller forces each to dig deep for emotional resilience, and all eventually find inventive ways to resolve wrongdoing. However, the character who commands most of the critical attention is McCone, and rightly so.

The articles included here take as a given that Muller's Sharon McCone stands as a break-through personality in detective fiction. These critical read-

179

ers note a few inconsistencies in McCone's personality from book to book. Yet by following changes in Sharon's profession, living arrangements, relationships, and values, the consensus is that McCone's evolution over the past three decades results in an emblematic woman character. Sharon shows both enough flexibility to endure whatever formula twists Muller envisions and the depth of personality to convey complex literary and cultural ideas. By solving cases, she also becomes adept at figuring out life. With the invention of McCone, Muller leaves an undeniable legacy, as witnessed by the legions of novels featuring women detectives, sleuths, and crime fighters from every corner of the justice system.

The articles also judge that, in places, Muller's work falls short. Walton notes that Muller pulls back from the international thriller hybrid that she is starting to move toward. Reddy faults Muller for not doing more with Sharon's "double outsider" status, both as a woman in a man's profession and as a woman of color. My article on the Soledad County novels sets up expectations for a mythic subgenre rooted in the landscape that Muller fails to develop.

The Ever-Running Man (2007) is the twenty-fifth McCone feature, and most recent book as of this writing. All the articles in this collection offer the reader accessibility to this latest Muller offering. Ideas from at least three of the articles are sharply relevant, finding expression with Muller's new examples, if not more elaborate developments. Harriette C. Buchanan's discussion on the lost child motif, Priscilla Walton's assessment of McCone as an anti-terrorist, and Alexander N. Howe's development of a theory of voice and silence all prove to be invaluable methods for assessing this latest McCone adventure.

The international security firm partly owned by McCone's new husband, Hy Ripinsky, is under siege. Explosions at several offices of Renshaw and Kessell International, or RKI, have raised the specter of a worldwide terror campaign designed to cripple RKI's surveillance and safety operations on behalf of corporate clients. The situation prompts Hy to take an unprecedented step. He wants to hire McCone Investigations to find out who or what is behind the bombings.

Sharon typically keeps her distance from clients like RKI. The company provides services to people who tend to operate outside boundaries, both geopolitical and moral. In a previous case, McCone had worked for Gage Renshaw, one of RKI's principals, but she has adamantly refused to take on Hy as a client, due to conflict of interest. Still, never say never. The book's opening scene starts with Hy dropping the case file on her desk and closes as McCone accepts the case but tells him, "I'm going to have to ask for more than the usual retainer" (9).

This book both relies on formula and breaks it apart. Sharon's network of associates, friends, and family from previous books are on board. Rae Kelle-her, Ricky, Mick, Patrick, and others formerly from All Souls all contribute to the investigation, although Mick is going through a wrenching separation from Charlotte. The office for McCone Investigations remains in the same converted warehouse on the waterfront, except Sharon spends little time there. Hy Ripinsky makes many appearances as her emotional touchstone, yet Sharon's painful discovery about his past leads to a terrible fight and separa-tion for the couple. The "safe house" where they are staying is bombed, and McCone later dreams that the foundation under their house named "Touch-stone" is cracking (181). Muller does more than shake up the familiar. Through the book's title image, Muller gives us a strobe-lit glimpse of herself as an ever-running artist, breaking down structures of gender and subgenre. Indeed, she includes a long scene of Sharon demolishing a treehouse in the backyard of her childhood home: "…the first thing I saw was a loose board on one side of the treehouse. I crawled over there, pulled it free, began to smash at the other boards. When I had destroyed that wall, I took on another. Then I began punching shingles from the roof" (147). Her wrecking-ball behavior contin-ues until only a few timbers of the small house remain. These actions pro-vide more material for Harriette C. Buchanan's examination of the "lost child" motif.

Priscilla Walton's discussion of a hybrid genre, with McCone as a PI turned terrorist fighter, is most obviously applicable to the series of bomb-ings that Sharon investigates.

Muller again reconnoiters international thriller territory. The explosions at RKI could involve a worldwide conspiracy against RKI's top secret clien-tele. The ever-running man is spotted detonating explosives in over five loca-tions in different countries, which demonstrates the command of resources that the villain has at his disposal.

To fight organized corporate powers, McCone has her own considerable agency. She asks Mick to analyze cyber break-ins and calls in favors to ask friends of security guards for tutorials on glitches in a surveillance system. She herself tracks down off-duty guards for information and spends an entire night following one on his rounds. She travels by plane and covers the Cal-ifornia coast, from San Francisco to San Diego and north again to Mendo-cino County. George N. Dove's analysis of *Suspense in the Formula Story* characterizes a "thriller" as a narrative featuring a "Giant Conspiracy Against Civilization" (2). *The Ever-Running Man* meets this criterion. If RKI is out of business, the dark forces could win. To combat this amorphous villain, Sharon gathers substantial resources, more than would be expected from a lone detective, but she mounts a hardly adequate offense against a global network wielding near omnipotent force. More breaches of security ensue, and Sharon seems powerless to stop them.

Muller uses some parts of the thriller formula in service to the story but lops off others. She sacrifices a globe-hopping protagonist and adds a dual strand of personal conflict to the case — Sharon's terrorism of the heart. The paranoia factor looms large when Sharon suspects that Hy could be part of the Giant Conspiracy. She may indeed be sharing a bed with the enemy. In this way, Muller blends action/thriller component with the more dainty "if I had only known" subgenre of the type construed by Mary Roberts Rinehart or Phyllis McGinley. While we cannot fully accept this view of McCone as the naïve woman who has unknowingly married an illegal arms dealer, Muller makes it credible that McCone cannot speak for certain as to the truth of the allegation against Ripinsky. McCone has always known vaguely about her husband's shady background, but she has overlooked it because she trusts him. His is one case file she refuses to read. Again, Muller stretches the subgenre, making the formula do her bidding.

As Walton notes, Muller has been adding potential terrorism to McCone's case load since 1993. With this focus on hostage negotiation, corporate security, and high-tech surveillance, Muller continues to stand in the forefront of literary trends. Post-9/11, political and international thrillers are increasing in popularity. As a corollary, thriller writers are gaining a stronger voice in the writing community. The International Thriller Writers Organization, established in 2004, draws influential authors, publishes a webzine, and hosts ThrillerFest, the hottest new conference on the writers' circuit. The conference offers features such as CraftFest, a segment geared specifically for writers, and AgentFest, a forum for conference goers to interact with publishers, agents, and editors. The website, www.thrillerwriters.org, presents a number of firsts, including a serial audio book and "Killer Year," an organization giving voice to newly published writers. ThrillerFest 2008 will be held, for a second year, in New York City.

Now that a thriller component to detective fiction has become more mainstream, is Muller content to stay with this hybrid subgenre? Is she a standard bearer for this trend? She says, "I've kind of made a career of blowing things up, but now I think I've finally gotten it out of my system" (Muller, "Happy Summer!"). Predictably, McCone's creator shies away from joining the crowd. Not resting on past successes, Muller rushes off to try something else. The title of her next McCone book, *Burn Out* (2008), however, suggests that the reader should not take the author's sunny claim of catharsis too seriously.

Despite the concussive blasts of the crimes, Muller continues to plumb the possibilities of silence and voice as metaphor. Alexander N. Howe's article on "the object voice" sets out an intriguing inquiry. *The Ever-Running Man* adds more provocative evidence to Howe's theory on the role of voice in deciphering the world. When McCone returns to Touchstone, the house "hummed with silence," yet the answering machine blinks with an unknown number of metallic voices conveying messages (59–60). McCone pegs one telephone message as a voice "identifiable as neither male nor female" (66). And what do we make of a witness who makes a hobby of comparing people's phone voices to their actual selves? When McCone interviews the witness, a psychiatrist, the woman tells her, "You don't look like you sounded on the phone" (95). As Sharon begins to question Hy's truthfulness in telling her about his past, she notes that he hasn't actually lied. What he has used is silence (152).

This development of voice/silence binaries presents a thematic that dramatizes the impossibilities of communication. In questioning how she and Hy had segmented their relationship from their working lives, McCone remembers Hy's account of an early hostage negotiation. Hy told her that he had defused a dangerous situation, getting the message across in a "bastardized version of Thai and English. It was like I'd been doing it my whole life" (159). Hy's voice is highly inflected. His use of silence to set his emotional distance from McCone adds yet one more dimension to his linguistic skills. In *The Ever-Running Man*, Muller continues to find new ways to convey the epistemology of voice.

This novel deals from the same deck as previous McCone adventures, but it ups the critical ante. Muller lays on the table yet another series of developments to Sharon's character, to the genre, and to the list of motifs embedded in the narrative. The novel includes enough re-conceptualized material to send commentators scurrying for addenda, if not outright reappraisals. Muller continues to locate new ways to subvert previously established textual certainties, thus breaching a network of insecurities: McCone's, the reader's, and the critic's.

Muller's substantive body of inventive work demands more attention from commentators. Her coverage of an array of hot button topics and a consistently solid critical reception keep her as a vital presence on the detective fiction scene. She is mostly innovative, continuing to re-define herself and readers' expectations. While an in-depth judgment of contemporary American literature is beyond the scope of this study, we must begin to address the issue of Muller's place in the American literary tradition.

Does Muller's work in a genre primarily regarded as "popular" prevent the work from attaining "literary" status? In an article calling for a redefinition of popular and "aesthetic" literature, Morris Dickstein notes the slippery nature of these two categories.

Frequently, Dickstein notes, innovation is the distinguishing feature between popular and literary fiction. He emphasizes that since the rise of the eighteenth-century novel, the marketplace has insisted upon what was new and different because "artists are forced to differentiate their products from those of other artists and even from the things they themselves have already produced" (34). Being "different," then, is a key to the so-called artistic novel.

Or is it? Dickstein goes on to note exceptions. "Sometimes this balance of innovation is reversed. For reasons that also relate to the marketplace, popular art is often more conservative than vanguard art, wary of drastic innovation, given to repeating formulas that have worked in the past" (35). Innovation, therefore, cannot be the sole determinant of artistic quality. Perhaps the degree of innovation, or even the locus in the text where innovation may be used to avoid upsetting the formula, characterizes the artistic quality of the work.

John Cawelti echoes a criterion of consistency similar to Dickstein's. In *Adventure, Mystery, and Romance*, Cawelti concludes a discussion on Hammett, Ross Macdonald, and Simenon by considering long-term critical evaluation: "To effectively interpret and evaluate their work requires a clear conception of the set of conventions they chose to observe, for it is from the interplay between the detective formula and their own personal concerns that their artistry arises" (299). Applying this standard to Muller's work is problematic. Given the shifting conventions she utilizes, we may not yet have a clear idea of the textual properties she has elected to keep.

A tough McCone would be a safe bet as one of the mainstays of the formula. But with each new adventure, Muller shows us that Sharon does more than change clients. McCone leaves comfortable situations, as in her job at All Souls, to challenge herself, opening her own agency. She earns a pilot's license. While the circumstances of McCone's life have changed, so has Muller shaded in Sharon's emotional and personal qualities. Her sense of identity takes on new dimensions, with the discovery of a Shoshone ethnic heritage. Her love life gains depth. She marries Hy Ripinsky. And in *The Ever-Running Man*, Muller teases the reader with hints that McCone, terrorist fighter, may be (gasp!) with child. How else to explain that she needs to refill her birth control pill prescription (20)? Or that she indulges in two long bouts of crying (26, 38–39)? Or that she has no appetite and has vomited twice (35, 37)? After this intriguing line of clues, we are assured that McCone does in fact renew her prescription (79), so the suggestion of pregnancy may be a red herring. Still, McCone's hunter instinct continues to miss the mark. During a crucial chase, she berates herself: "Dammit, why had I fallen asleep? Why had I sat here instead of moving around? I should have known he'd search the area" (220). Muller's idea of conventions of character is that they exist to be upended.

The narrative arc of suffering and redemption may be another constant that Muller keeps. McCone's file cabinets overflow with cases involving clients from an array of income brackets and of many ethnicities. The cases open up for scrutiny a wealth of human issues involving domestic violence, alcoholism, and mental illness. In addition, Sharon takes on broader social issues such as illegal immigration, political corruption, gender inequality, and extremist environmentalism, to name a few. Sharon McCone's interactions with her clients and the sacrifices she makes to solve their cases reflect an American story. In each book, McCone rebels, suffers, and redeems herself by validating the issue with a successful resolution of the case.

With a thirty-plus-year sterling reputation and still ever-running, Muller is clearly no literary flash in the pan. However, does her accumulated work achieve a level of universal artistry? Do the novels make a profound statement about the human condition? Without a doubt McCone is a major figure in detective fiction, and Muller deserves credit for being first, but fifty years from now, will her creation stand with the likes of Hester Prynne, Edna Pontellier, Lily Bart, or Daisy Miller?

Although we may begin this discussion, it is too soon to define with certainty Muller's place in the history of American literature. Cawelti raises another thought on work that "achieves extraordinary popularity at the time of its creation, yet turns out to be largely ignored by later generations ... [the writer's] initial popularity is a kind of aesthetic mistake on the part of the audience that is deceived by topicality or by appeals to temporary or fleeting states of mind or mood" (299–300). Thirty years is hardly temporary or fleeting, and publishing twenty-five books cannot be considered a mistake, but will McCone have what it takes to hold audience interest over time?

Carolyn Heilbrun, better known to detective novel readers as "Amanda Cross," bristles from the many times she faced the annoying question of why a writer would choose to produce a detective novel rather than a "real" one. Not a little defensively, Heilbrun responds that "with the momentum of a mystery and the trajectory of a good story with a solution, the author is left free to dabble in a little profound revolutionary thought" (300). The best formula fiction, then, has moments of challenging the status quo. Marcia Muller's writing has given us many moments, indeed, hours, of these dangerous, ground-breaking thoughts. For now, it remains for future critical collections to continue examining the value and artistry of the works framing these thoughts.

Works Cited

Cawelti, John G. *Adventure, Mystery, and Romance: Formula Stories as Art and Popular Culture.* Chicago: Chicago University Press, 1976.

Dickstein, Morris. "Popular Fiction and Critical Values: The Novel as a Challenge to Literary History." In *Reconstructing American Literary History*, ed. Sacvan Bercovitch, 29–66. Cambridge, MA: Harvard University Press, 1986.

Dove, George N. *Suspense in the Formula Story*. Bowling Green, OH: Bowling Green State University Press, 1989.

Heilbrun, Carolyn G. *Hamlet's Mother and Other Women*. New York: Ballantine Books, 1990.

Muller, Marcia. *The Ever-Running Man*. New York: Warner Books, 2007.

_____. "Happy Summer!" Newsletter, July 2007. www.marciamuller.com (accessed March 20, 2007).

About the Contributors

Pamela E. Bedore is an assistant professor of English at the University of Connecticut. She coordinates the writing program at the Avery Point campus, and teaches classes in popular fiction, Canadian and American literature, and gender theory. She is currently working on a book entitled *Open Universes: Feminist Science Fiction and Gender Theory.*

Hariette C. Buchanan is a professor of interdisciplinary studies at Appalachian State University, Boone, North Carolina. She has published numerous articles on women writers, especially such Appalachian writers as Lisa Alther and Lee Smith. Other research interests include contemporary Southern writers, including Daphne Athas and Margaret Maron, material and popular culture, and women mystery writers.

Patricia P. Buckler is professor emerita at Purdue University and is on the English faculty at Indiana University Northwest in Gary. For many years she has been an active member of the Popular Culture Association's Mystery and Detective Fiction Area caucus and served as its co-chair in 2004 and 2005. She has written on detective novelists ranging from Canada's Gail Bowen to Indiana's Terence Faherty to Michael Dibdin. Her other research interests include scrapbooks and composition pedagogy.

Chin-jau Chyan is a Ph.D. candidate in the Department of Literature, Film, and Theatre Studies at the University of Essex, UK. Her research focuses on contemporary American crime fiction with particular emphasis on the intersections of gender and genre in the female private eye novel. She has presented papers on women crime writers, including Marcia Muller and Sara Paretsky.

Kelly C. Connelly is a Ph.D. candidate and adjunct professor in the English Department at Temple University in Philadelphia, Pennsylvania. She is also an attorney for the federal government. She is currently completing her dissertation on the origins of the dissolution of certainty and identity associated with the postmodern detective novel.

Jessica V. Datema received her Ph.D. in the Department of Comparative Literature at the State University of New York at Binghamton in 2003. She lives in Brooklyn and is a full-time instructor at Bergen Community College. Her specialties are modernism, philosophy, and psychoanalysis. At present, she is working on a book about modernist techniques of mimetic and anti-mimetic representation in Gertrude Stein.

Winter S. Elliott is an assistant professor of English at Brenau University in Gainesville, Georgia. She holds a Ph.D. in English literature from the University of

Georgia. She teaches medieval and early modern British and contemporary multicultural literature courses, often focusing on the intersections between gender, race, and identity. She has presented at numerous conferences and has published papers on Medieval literature and science fiction.

Alexander N. Howe is an assistant professor of English at the University of the District of Columbia, where he teaches courses on American literature, literary theory, and film. He is the author of *It Didn't Mean Anything: A Psychoanalytic Reading of American Detective Fiction* (McFarland, 2008) and various articles on Raymond Chandler, Mickey Spillane, and Philip K. Dick.

Christine Jackson holds a Ph.D. in American literature. She is a full professor in the Division of Humanities at Nova Southeastern University, Fort Lauderdale, Florida, where she teaches writing, literature, and music history. Since 2001, Chris has been active in planning SleuthFest, the mystery writers' conference sponsored by the Florida Chapter of the Mystery Writers of America. Chris has published *Myth and Ritual in Women's Detective Fiction* (McFarland, 2002). Her short story "Cabin Fever" was a finalist in the Winter 2006 "Cozy Noir" contest sponsored by the online mystery writing journal *SpineTingler* <www.spinetinglermag.com>.

Patricia D. Maida is a professor of English at the University of the District of Columbia. Her interests include American literature, works by women authors, and mystery fiction. She co-authored *Murder She Wrote: A Study of Agatha Christie's Detective Fiction* (Bowling Green University Press, 1982). Her research on Christie led her to explore the background and works of pioneering American detective fiction writer, Anna Katharine Green, in *Mother of Detective Fiction: The Life and Works of Anna Katharine Green* (Bowling Green University Press, 1989). The essay included in this text is the product of Maida's long-term interest in Marcia Muller's work.

Maureen T. Reddy is professor and chair of English at Rhode Island College. Her books include *Traces, Codes, and Clues: Reading Race in Crime Fiction* (Rutgers University Press, 2003), *Crossing the Color Line: Race, Parenting, and Culture* (Rutgers University Press, 1994), and *Sisters in Crime: Feminism and the Crime Novel* (Continuum, 1988). She is working on a book on race in Irish popular culture, parts of which have appeared as articles in several collections and in *Irish University Review*.

Priscilla L. Walton is a professor of English at Carleton University in Canada. She is the author of *Our Cannibals, Ourselves: The Body Politic* (University of Illinois Press, 2004), *Patriarchal Desire and Victorian Discourse: A Lacanian Reading of Anthony Trollope's Palliser Novels* (University of Toronto Press, 1995), and *The Disruption of the Feminine in Henry James* (University of Toronto Press, 1992). She is the co-author, along with Manina Jones, of *Detective Agency: Women Rewriting the Hardboiled Tradition* (University of California Press, 1999), and, along with Jennifer Andrews and Arnold E. Davidson, of *Border Crossings: Thomas King's Cultural Inversions* (University of Toronto Press, 2003). She co-edited *Pop Can: Popular Culture in Canada* (Prentice-Hall, 1999), and edited the Everyman Paperback edition of Henry James's *The Portrait of a Lady*. She is presently at work on a new study, with co-author Bruce Tucker, on post–9/11 America.

Index

A Is for Alibi 1
The A.B.C Murders 94
Achilles 165
activism (social and political) 13, 14, 15, 17, 18, 19, 44, 114, 168
"The Adventure of Charles Augustus Milverton" 177n
adventure genre 80, 87, 91
adventure narratives 176
adventure novels 90
adventure story 80, 90, 91
Adventure, Mystery, and Romance: Formula Stories as Art and Popular Culture 80, 85, 90, 184, 185
aesthetic literature 179, 183
affirmative action 44
agency 7, 18, 25n, 90, 91, 181; see also women's power
All Souls Legal Cooperative 6, 16, 17, 18, 19, 23, 33, 34, 35, 36, 71, 72, 73, 75, 76, 80, 81, 82, 83, 84, 85, 97, 102, 103, 106, 107, 108, 109, 111, 114, 143, 144, 145, 148, 181, 184
"Alphabet Series" 34; see also Grafton, Sue
amateur detectives 40, 58, 66,
American detective fiction 51, 65, 162
American dream 19, 30
American hard-boiled detective fiction 70, 100
American history 137
American identities 32
American Indians 41
American literature 32, 163, 183, 185
Ames, Katrine 79; "Murder Most Foul and Fair" 79
Anglo culture 41
Anglo detectives 102
anti-detective 55, 59
anxiety 121–130, 130n, 131n
Archer, Lew (character) 7
archetypal criticism 135
architectural spaces 160, 161
Aristophanes 165

artist (as motif) 58, 129, 150, 156, 159, 181, 183
As I Lay Dying 158, 163
Asian-American literature 31
Asian immigrants 31
Ask the Cards a Question 1, 21, 22, 69, 73, 108
askesis (Lacanian concept) 123, 131n
authorial anxiety 122, 124, 130, 130n
authority 2, 16, 18, 19, 20, 35, 42, 45, 113, 149, 162, 164, 167
autobiography 121, 129
The Autobiography of Alice B. Toklas 122, 123, 126, 127 129

Bachelard, Gaston 160; The Poetics of Space 160
Baja, California 96
Barnes, Linda 70
Barr, Nevada 150, 163
Beat Generation 4
Bedore, Pamela 179,
behaviorist criticism 179
Bentley, E. C. 59; Trent's Last Case 59
Berkeley, California 18, 71, 84 87, 100, 106, 107, 111, 114, 157
Bertens, Hans, and Theo D'haen 7, 34
Beyond the Grave 40, 58, 59, 60
The Big Sleep 95
Bilignin, France 126
black women writers 41
Blood on the Common 121
Blood on the Dining Room Floor 9, 121, 122, 123, 124, 126, 127, 129, 130, 130n
The Bluest Eye 156
body (as text) 17, 20, 33, 154, 155, 174, 177
Bond, James (character) 85
Bookstaver, May 127
Borden, Lizze 127
Both Ends of Night 84, 89, 90, 91, 113, 135, 171, 175
Boundary Waters Canoe Area, Minnesota 171
Bowles, Paul 122, 126